THE LIVING INDIA

ITS ROMANCE AND REALITIES

THE LIVING INDIA

ITS ROMANCE AND REALITIES

BY

GEORGE MACMUNN

GYAN

Published by

GYAN

Gyan Publishing House
5, Ansari Road
Daryaganj, New Delhi-110002
Phone: 011-47034999, 9811692060
E-mail: books@gyanbooks.com

Distribution Network
gyanbooks.com
India, USA, Canada, UK, Australia

ISBN: 978-93-6433-638-3 (HB)
First Published, 1934

2nd Impression 2024

Printed at: Gyan Press, Delhi.

THE LIVING INDIA ITS ROMANCE AND REALITIES
Author: GEORGE MACMUNN

THE LIVING INDIA

By courtesy of Indian Railways Bureau

Modern India. Victoria Railway Terminus, Bombay

THE LIVING INDIA

ITS ROMANCE AND REALITIES

BY

LIEUT.-GENERAL

SIR GEORGE MACMUNN

K.C.B., K.C.S.I., D.S.O., p.s.c.

Colonel Commandant, Royal Artillery

LONDON

G. BELL AND SONS, LTD.

1934

PRINTED IN GREAT BRITAIN
BY R. & R. CLARK, LIMITED, EDINBURGH

AUTHOR'S FOREWORD

DURING the last few years I have been constantly invited to lecture on some aspect or other of Indian life and conditions, and have found a very great desire among my hearers for a book on India that is less serious than a history and less formal than a guide-book. To stimulate the interest has now come the White Paper, with the uprising against some of its provisions which has been indeed a phenomenon of 1933.

The classes who have given their sons to the rebuilding of this crashed sub-continent for many generations are now abstaining, or seeking to probe the conditions of the future before following what has hitherto been the family destiny.

The Living India aims at helping this spirit of inquiry, of giving a *coup d'œil* of history and peoples, the life of the Europeans and such matters as the winter visitor may care to take cognizance of at opening the shutter for a few seconds.

The spelling of the Indian names herein is the illogical British spelling, that we all know from the days of *Little Henry and his Bearer*, and no attempt has been made to follow scientific rules. Many of the photographs have been lent by the unlimited courtesy of the Indian Railway Bureau; others have been taken by the author so recently as 1933.

Where figures and data are given they are taken, for the most part, from the official publication, *India in 1930–31*, the latest available.

G. F. M.

CONTENTS

BOOK II. THE SERVICES AND EUROPEAN LIFE

BOOK III. LIFE AND SPORT

BOOK IV. THE SEEING OF INDIA

ILLUSTRATIONS

BOOK I

THE INDIA OF FACT

CHAPTER I

THE COUP D'ŒIL

What is India?

While lesser Europe and not too numerous circles in India agitate themselves over matters political, and the lesser statesmen take them all too seriously, the great sub-continent of India remains under the stars and the sunlight, and beneath the great snows of the Himalaya. With its stress and its duress, and the difficulties that appertain to its conditions, which the British have striven so manfully to rebuild and amend, expending many good young lives in the process, she has been aptly termed by Kipling, 'The grim Stepmother of our kind'. Rather indeed is she the grim stepmother of all and sundry, to none less than to that other white race which almost before time was, impinged from the steppes of Central Asia upon the civilizations and savageries of older folk still.

Much has been written by the West of the East especially in these times of change . . . change because all the world is changing, outwardly at least, in the profusion of new things that science has given us. But in all the procession of books, of books about India, many of which are more than able and more than beautiful, there seems to be no clear picture before the West yet, of what this sub-continent really is as it stands to-day before the world, and of its wheel of life. Nor does the rush of tourists tell much, since such must of necessity hammer out the track already beaten, and that too in the cold season, the cold season that is shorter than the hot which is the real India. This book is written, not because of the making of books there is no end, but to try and picture this India of all seasons, and all climates, and to see how far life in India of to-day is changed for East and West in its appearance and its promise of days gone by. It was the constant demand of Napoleon to his staff that they should show him where they really were—make him see into the enemy's lines and minds, and into the realities of his own communications and means of supply. '*Faites-moi voir!*' was his insistent demand, and it is not too much to say that the cry of the British and even of other Western peoples, as regards India, is still '*Faites-nous voir!*' That is the ambition that lies behind these printed lines.

To talk of the 'British' is to use a big portmanteau word. Do we mean the thoughts and ways of the proletariat, the sour ways of the introspective labour fanatics, the bustle and efficiency of business folk, the staunchness of the country gentry, the culture of the universities, the still more practical way of the Scotch, the Irish genius of those whom Mr. Cosgrave represents, the sour venom of the De Valera obsession? All are 'British', let alone the folk of that land that is free of vowels. How much more then are we to wonder what we mean when we talk of 'India', the land of over 350 millions of varying races, warring religions and strange inhibitions.

The Vastness

India is such an inscrutable subject not only to the West but to the United States across the water, that before any attempt is made to explain the living India, the India of to-day, the child of history, and in recent time the plaything of politicians, it would help the human mind if some figures are given illustrating the vastness of the problem. When that is grasped, turn aside to think of your fellow-countrymen, the eager lads from your schools and colleges, and usually the best of them, who have spent their lives during the last century and a half in achieving the miracle of making this huge derelict into one of the most amazing pieces of constructive government that the world has ever dreamed of. Pause for a moment to think of the many of them who died in their prime in the services of India, who have left their young wives and their children to lie in those dusty pathetic graveyards that are scattered over the whole of India. They are the graves of the British middle class, the everyday intelligentsia, the plain men who tried to do their duty; remember also, that the proportion, who fail to creep home when all the world is brown, is far larger than in the ordinary walks of life.

India, whose pear-shaped peninsula we know without much idea of size, is in rough figures for the purposes of memory, 1800 miles from north to south, viz. from Cape Comorin to the Khaiber, and 1800 miles across from Assam to the coasts of Sind, and the area is 1,800,000 square miles, and lest the figure eighteen be not sufficiently emphasized note also that it was in the eighteenth century of blessed memory that British India took definite form, and the reconstruction began of the mess which had accrued from crash of the great Turkish overlay, yclept the Mogul Empire.

By the census of 1931 the population is 353 millions; here pause, those who live in forty million Britain and wonder how we all live even in these little islands. To make the problem easier let it also be stated that this is an increase of 11 per cent or thirty-four millions (34,000,000) in ten years! And again take off your hat to the great rule that goes on while even our Press Correspondents sleep, and makes life and peace and order possible. Incidentally let it be remarked that the population of Europe, less Russia, is 375 millions and its size about the size of India.

The Terrain

What like is this immense land? As well ask what like is Europe! It is an ancient land covered with the ruins of ancient peoples, of great kingdoms and empires, and of romantic histories. It has been the home of learning before Rome was; it was old and highly cultured when Alexander of Macedon came out of Persia. It has every climate in the world within its area, and can grow all the fruits of the earth, between those 29,000 feet of Everest and its seas. In some parts it has a yearly rainfall of 500 inches, in others but 6. On the west is a great wall of plateau edge that faces the sea, and from that edge vast plains slowly fall away to the deltas and flats of the eastern snow-fed rivers. The great rivers, the Ganges and the Indus, and their tributaries carry a large sailing marine of country boats, and before the railways came carried numerous steamers. Down in the south, the lands break into great mountains of good rainfall and cool winds, and there grow tea and coffee, and there too gold is mined.

In the romantic country north of Central India the deserts, rugged raw-red hills, and fertile oases of Rajputana hold sway. The Punjab is a great and often arid plain, through which the *Panj-ab*, the five waters, the *funf avon*, bring down the snows of the Himalaya, now spread over the lands by the astounding irrigation systems of the British engineers. The Ganges and its tributaries flow for hundreds of miles through fertile arable lands, rich also with the waters and silts of the Himalayas. Under this great wall, which forms the north-eastern boundaries, the submontane tracts grow again the teas and fruits of the more temperate zones. Here are scattered those pleasant retreats that the Europeans first built to escape from the summer heat, and which the Indian has now learnt to appreciate. The southern seasons are always warm and often moist, the centres have a pleasant winter and a hot summer tempered by an early rainy season. The north has a magnificent winter with frosts and cold nights, and a scorching long summer to make up for it, with a rainy season that is late in coming, and brings little, if any, amelioration of temperature. But the north breeds men, and some contemptuous North Indian folk will tell you that the south breeds monkeys, which is but a way of saying that heat, malaria, in-breeding, premature marriage, and short commons combine to make something very different to the great wheatmeal-fed men of the Punjab. The semi-historical myth of the war with the Monkey God and King of the South is but the expression of Aryan contempt for the lesser races of Dravidian India.

A Few Figures

Here are a few of the figures that assist the *coup d'œil.* There are, as has just been said, 353 million inhabitants, according to the census of 1931, which is an increase of no less than 34 millions in ten years. That alone is making the economists anxious, and the contraceptionists active. This too when baby clinics and welfare is likely to decrease the heavy infantile mortality, in spite of which this vast increase has taken place. So fertile can this land be, where there are no unmarried adult women, that a few years ago a farmer's wife near Delhi gave birth to five perfectly good sons.

The population of Europe less Russia is 375 millions, that of the United States 125 millions, of Russia 147 and of China 342. The population of the world has been estimated at 1849½ millions, so that India represents one-fifth of the whole. That fact alone should make us wonder and marvel.

The different languages of this continent of 353 millions are 222 of which twenty are spoken by over a million people, and twelve of them by over seven millions each.

India is a country that lives by agriculture, and British India alone has an area of over 1166 million acres of which less than a quarter are unculturable. Its live-stock, of which, however, a good proportion is inferior and a loss more than a gain, is 218 millions, over 154 millions being bovine.

Ninety-five per cent of the population is purely rural as compared with 21 per cent in England and 70 per cent are actual cultivators. The birth-rate is the exceedingly high one of 35 per cent. With these few figures to stimulate our imagination we are the better prepared to see what living India really is.

Some Fundamental Conditions of Life

To even begin looking at India with the eye of discernment there are a few great facts of Indian life worth understanding which will materially alter the outlook of this country for all who think of it at all. In the first place, save to a limited extent in Calcutta and the big seaports, or the largest of up-country towns, there are practically no shops as *we* understand the word. Such as there are, are entirely for the use of the small proportion of Europeans, and the wealthier of the westernized Indians. There are, of course, countless booths, all over the land in which goods are displayed at tiny windowless fronts. They are largely cotton and woollen piece goods, locally grown foods, and copper or leather workers' shops and kindred industries. But since there are practically no shops, there are no shop assistants as we know the word, there are no accountants, no jobs for Indian young ladies behind glass screens. This means that there is no employment in this sort of life for all the countless young men of the lesser intelligentsia who crowd out with a European education, as would be the case in the West. The little open booths may sell and do sell European goods, drugs, etc., but in almost every case the shopkeepers' sons or relatives give any assistance that is required.

There are practically no banks, except in the great cities and they are largely for the use of Europeans and of big Western business. The ordinary Indian does not bank or invest. His savings are on his wives' ankles, arms and necks, in the shape of ornaments of silver and gold. Banks, as we understand the word in the West, do not exist in the interior. There is, of course, an immense indigenous banking and financial system for trade purposes, that has existed for countless years and has spread all over the East. Many of the bankers' words and bonds are famous far outside India, but they do not bank as we bank; they do not need hosts of neatly dressed westernized clerks or branch managers. The wealthy financiers and bankers who can draw bills of exchange on Kashgar or Samarkand for vast amounts, work underground with a few iron-shod chests, with a clerk sitting on the floor, a reed pen in his hand, writing in a language and a script chiefly used by bankers. It serves the Eastern purpose but it does not employ the lesser intelligentsia. The transactions may be immense, the overhead charges are almost nil. This again is because the economic system of the country cannot support our costly way and does very well with its own.

Then again, there is very little piped water supply, and certainly outside the westernized portions of the great cities there is no house-to-house supply. The stand-pipes in the city roads appear the height of civilization, but all the half-million villages are supplied by wells or from tanks, or the passing stream.

There is no waterborne sewage at all, outside a very small portion of the very latest seaport towns. Even in the European portions of New Delhi there is only hand removal. The mass of better-to-do Indians have hand removal from their houses, the women from the roofs. The ancient racial construction of society has produced a race of professional and exclusive 'night soil' removers. The millions have no conservancy at all. In the villages all sexes and ages use the fields to the great boon of agriculture.

The meaning of all this is, that the scale of production of the land cannot carry much more comfort. The East gets what it can afford and what suits its needs.

A few years ago a very humane zealous British magistrate and his wife spent several years working at the social uplift of a district. They organized 'guides' who should tell the villagers of all that Government was doing, of agricultural and veterinary benefits, of medical and midwifery help; they taught them to bury the village refuse, to use latrines . . .

the local schoolmasters composed odes in the praise of the latrine and those who taught them to use them. The *sahib* and his lady spent much private money on their work of love and sympathy. Pamphlets were written, others urged to do likewise. But alas when the couple went elsewhere it did not take long for the district to slip back into its own simple insanitary no-bother-at-all way. An equally sympathetic and even more experienced officer, who has recently traversed this district, records that now only if a European is seen approaching are refuse trenches and latrines hastily dug. The people recognize and approve, but inertia and ways they know, suit them best. That was in the north, where the heat can be so great for months on end that nobody cares about anything—an aspect of India that the visitors never see. It was Mr. Pagett, M.P., who was cozened to stay, when 'mosquitoes found him a treat', and learn.

Then think! there are no hats worn in India; a small number of Moslems wear the crimson fez, a few thousand Parsees have a special hat. The hundreds of millions wear a cotton cloth over the head in the case of women, a longer or shorter whisp of rag round the head in the case of men. Think of it! Not one single hat-shop in our sense of the word. Where are the travellers, salesmen, and designers, among these millions? They are not needed.

This curious fact will bring you back to the old truth, that you can't get more out of life than the land will let you get. You cannot grow richer if a day's hard work will barely feed you and you have no cash crops, or if you can grow cash crops, and nobody wants them, which is the strange position of so many agriculturalists all the world over. Truly India is a grim stepmother to all her people, so that many by working all day on their land can only keep body and soul together, and have not the energy to do more in their climatic range even if you can show them how.

The tragedy of the contact between East and West as the foolish old Gandhi does in this case clearly see, is that you are teaching people to want more than they can get. It is no good producing or trying to produce gramophones for the Indian million or even the more comfortable necessaries, if by no stretch of imagination and no exercise of energy they can possibly earn the money for them.

CHAPTER II

INDIA IN LEGEND AND HISTORY

It has well been said, that as a man cannot get away from his shadow, so a country cannot get away from its history. Even the modern super-progressive West is inseparably wedded to its past, perhaps most so when it leasts suspects it. In India, however, this anchoring is quite inexorable, and it is impossible to follow any of the problems of India or understand and sympathize with her religions, and marvel at her disabilities, without a bowing acquaintance with the historical outline whether as a visitor or a sojourner.

The controversy of the untouchables is as deeply mixed up with the last five thousand years as any of the problems of India. The unbridgeable rift between Muhammadan and Hindu is but the survival of a thousand years. The dissensions of Hinduism itself were old when Christ was born into the world, and some of its Princes trace their descent and the privileges which they are in no wise prepared to relinquish, to happenings of long before Caesar crossed the Channel, or even Xenophon marched to the sea.

That being so, a brief outline is given here as a fit and proper or indeed the only gambit with which a book which aims at showing the India of to-day, the Living India of the fields, the jungles and the bazaars to the anxious but sympathetic eyes of the West, may open.

The Coming of the Aryan

The known history of India is one of the most astounding stories, and told in detail would fill innumerable complex volumes. Yet India's history of precision, and that only occasional, probably dates from the writing of the Alexandrine historians,[1] they who knew the men who made the Alexandrine legend. But now, just as we thought we had some finality, lo! the spade of the archaeologist has found that a civilization rivalling and contemporary with that of the first Babylonia—a very different thing from upstart and recent Nebuchadnezzar, and perhaps even more powerful—was existing in India. It has incidentally disposed of the pleasant Aryan fiction that out of their great desert-minds the civilization of India grew, when in reality as the Goth learnt civilization from conquered Rome, or the Saxon from civilized Britons, they may have got it from more ancient Dravidia. However that may be, the whole story is so complex that only sufficient can be said here to explain some of the phenomena of modern India, and Britain's share in the restoration.

It is to be realized that somewhere in Central Asia some happening—probably a gradual change in the climate or even a dry cycle in which steppes grazing disappeared, or contrarily some excess of rain that filled the valleys with sand from the mountains for the winds to scatter to the smothering of plough—set tribes a-moving.

Thence came, it would seem, separated perhaps by generations, three great waves of a white race, or group of races, seeking for new and better lands and a better scale of existence. One wave apparently went to Persia, one over the Caucasus to Europe, and the third into the Oxus valley and over that mighty river, swirling up and round the valleys of the Afghan highlands. Thence eventually, in how many centuries or how many generations we know not, the migrants crossed the Indus and swarmed into the valleys of the five rivers of the Punjab. From thence by way of Sirhind, the 'Head of Hindustan', they came to the great plains of the Ganges and the Jumna, and swarmed up into the more habitable valleys of the Himalaya. Nor need we marvel at the distance of any of the treks of ancient times. To folk who travel *khaneh per dosh* (house on back) with nothing to do save fish

[1] Arian used the last history of Ptolemy.

and hunt and see the day in and the day out, thousands of miles are as easily covered as hundreds. It is as easy as the moving motor caravan and eventually as long-ranged in its result.

Now the years and the dates of these moving waves is lost in the mists of time, but it seems probable that the early part of the third millennium before Christ might be about the period.

They swept into India a simple patriarchal people and they had a simple faith in the owners and masters of the elements, and they did not think very deeply. But when the stress of the conquest was over and the main lands of the rivers, the Punjab and the Gangetic plains were colonized, perhaps before, their active Aryan minds began to think and to form theories of life, and to formulate beliefs, and their priestly duties became more complex and the priestly status hereditary. Thus the faith that we call Brahminism and its popular shape of Hinduism evolved.[1] Now let it be realized here that Hind, Sind, Ind are the same, and Hindu and Indian are equivalent or rather identical words, and that Hinduism is not a word that the people of India, except so far as they have accepted Western nomenclature, use of their own religion. The Aryan invaders slowly climbed the Aravalli mountains that bar North from Central India, penetrated the jungles, went round by the coast, and eventually brought into some form of temporal and religious suzerainty the peoples of India. When the great caste grouping took place in a manner to be outlined hereafter, the country became Indianized. The people were Hindu, viz. Indian, of intertwined races, and there was a very comprehensive religion in which thousands of deities were accepted as local manifestations of the presiding deities of the Aryan conception. All of these could be thought of anthropomorphically to the *n*th degree. Hinduism is therefore the polyglot religion of the people of India, before such disturbing things as Islam appeared on the scene to upset the great network that the Brahmin had woven.

[1] Explained more fully in Chapter V.

That network was rudely torn in the height of its complexity, torn to ribbons for centuries, by the rise of the Kshattriya Prince, Gautama Siddartha, an Aryan of Aryans born at Kapila-vastu in the Hindu state of Nepal. He it was, as the *Buddha* or 'Enlightener' born in 557 B.C., who, disappointed at the evil of the world and the helplessness of the Brahminical teachings to show an effective way of life, after seeking far and near for enlightenment and truth at the hands of many disappointing teachers, evolved the famous holy 'Way'. The influence of 'The Way' grew and grew, and about the time of the birth of Christ had spread nearly over the whole of India. During these centuries, however, there had been in the North many more waves of migrant tribes and invasions of Tartars and Huns, some of whom too learnt to follow 'The Way'. The Buddha lived and taught till 477 B.C., dying in his eightieth year.[1]

The Invasion of Alexander

In 327 B.C.—a century and a half after the death of the Buddha—came Alexander of Macedon seeking to recover a satrapy of Darius, which had extended east of the Indus. India was then divided into many Aryan kingdoms usually at variance, and Alexander conquered some while others sought his alliance.

The history of Alexander is well known, how his men refused to go further than the Hyphasis, which men now call the Sutlej, and how he was compelled to march down the rivers to the Western sea to meet his fleet. He left behind colonies of what we should now call his 'C3' men, but they and his governors endured in India but a little while. The Greek influence that we hear so much of came years later, when the large Greek colonist kingdoms of Bactria in the valley of the Oxus were driven before fresh incoming waves of Jats and Tartars to the Indus. There and in Swat they established that civilization and control which is spoken of as Graeco-Buddhist, and which endured for several genera-

[1] The story of Hinduism and the Buddha is told in brief in Chapter V.

tions. We may realize that Aryan Greek and Aryan Indian were not so greatly removed from each other in affinities. What this civilization meant, the remains of Taxila not far from Rawalpindi, with its magnificent museum, explain to modern eyes eloquently enough, especially when we also realize that this Taxila, a century or so before the Christian era, had a million inhabitants.

Buddhism and Asoka

Within a century of Alexander's departure, one of the large Hindu states that the invader had failed to reach, fell into the hands of the greatest of India's early rulers, Asoka. His dominion approached in its vastness that of Britain in India or of the Mogul Emperor Aurungzebe, nearly two thousand years later. Asoka's rock edicts prescribing laws and rules of life stand to this day over the length and breadth of the land, and more are constantly being discovered. He eventually adopted Buddhism, becoming finally a monk.

Never again has a Hindu or Buddhist monarch been able to exercise such wide world dominion in India, and after his death the kingdoms soon separated. The Tartar invasions added their discords, though many of the newcomers were absorbed as related, into the northern Buddhist kingdoms. After Buddhism had become the almost universal faith, it gradually became as complicated, with its cathedrals, its abbots and its ceremonies, as the Brahminism and Hinduism that it had displaced, and slowly it faded away over the Himalayas, to Tibet, and to Central Asia. By about A.D. 500, the whole country had become Hindu once more with the Brahmin priesthood in full control. The continent remained for many years broken up into Hindu kingdoms, each as large as the great principalities of Europe, and all quarrelling with each other. The rulers almost all came of the old Aryan princely or baronial classes, the Kshattriyas of the Aryan dominations, although in the north Jat and Tartar blood must have been freely mingled therewith.

Eventually Buddhism died out of the land, and in the first thousand years of the Christian era Brahminism succeeded in remodelling the whole of India. It may be said that the old caste system was reaffirmed, having apparently retained much of its vitality. The Brahmins were always there, the children of the hereditary priestly class, far more numerous than the priestly service required and available as soldiers and cultivators. How this came about and its results will be explained in Chapter V.

The Muhammadan Conquest of Sind

In the eighth century came the first sign of the storm that was to alter entirely the face of Indian history. Indeed India was as yet to feel but lightly that great blast conceived in the pot-holes of the desert, that was to roar over half the world like a forest fire, destroying both the wild grasses and trees of the prairie as well as the forest and plantations of civilization. The astounding furore of the desert tribes which had followed the evangel of Muhammad, had swept down to the sea of the Persian Gulf, as well as far inland to Persia and Central Asia, and to the plateaux of Afghanistan.

In the year 712 Muhammad Ibn Qasim brought a great Arab fleet from the Gulf into the mouth of the Indus, and fought desperately with the Rajput chiefs of Sind, conquering their territories and permanently acquiring dominion over Sind, the Indus and its tributaries being especially welcome to the river boatmen from the Tigris.

But with the Conquest of Sind the Muhammadan invasion and conquest stopped for the time being. Within Sind, temples were destroyed and priests slaughtered, and thousands forcibly converted to Islam. After that the land had peace from Muhammadan invasion for nearly four hundred years, while the sons of the Prophet were overcoming the hardy races both Tartar and Aryan of the temperate highlands of Afghanistan and Central Asia. It was not till this was thoroughly done that the movement had gathered sufficient momentum to flow through the

Mountains of Solomon and cross the mighty Indus. Before that came to pass, the Hindu states and their Brahmin spiritual directors had these centuries wherein to consolidate their new order, viz. the general reconstruction of society, already described, that followed the fading of Buddhism. From their own point of view they failed lamentably, for India, just as Europe could not and would not settle down into the bond of the Holy Roman Empire, could not form a bond of Hindu kingdoms in friendly alliance that could stand four-square to the invader. She was to rue her failure in blood and misery and humiliation untold.

The Coming of Turks and Moslems from the North

While the Hindu kingdoms were re-forming and quarrelling one with another over a period of several centuries, and while the lesson of the Conquest of Sind was forgotten, the roaring of the forest fire of Islam across Asia was in full blast. The wild desert swordsmen had bred countless soldiers from among the women of the conquered, and the hordes thus increased had surged round the mountains of Persia and converted many of the Turkish and Tartar races to their faith. Half-Arab, half-Turkish kingdoms opened up at many of the old centres and capitals of the trans-Oxus states. The same waves were surging round the mountain valleys of the land between the Oxus and the Indus that we now call Afghanistan, where Turkish principalities rose and fell and the remnant of Buddhism succumbed before the faith of the Prophet. The Arab and Turkish dynasties thus flourished and fought for several centuries before they thought of crossing the Indus. The old practice of slave-boy *huscarle* was in being and from this custom arose a race of slave-kings in Ghuzni. About the year 1001 one Mahmud, son of Alptagin, slave-king of Ghuzni, hearing much of the wealth of Ind, suddenly led his bands across the Indus into India. He came not to conquer but to ravish, to plunder, and to slay the infidel and destroy his places of idolatrous worship. Times and again he came down; times and again the Hindu princes failed to combine or combined too late, and even so far down as Muttra on the Ganges were the temples destroyed and the priests slain. Times and again too, the Turk went back with long strings of slaves, of looted cattle laden with Hindu riches. At last his son came to stay, and in Upper India, the India of the five rivers, there arose a Moslem kingdom of Northern India and Ghuzni, which lasted for close on three hundred years and which was in turn succeeded by another Turkish dynasty of very similar origin. Both of these conquered more and more of India, till at length the Rajput city of Delhi was captured, and then the disgusted Rajputs 'upped sticks' and fled before Islam and the Turk, and finally settled amid the inaccessible mountains and jungles and occasional fertile valleys of what is known as Rajputana or Rajasthan. Then the rule of Islam and the setting-up of baronies and states by Turk and Afghan leaders of horse took place all over India, down to the Deccan and *far Bengal. Except in the fastnesses of Rajputana and in* the far south, the green flag of the Prophet and the Crescent ruled supreme. And so it lasted so far as Northern India goes, through Slave Kings, Tuglaqs, Lodis, Sayads, Afghans and all the well-known kaleidoscopic phases of Delhi and its seven cities. Such Moslem states as Bhijapur, Golconda, Ahmednagar, Patna, Murshidabad and Dacca sprung up in the south and east, often more or less independent of Delhi. Then when Tudor Henry reigned in England, with the last Delhi dynasty tottering, there came out of Ferghana in 1526 a Chagatai Turk known as Baber the 'Tiger', claiming India as a descendant of that Timur who had once conquered her. And he won the crown of Delhi on one of those battles on the famous common field of Panipat.

The Mogul Empire

How Baber's dynasty rose and fell for a while does not matter here; suffice it to say that in the days of our Elizabeth, Prince Akbar a youth, grandson of Baber, son of Humayun, a minor in charge of guardians, seized the power into his own eager hands and consolidated the foundations of the Mogul Empire. Mogul or Mongol was an incorrect name, for they were Turks not Mongols, but since Baber's mother was descended from Ghengis Khan the great Mongol conqueror, and because Mogul was a name of fear in Indian eyes, they did assume that appellation.

Akbar was the most enterprising soldier and the most humane administrator since the days of far-off Asoka. He *tried to blend his Hindu and Moslem subjects, the latter* Afghan and Turkish colonists and both Hindus converted by the sword in the past centuries. Then came three more great Moguls, whose titles, by which they are known, sing themselves as they go, *Jehangīr*, *Shahjehān*, *Alămgīr*. Alamgir is more often known by his own name of Aurungzebe, and he by conquest absorbed all India and ruled over almost as much as the British. After a long reign he died in the reign of our Anne, an intolerant fanatical Moslem; and with him died the Mogul Empire. It tottered on through rebellion, schism, fission and feebleness, for close on a century, and nominally for a century and a half but Alamgir the 'World Grasper' was the last of Great Moguls to be great. They were great names to conjure with, these three, the 'World Encircler', 'The King of the World', 'The World Grasper', and their fame, and their might, and their magnificence dazzled both East and West, and lasted when their names were but a fable. Even till 1835 the British cast the coinage in their name, and now 'None so poor to do them reverence'. They built on sand and they have gone. But let it be noticed that since about 1100 not only has the greater part of India been ruled by stranger dynasties, but mostly by Turks at that.

The Growth of the Ruling Princes

During the fall of this dazzling Empire arose the States and Princes of India. The old Rajput princes whose daughters Akbar married so frequently for peace's sake, were always rulers, even if vassal rulers, but most of the others are descended of barons, governors of provinces, or leaders of horse summoning to themselves every masterless man, who carved out principalities, with their hands one against the other. The Mahrattas whose little baron Sivaji carved out a tributary kingdom in Alamgir's time, are in a class by themselves.

It should be realized that some two-fifths of India is in the hands of the ruling Princes, who number some six hundred, and whose subjects number approximately a fourth of the population of 353 millions. How do they come to be, in view of the fact that the Mogul Empire extended over practically the whole of India? The answer is a complicated one. The Princes may be divided into five general categories. *First* those Princes who ruled their own states as tributary to the Empire, though these states were far older, and who had only bowed the head by force of arms. The *second* are those governors of districts and provinces who broke away from a weakened Empire in the stage of crashing and set up on their own. The *third* comprises those leaders, captains of horse and the like, who in the great anarchy in the wild Central India and Khandeish set up for themselves merely by force of arms. The *fourth* are those whom the British themselves have created, either in preference to annexation of a derelict state, or as rewards for services, while the *fifth* are those who voluntarily sought our protection after the Company had assumed control of the Mogul area.

In the *first* category come the majority of the Princes of Rajputana, who, as already related, had for the most part been driven to migrate to that inhospitable country to escape from the conquest of the Turkish and Afghan invaders from the North. For long they had retained their independence, had fallen to Akbar's arms and conciliatory policy, and in the break-up of the Empire were saved by the British from ruthless conquest at the hands of the Mahrattas. In this category would also have come the Mahratta Kingdom of Satara the relict of Sivaji, had it remained.

In the *second* category comes first and foremost, the great ex-viceroy, the Nizam of Hyderabad, not only a Mogul governor by descent who had broken away, but a real Mogul or Turk. The Kingdom of Oudh, another Mogul Vice-royalty, similarly lasted, but after years of misrule and generations of warnings its ruler was deposed in 1856 and his country annexed. The title King of Oudh was granted indeed by the British, the last effective Mogul ruler had been the Nawab Vizier of the Empire, who was of Persian origin. Had the kings listened to the British advice, and ruled with moderate efficiency or conducted their court with even moderate decency, they would have remained as does the Nizam to this day.

In the *third* category come those chiefs of the Mahratta confederacy, who started kingdoms of stolen lands in the crash, who fought the British constantly, who finally accepted British suzerainty and abided by their treaties. Of the famous five, the Peishwa fell of his own folly, the Bhonsla through want of heirs, but Sindiah, the Gaikwar, and Holkar remain.

In the *fourth* come those actually created or recreated by the British, such as Kashmir and Mysore, for various reasons. In the *fifth* category would be what are known as the Phulkian States of which Patiala is one, whose rulers readily preferred an alliance and took British protection to save them from an acquisitive and powerful neighbour. All these states, large and small, were and are in direct treaty with the British Crown. At one time these treaties were very divergent, made by separate authorities and at varying periods. By mutual agreement these have for the most part been remade and drafted to make the general relationship much the same.

It is possible to have many legal arguments about these relationships and what they perpended in the past, but the one clear point that governs the problem is that the British stand exactly where the Mogul stood, as the overlord or paramount power of India. If anyone asks why, or how, there is no need to go further than to say, by exactly the same title as the Mogul, the excellence of that title being thrice strengthened by the general justice and benevolence and evolutionary nature of the rule.

The Princes of India, especially all those who owe their preservation to the British, have always been loud and active in their loyalty. Similarly, justice and neighbourliness have made those who had to be conquered equally firm in their devotion to the Crown. It is this fact of their alliance that makes them so jealous of their position *vis-à-vis* any attempt to make an all-India Government.

All the 'Princes' States' are romantic and interesting and some of them present in their life many of the features of a thousand years ago, which in no way minimizes the general content of their people.

The Coming of the Western Traders

It was not till the Mogul days when Western sailors were well versed in sail, and took the courage in their hands that brought them round Cape Horn and the Cape of Good Hope, that the first signs of the modern state of affairs in India came into evidence. The early Portuguese and other traders who came to the Indian coast did so during the days of the Great Moguls, though the Mogul jurisdiction was not yet spread over all India. But Mogul India then, barring local rebellions, was an organized Empire with its admirals on the sea, and a great centralized organization, with its provinces and Governors. Soon the trading powers of the West sought concessions for their nationals, and the chartered companies arose merely to secure rights and ventures without which authority and usually monopoly, private capital would not venture so far afield. When the trading ventures became organized and partly national, it was by the general licence of the Mogul Government. Had that Government remained in being, the companies trading to the East would be in very much the same position as the traders and powers are in Shanghai to this day, viz. as a local settlement existing under licence and treaty with the Chinese Government.

Calcutta would even have been as Shanghai, had the Mogul Empire survived as an effective Government. Because that Government crashed, the French and British traders had to fend for themselves. Portugal had already exhausted its colonizing and sea-faring petrol. Then England and France began, to save themselves, to acquire territorial influence and even possession. What had originally been night-watchmen and caravan guards developed into companies, companies then grew into battalions, and factories into Government houses. Allies sought their protection and assistance in the general smash-up of central authority. Thus began almost independently the three British Presidencies of Madras, Calcutta and Bombay, the Island of Bombay coming to Britain as part of the dowry of Catherine of Braganza, Charles II.'s Queen, another of the many things that maligned monarch brought us, and perhaps the greatest that the world has ever dreamed of as dowry.[1]

The French more than the English rode the more jealous, and for close on seventy years the two nations quarrelled as to who should be predominant in India. When France went to war with Britain, the trading companies and their troops fought in India, and the sea power of Britain clinched the argument.

The Rise of the British

To Britain, far more by chance than design, fell India after the ousting of the French. That solution of the British difficulties only applied to the South and Lower Bengal. There Britain now reigned as paramount among the extremities of the falling Empire, whose control had always been least felt far from the nerve and power centre. The story of how power grew, how it fell into our hands, and how hostile combinations that should more wisely have let us alone, but served to aggrandize the British Raj, is a long

[1] It is an open question whether under the provision of the White Paper the Island of Bombay, like Aden, should not return to Britain, who lent it to India.

romantic story, and not to be retold here. It was not till the days of Warren Hastings, so late as 1774, that any attempt was made to put the independent settlements of the distant company in London under the general control of the Governor of what was becoming the major one. It was not till the coming of the great Governor-General of the Wellesley family, Lord Mornington who was later the Marquis Wellesley, in the end of the last decade of the eighteenth century, that his clear vision saw what was inevitable in India, if India was to have peace, and British and world trade to progress. Even he but planned a small British India, with the Princes connected by alliances with Britain as the paramount power. Yet it is his dream enlarged that remains fulfilled to this day. His dream stopped at the Sutlej, with a line of inner and outer states between India and the Allies, France and Russia. Because the freebooting parvenu states of the Mahratta group endeavoured to oust the British he decided that their strength must be sufficiently broken to make them keep their treaties, keep within their own boundaries, and be guided in major outside policy by the advice of the British. They fought and they fought hard, with all the strength of their French trained armies, their French officers and their great artillery, and they were beaten, beaten by Arthur Wellesley and General Gerald Lake and an enthusiastic Indian soldiery with a European spear-head of the British line. The blinded, whimpering, old pantaloon who had once been a Mogul Emperor, if a feeble one, was rescued from durance vile and placed in pensioned comfort. The masterless territories around Delhi were annexed, the Mahratta chiefs brought into alliance, and the British frontier brought into touch with the nominal Afghan frontier which Afghan invasion and conquest had brought down to the River Sutlej. South of the Sutlej between the Punjab and the British lay the buffer Phulkian states protected by British support. Across the Sutlej the brilliant one-man one-life domination of the Moslem province by the small Sikh community was beginning, and the British plan aimed at the line of inner and outer buffers to India aforesaid, of which the Punjab under Sikh rule was to be one. An inexorable fate drove Britain on to the control of what was awaiting her—the whole or nearly the whole of the Mogul domain. After prolonged attempts to maintain a Sikh régime there, the Punjab fell from its own rottenness, to be followed by the Kingdom of Oudh. The almost inevitable policy of getting control of the Mogul province of Afghanistan failed through bad execution and bad planning, but by 1856 British India with all its tributary stars and satellites was accomplished, and since those days Britain by Crown and Company has worked to restore and improve a thousand-fold, the fabric that came to her by such a series of curious chances, and by the prowess of her sons.

The tragedy of the mutiny of the Bengal Army, which made the Crown resume its Commission to the East India Company, is outside the story. The change was not so revolutionary as it sounds.

This story of British India is a drama of which every chapter is worthy of study for its own sake, especially those studies which give the colour of the grand adventure. Lest anyone should think that the famous East India Company was a coterie of profiteers, the despatches from its courts and the wisdom and sympathetic outlook towards the people and the princes shown therein, are well worthy of study, and tell a different story.

That is the story, in a galloping panorama, of India's past. Before, however, trying to see the India of to-day, a little more history is unavoidable as we glance at the religions and the languages and the races that go to make up this complex continent, which the Moslems called Hindustan in the centre, and by various names elsewhere. India for the whole is the British name.

CHAPTER III

THE LAY OF THE LAND

Rivers and Rifts

Because here in England we cannot realize size, we who pack 40-odd million people into a country meant to carry half that number, it is no bad thing to attempt to grasp the main features of Indian geography, recounted in words of one-syllable metaphor.

First let us again envisage the main figures already given. Population 353 millions, length from north to south, from Cape Comorin to Peshawur 1800 miles, breadth from west to east from Karachi to the vicinity of Assam also 1800 miles. The shape of India is well known, and need not be descanted on, hanging out of the map like a blunted icicle. Those of us who see a good orographical or raised map know the look of the astounding great wall of the Himalaya, the 'Abode of Snow', that leaves the Indian Peninsula lying far below the great uplands of Tibet and Central Asia, and the strangled, torn, and tumbled ways that lead from the Afghan plateaux to the low-lying valley of the Indus. The great wall of the Himalaya has been an almost effective barrier to the infiltration of the Mongol races from that side, but through the more open and accessible, if grim and overhung, Afghan passes the great waves of racial tides have poured into India from the human matrices on the Central Asian steppes. Through the ages, almost before time was, have they come . . . Dravidian, Aryan, Jat, Tartar, Turk and Mongol . . . to make this strange warp and weft which the West calls India, from the people of Hind or Sind and the Indus.

The general geography of India is not hard to understand if we once fix in our mind's eye the lay of the great rivers. There are many rivers in India, and they are divided into two distinct classes: the first, those that are perennial, fed from the snow reserves of the Himalaya; and the second, those rising in the lower plains and hills of internal India, which rush through wide beds in the rainy season and drop to the merest trickle in the long dry months of the year, bursting into slighter freshets when some of the seasonal storms come by.

In the first class are the two mighty systems that give life to internal India, the Indus system and the Ganges system; the Ganges being that holy stream on which the invading white race of Aryans came to their final rest and developed their religions and their culture. Of the same nature, but almost outside India proper, is the Brahmaputra, which runs from the great table-lands of snowy Tibet down to India through Assam and enters the Bay of Bengal through the same delta as Mother Ganges tumbling off the high Tibetan plateau in an astounding succession of rapids. For the moment the former may be disregarded, and the Indus and the Ganges are the great features which should engage our attention. To understand them let us imagine the apex of India as a northern corner walled inside by the Suleiman mountains and their subsidiaries on the Afghan or north-west side, and the Himalaya on the Tibet or north-east side. Then we can understand the river systems, the Indus running down below the Afghan wall to the south-west and the Indian Ocean, the Ganges to the south-east into the Bay of Bengal. So close are the water-partings of these two great valleys, that there is a spot on a spur a few miles out of Simla at the old toll-bar, where if stood by on a wet day the drippings from one side of your umbrella would go into the Indus system, and from the other into that of the Ganges and finally enter the sea a thousand miles apart. There is something to think about! But though the Indus runs close under the Afghan hills, it draws its main waters, except for those of the Kabul River, from the Himalayan snows just as do the Ganges and her tributaries. The Indus is fed, in addition to its own Tibetan sources, by the famous five rivers of the Punjab, the word that itself is Persian for five waters. In fact '*Panj-ab*', and 'Five or *Funf avons*', are but the same Aryan words in different hats. The five rivers, the Jhelum, the mighty Chinab, which, as its name shows, is the 'River out of China', the Ravi, the Sutlej and the Beas, all bring down also the snow-fed waters. Time was when they but rolled away from the mountains to the sea, untapped save by a few inundation canals of the snow-flood season. Now, thanks to the amazing British irrigation engineers and their Indian assistants, each of them carries head-works equal in magnitude and skill to that of Assouan, and spread the waters over the arid grazing lands of the disappearing camel. Millions of acres of wheat and barley shine in brightest gold in early summer, by the soaking from thousands of miles of canals. Hundreds of thousands of colonists have been put into the plains that were so sparsely populated in the old time before. Never in fact has a 'satanic Government' been so saturnine! Under the eastern wall the Ganges and its principal tributary, the Jumna, rising among the great snows and the twin peaks of Gangotri and Jumnotri, hurry to the Bay of Bengal giving up, however, their waters also to great canal systems, so that not two blades of grass or corn grow where one grew, but a hundred. That is the real mark that British energy and planning have made for India, the millions and millions of acres that once were sand and desert and are now cornfields. Nor is it the work of the British engineer alone, but of the British investor who has lent money to poor India at a quarter the interest that any of their own investors would dream of doing. That, however, is part of the economic and not the geographical story, save that geography may brighten at the gold of the corn.

Into the Ganges and the Jumna come a few lesser streams such as the Gogra which also bring down the snows of the nearer Himalaya as the big rivers pass below the mountain wall.

The country watered by these two systems, the Indus and the Ganges, has one fundamental difference. The Ganges valleys are within the area of the full summer rains, and therefore are not devoid of water. The Indus rivers and their tributaries run through a country outside the regular relief of the rainy season, which gasps and pants for water. To the Punjab, the Land of the Five Rivers, the canal systems have given a new and teeming life. In the Ganges system they have but added to and made more certain the prosperity which the rainy season to some extent ensured. In the British Islands we cannot realize the effect of the long waterless months when the cattle show every rib to the counting, and can hardly even search for the lost blades of grass, nor the joy when the rains come and the grass grows again as a miracle in the night-time.

The Western Table-land

So much for the great rivers at this moment, and we have done enough if we can see in our mind's eye these two great mountain walls with the plains at their foot through which run the huge rivers, to the right hand and to the left, parallel to the mountains. Let us now turn to the western coast, and we shall see another and a different natural phenomenon of the hardening crust. Here it is as if the great pan of molten India had been tipped up at the west, and solidified thicker at the west and shallower in the eastern plains where the Ganges runs. The result of this tipping has been that when the casting came out of the mould as it were, there was a great and solid ridge of cliff and mountain facing the western sea, the shore of the Indian Ocean or Arabian Sea, for it carries both names at your fancy. This great wall that varies from one to two thousand feet in height is known as the Western Ghats or more generally as the Ghats. An up-ended line of rugged mountains, it runs from near Surat, north of Bombay far down to the south for many hundreds of miles. There it rises into great table-lands several thousand feet high. *Ghat* has many meanings, such as 'pass', 'ascent', 'steps', etc., but 'ascent' is perhaps the rendering that covers most cases. Between the Ghats and the sea itself runs a low-lying strip of fertile coastal plain, though here and there some spur or bastion of the Ghats runs actually down to the salt sea. While on the sea side the Ghats present a rugged line of steep mountain-side, often capped with cloud, on the inside it is otherwise, for the rugged line is but the edge of the plateau, the surface of the tipped-up pan of hardening crust. From the top of the Ghats it slowly falls to the low level of the Ganges plain or is up-ended again into coastal hills before it actually comes to the Bay of Bengal. Through the Ghats are numerous passes crowned with baronial and royal castles of the land-owners and freebooters, who have lived on the traders' tolls with or without authority. Now and again some small river comes through but the trend of the rivers is all to the east. These are the big river-beds that are roaring rivers or trickling streams according to the season, the Godaveri, the Kistna, the Cauveri (Kaveri).

Central India

With the trend of the rivers outlined we have the main features of the Indian borders, the two great snow-fed river systems, and the up-tilted western wall of the Ghats that sets the peninsula part of India draining to the east. Let us now glance at Central India, using that expression in general senses apart from the lesser area known as 'Central India' and the 'Central Provinces', to include everything between the Punjab and the Ganges Plains just described and the western table-land or Deccan.

It is the country that the navigable water-ways did not touch, and contains the great wastes and the rocky hills of Rajputana or Rajasthan to which the chiefs and clans be-took themselves to escape from Islam as related. The Ridge at Delhi, that little stony outcrop of heroic memory, is but the commencement of a long mountain range, the Aravallis, which rise and swell into considerable mountains in Rajputana, and run south-west almost to the sea. This range, often waterless and covered with dense thickets and forests, was the great barrier and bugbear to the Aryan colonists thousands of years ago, for whom the famous Aryan sage prayed that the mountains might be made lower, *i.e.* be penetrated and passed. South of the Aravallis the River Chambal drains any spare water to the Ganges, and carries off the rain floods.

These wide river-beds that we see from a-top the high steel bridges, as we rumble over them, often at night, have produced in our later days some of the greatest bridge-builders of the world. The great broad-gauge line to Delhi rumbles over the wide Chambal for all the world to see, and as the Chambal Bridge is, so are a hundred more in the land.

Between the Chambal and the Deccan we find Central India proper, with two rivers that run the opposite way—to the west. These are the great Nerbudda and the lesser Tapti, two that bear no snow, and like the rivers of the Deccan, are trickles in a wide stony bed, till the monsoon bursts and brings down the great spates. The Vindhya mountains separate the east-and-west-running Chambal and Nerbudda, and the Satpura hills, home of aboriginal Bhils and of tigers, divide the Nerbudda and the Tapti.

A glance again at the map will show how some 700 miles from the southernmost point of India, the rocky wall of the Ghats breaks to let the Nerbudda and Tapti through into the Gulf of Cambay, and we have a series of flatter countries, the curious pear-shaped isthmus of Kathiawar, the Raun of Kach and the like. At the mouth of the Tapti lies Surat the old Mogul seaport, where the earliest and more important of the merchants and factors of the East India Company first set up their establishment. The old port is one of the most interesting places in India, and only too few stop to rummage there. The map of India shows that here was the shortest road from Delhi to the West, and that Bombay had nothing like the same facilities, save its magnificent harbour. The glories, tragedies and crimes of the earlier merchant adventurers, rovers and free-lances, and the regular ships of the Company, revolve round old Surat. On a line 700 miles from the mouth of the Nerbudda, at right angles to the 700 miles of the coast, lies Calcutta, and for three-quarters of that line runs that great river itself. Near to its head-waters is the big military centre of Jubbulpore, famous for its gorges and its marble rocks, but in 1933 coming to great geological fame by reason of the discovery of several dinosaurs lying in the hard clay close by the modern gun-carriage factory. It has, of course, long been known that geologically this was the oldest part of India, formed long before the Himalayas were thrown up. Curiously enough these dinosaurs are of both the carnivorous and the fish-eating varieties.

The Nerbudda, the centre for long of impenetrable jungles, developed in the eighteenth century a terrible reputation. There in the collapse of Mogul power and authority, rose a nest of land-pirate leaders, to whom went every masterless man, broken moss-trooper or dispossessed freeholder, in large numbers, with their women, captured, light-o'-love, or otherwise. From their jungle fastnesses they issued forth each autumn, the traditional raiding season, spreading over the land for hundreds of miles to pillage, rape and destroy. For generations all India prayed for relief to high heaven, as from the impudent forays of the Mahratta hosts. Perhaps one of the greatest works of mercy that England did for India was to root out this poison, which had grown up during the crash of the Mogul power. When the great *Book of Days* is opened, it is the destruction and uprooting of the Pindari, and the destruction of the astounding cancer of Thuggee, that will bulk among the greatest of the benefits that the British have conferred on India. It was just as are many parts of China now, in the welter that has succeeded the crash of that other great Tartar dynasty, that of Pekin.

In the Kipling metaphor these are other stories, but stories well worthy of study, of all those who would nullify the shameless venom that Mr. Gandhi used to purvey, and has later perhaps abandoned.

So much for the Nerbudda. It is now worth while to remember how this mass of tumbled mountains and jungles have affected the political and also the ethnological side of the Indian story. Out of the mountains came the white races far back in the mists of time. Down the easy roads of the Indus valley and across and along the rivers of the Punjab swept the herdsmen, with little perhaps to hinder them save the walled cities of the Dravidians whose civilization, long considered non-existent, is now springing to light as aforesaid, under the spade of the archaeologist. Then the warrior graziers with their swords and their herds came on as the generations waxed, down the Jumna and the Ganges by the easy ways of the Plains. And then it was that the impenetrable jungles and the rugged mountains of the Central zone stopped them, save when young men, crowded in their patrimony, sought conquest and adventure as the Norman in Ireland, and penetrated thereto. How the Aryan came south and how he guarded himself by what are now the rules of caste—little more rigid than those of white against negro in the United States—against miscegenation and the results of his young men's love and lust, will also be outlined later. Suffice it here to point out that, because the snow-fed water-ways were navigable, up and down the rivers grew the market towns and capital cities the Stokes and the Chipping Camdens and the like, each to each. In our own times for the same reason before the railways drove away impenetrability as they are driving away untouchability, it was up the Ganges and the Jumna that our cantonments and arsenals arose in Hindustan, and on the Indus system. For the same reason Moslem domination followed the water-ways, and it is this geographical and physical condition that accounts for the major portion of the ruling Princes and their states being in this, at one time, inaccessible region. There they could defy Delhi or at most enter into liaison with the Imperial power, or appeal to the common sense of the British successors to the Mogul, and were out of reach of navigable penetrating water-ways. How the Aryan Rajput left his original Hindustan for the inaccessible and arid tracts that we call Rajputana also before the hosts of Islam, in the northern portion of the inaccessible tract, will also be told. Geography and politics are inseparable and that must explain the brief allusion here.

The outline now given should be sufficient for those who dash over the surface of modern India.

One more rough explanation is needed. The surge of the tip-tilted pan of cooling earth referred to which made the wall of the Ghats, here and there bulged into plateaux within the central areas. These plateaux, in addition to affording culturable zone, for the less tropical products of India, produce forests and timbers of great value, climates in which the summers are bearable, rain-fall regular and constant in due season, and a fair park-like land that is good to live in. They also produce many of the minerals of modern needs, notably coal and manganese. It is in this jungle district too, that the old story had its apocryphal origin, of the Indian telegraph clerk at a small wayside station who wired, 'Tiger on platform stationmaster on roof. Please arrange and accept my resignation.' For it is a land to this day where tigers abound, despite the constant clearing of jungle which has so markedly changed the surface of much of the old wild realm.

The Mountains of the South

The mountain ranges of India are, as mountains, nothing to write home about in point of size, till we come to the Himalayas, save perhaps in the far South. The Ghats, the Vindhya mountains, the Satpuras, the Aravallis are no great height, running from 2000 to 4500 feet above the sea, where snow falls not nor hardly ever frost is known. But in the far South the Ghats suddenly surge into great downs and plateaus of surprising height and with an almost European climate. Best known of such are the Nilgherries, the 'Blue

Mountains' and downs, over 6000 feet with some peaks of over 7000. Other outlying ranges are of similar if somewhat less lofty type, the Adamallies, the Pulneys and the Cheveroys, all growing tea and coffee and products requiring a moderate and cool climate. Here, too, snow falls not and a mild frost is the severest drop.

In the Punjab, however, there is a peculiar and romantic range which belies the statement that the lesser hills of India see no frost and snow, for the Punjab is the land of scorching summers and contrasting English winters. There the plains, let alone the low hills, see frost, and this raw red Salt Range even sees snow at times. It flings its way out from the great hills and is but just detached therefrom, and runs along the north-west banks of the Jhelum. Among its rugged spurs and valleys are to be found temples and fort ruins of a long-dead Hindu Raj, temples of perhaps the fourth and fifth centuries A.D. Among modern sights is the great network of caves and galleries cut out of the red rock salt at the Kuti-Kura mines, caves of red glowing pilasters that are lit with electric light on occasions so that the visitor may find himself in fairy-land.

But the glory of the Salt Range is its people—the strapping, hard-bitten Rajput peasantry, who long ago embraced Islam. Primest of soldiers in horse and foot do they make, but are farmers *par excellence*. Here, too, is some genuine remnant of invaders, in the existence of a pocket of true Moguls, Moguls that are born and not made, with a trace of the almond-eye at times, that almond-eye which in most of India has disappeared. There are some racial traits that live for ever, and others that fade.

The mountain folk in the centre of India are often far removed from the Aryan races, and those in the great hilly plateau of Orissa are actual aboriginals as the Sonthals, or even folk such as the Todas who lie far down in the south in the Blue Mountains. In any case all mountains are full of jinns and sprites, of demons and *rackshas*, and *bhuts*, for India is still the most fear- and ghost-ridden country in the world.

There the evil eye is a commonplace, and *churels*, the ghosts of women who die in childbirth, and haunt young men, with their toes turned backwards, are to be watched for and guarded against by high and low alike, for all are fish to a *churel's* net.

CHAPTER IV

THE RACES AND TONGUES OF INDIA

Aryans and Pre-Aryans

In Chapter II. an outline has been given of the amazing history of India, and that history alone must give us the clue to the varying races. The white race, whose influx has been described, soon found that its eager young soldiers were mingling freely with the women of the country they overran.[1] If steps were not taken, ere long the white race and strain of which they were so proud, and which was so mixed up with their traditions and the religious conceptions which were developing, would be lost and drowned in the darker. On the other hand the fertility of the race if kept in its proper channels would soon produce a dominant white folk who might overrun the whole of India. It appears that this is the real origin of the depressed and outcaste races, and in fact of all castes below the three that were the original groupings of the incoming whites, viz. those of priest, which became hereditary and in time racial, warriors and traders. In those classes people who kept the rules remained in them, and those who didn't went down. We see the same thing happening in many countries where white and dark races have mingled.

The result of these invasions was that the races inhabiting the river valleys, where cultivation was possible, viz. the Indus valleys, the valleys of the rivers of the Punjab, the Ganges and the Jumna, are largely Aryan. The earlier races are usually and conveniently called Dravidian themselves and represent, as is believed, an earlier migration still

[1] See Chapter V. for further consideration of this point.

from much the same direction. They, too, must have ruled and mixed with aboriginals some of whose less accessible tracts remained, and indeed remain to this day, not only non-Aryan but non-Dravidian. It now seems probable that it was the Dravidians who may have been the civilized builders of the cities of the new discovery referred to, and that the chapter of early India in the world's histories may some day be written far more fully than is at present the case; in fact many of our imaginings regarding pre-Aryan India will need recasting.

The Aryan race in the Punjab suffered many attacks and invasions subsequent to their settlement by Jats, Tartars, Mongols, and indeed all those peoples conveniently talked of as Sakae or Scythian. It seems to have come to its major colony on the fertile plains of the Ganges and its tributaries, and indeed that is where we find them to this day in their purity, so kept by the caste system, but with plenty of conquered races to their hands as serfs and slaves, such as *Kas* and *Dom* and *Mhar*. From this province of which Ajudiya in Oudh may be considered the centre, warrior colonies pushed far into India, held back to a great extent by the mountains and jungles of the Aravallis and the more southernly forests.

The reconstruction after the waning and death of Buddhism has been explained, and we have now in historical times, of about let us say the Norman Conquest, an India consisting of the priestly class, the Brahmins, spread and spreading all over the land. Then below them is the great warrior class once known as Aryan Kshattriyas, now, with a good deal of blending and additions, known as Rajputs. Next to them the high-caste Aryan trading classes, divided it is true with many inhibitions of their own makings, but as pure white as the Brahmins. Below them again are the countless castes of the Sudras which include the results of miscegenation, and those who, while being Dravidian, had come under the Hindu umbrella and accepted a caste status and the reverence of Brahmins and the cow. By so doing they became, however, lowly and part of the warp and weft of a Brahminized India, and this would include the depressed classes and their extreme left wing, the untouchables. Ethnologically, you have then the scrupulously pure-bred Brahmin, as white as ourselves, as is noticeable in some cases to this day, expecially among the secluded women. In the same category you have the pure trading classes, all of the old white immigration. Thirdly, there is the Rajput class often as white as others but needing a whitewashing so far as the Tartar or Scythian blood in their veins goes. Since the reconstruction, their rules of marriage have kept the legitimate stock as pure as can be for the last thousand years. Nevertheless since military men, as Francis Bacon said, are given to woman as they are to wine, the Rajput blood flows in many by-blown lanes. Apart from that, the old traditional white India is to be seen and recognized easily enough. Below it the variety is immense, and the Dravidian blood predominates. Among them, too, are those pre-Dravidian races who by prowess or the intrigue of ambition have managed to reach within the 'Umbrella' by various processes of climbing.[1]

Quite apart and distinct from these are the eleven million 'animists', the non-Hindu, now partially Christian, tribes of the jungles and plateaux that were formally inaccessible, described in the next chapter.

Ethnologically these aboriginal races belong perhaps to more than one race, there has been Mongoloid infiltration from the Himalaya and there are races that can only be Negrito, races that are as black as any in Africa. They are people whose religious ideas are of the very simplest, and indeed among them it is possible perhaps to learn much of the dawn of civilization, the evolution of religion, and the forming of *homo sapiens*.

The Semite Races

The Moslems of India divide themselves into two kinds, those who are immigrants and those who are merely Indians

[1] This is treated of more fully under religions in Chapter V.

of various castes and peoples who have adopted Islam either under pressure or, as also often happened and as still happens, from conviction. This conversion goes on slowly, usually among the humbler[1] outcaste folk who get as great an uplift in their own consciousness as did slaves who became Christians in the Roman Empire. Theoretically all Moslems are equal before God and man. In India, however, the trammels of caste are so strong that many of the caste prejudices remain among Moslems. In fact, in the villages of the North where many Rajput clans became Moslem hundreds of years ago, a Hindu family priest is necessary to many domestic ceremonies and services.

The incoming colonists, some of whom at the time of arrival were not even Moslem, come roughly in six racial classes, Arab, Aryan, Persian, Tartar—in which are included Turk, Tartar or Mongol[2]—Afghan and Pathan. Their descendants still remain and are known by these racial origins, though since Moslems do not restrict marriage to the same races, but marry where they please without religious or social ban, the Moslem community always tends to be far more homogeneous as the years roll on than any other, save where women of one special race only are available.

In the phraseology of India, the Moslems are divided into four classes, Sheikh, Sayad, Mogul, Pathan. The *Sheikh* is a general title of euphemy, and sheikh or 'chief' applied to all who have been converted, carries no significance, save that it is usually in practice borne by those who can claim no more specific and worthy ancestry. For instance those of the Sheikhs of the Punjab, who are converted Rajput tribes, would call themselves nothing less than Rajputs. *Sayad*, the descendant of the Prophet, is the name by which all Arabs of ancient arrival are known in India and Afghanistan. The claim must be an epynomic one, almost equivalent to being one of the original conquering proselytizing

[1] In the spring of 1933 in Lahore two Indian gentlemen of education, both Hindus of status, embraced the Muhammadan faith, and were publicly received into the Moslem community.

[2] Quite separate from the earlier prehistoric Tartar strain.

Arabs who acquired land in pockets in Central Asia and Afghanistan, and thence came into India to carry on the good work and acquire better lands. *Mogul* stands for all of recognizable Tartar or Turkish origin, and *Pathan* for those just referred to as Afghan as well as Pathan. This distinction is made because, whereas both Afghan and Pathan speak Pushto or Păkhto, and Păthăn means Pakhtan or he who speaks Păkhto, there is a very distinct difference. Into southern Afghanistan, before even the coming of Islam, came an Arabic or Hebrew people calling themselves the Children of Israel who acquired lands and domination in the country now called by their name, the country of the Afghans. These Afghans who are of Semitic countenance call themselves the Ben-i-Israel and claim descent from one Afghana, said to have been a son of Saul of Israel.

On the other hand many of the Pushto-speaking tribes are of perhaps Aryan, Jat or Tartar origin. Hence the difference between Afghan and Pathan. All Afghans are Pathans, all Pathans are not Afghans. The new-comer to India will soon notice the many Pathans and Afghans of the Frontier who are to be seen about the ports and the northern cantonments, by their distinctive dress, and as knowledge comes will even tell their particular tribe. Those Pathans, however, who have been centuries in India, have long adopted the usual Moslem dress of India and are not easily distinguishable. An analogy which may be followed in a good many facets with reference to the domiciled Pathan, would be that of a Scottish Highlander settled in the south for generations, as compared with one down from his glens for the day.

The Semite blood in India then is the descendant of the Arab and Afghan invaders and colonists, who indeed to this day cherish the tradition of origin.

The only trace that the eye will gather of people of Tartar origin will be high cheek-bone and the ever-mysterious almond-eye. But in India the almond-eye even among the Mogul nobles has largely gone, though it is slightly in evidence in agricultural tribes of the northern Salt Range.

By courtesy of Indian Railways Bureau

A Rajput priest and his son

By courtesy of Indian Railways Bureau

The hardy folk of the southern coast A surf boat

Incidentally, it may be said that many an outcaste who has adopted Islam will call himself 'Mogul,' for the sake of a tag of credit attached thereto.

From the foregoing it is not hard to realize that the ethnology of India is of a complex nature.

The Jăts

Among the Hindu cultivating races whose reputation as warriors has always been high, are the Jăts, a great race distinct from the earlier Aryans, who must have entered India as pastoral nomads centuries later. They hold high positions among the castes, yet are not within the Rajput fold, possibly because they were not in the general grouping at the time of the Brahminical reconstruction aforesaid. They will be found in force round Delhi and in the southern Punjab. Their kinship with the people of the west is interesting in that they are very possibly one with the Jut or Jutes of Jutland, and the folk who colonized Kent when the Saxons came. In fact the famous Indian political officer, Colonel Sleeman, wrote to young Prince Dhulip Singh who was a Jăt Sikh—after the British annexation of the Punjab, when he was going to be brought up in England where a house in Kent had been taken for him—'You will be among your own people there for they are all Juts too'.

The Jăt or Jut race in India is a remarkable illustration of the complexity of the Indian ethnological problem and its mixture with the religious one. In Delhi and Gurgaon they are Hindu and the name is pronounced Jăt. In the southern and eastern Punjab they are almost all Sikhs, having adopted Sikhism and Singhism when that faith was acquiring strength.

Again in the western Punjab there are many of the Jăts who have adopted Islam through the centuries. Indeed since all Jăts are cultivators, the term has almost become a name for a cultivator, and many cultivators who are Muhammadans call themselves by the term Jăt without any racial claim thereto. Again in many parts of the Punjab there are

Jăts who are neither Sikh nor Moslem, but are Hindu of ordinary type and fair social status.

Thus we have the southern portion calling themselves Jăts who are all Hindus. We have the northern branch, those who live in the Punjab, calling themselves Jăt, and they may be Hindus, Sikhs or Moslems but are chiefly Sikhs and form the backbone of that community.

A word here of the Sikhs, who will be also treated under religion. The Sikhs are not a race, but are a community, though no doubt the isolation of their religion, if it continues, may some day entitle them to be a race, since races grow by methods of insulation. Anyone may be a Sikh, but the conversions to the reformed religion first preached by Baba Nanak, a high-caste Hindu in the days of Martin Luther, is practically confined to the Punjab and very largely to that magnificent sturdy peasantry of the Jăt race aforesaid. Their sturdy qualities are immensely stimulated by the tenets of Singhism, the militant brotherhood of the faith to which the Sikhs, *i.e.* disciples, were brought in the days of their famous tenth Guru or successor to the leadership of Baba Nanak.

The Languages of India

Though language is no definite proof of racial origin, yet language is inseparably bound up therewith, and an outline of the languages of India may best be included in this chapter on race.

The tongues of India are infinite, some being but ancient developments from a common stock, others of entirely different origin and matrix. The number of different languages, and even those of a common stock are so divergent as to be entirely distinct, is well over two hundred. It is perhaps only the amazing diligence of German linguists that can fully probe the problem. Apart from the general interest of so important a subject, there are the phenomena of derelict and island tongues, much as the Basque and the Etruscan in Southern Europe, which are full of romantic suggestions of a still unprobed past.

The main division of the languages is into those of Dravidian and those of Aryan origin, while into these come the entirely divergent vocabulary of the Arabian and Persian infiltration.

Not only are the languages very different but there is a great variation in script, some that of local development, others varying of design, where as in the Gurmukhi, the Sikh variant of Punjabi, different values are given to existing symbols as in a cypher.

Speaking very broadly, the tongues divide themselves into three following main groups:

(1) Aryan tongues, with great differentiation and eccentric modifications.
(2) Dravidian tongues.
(3) The lingua franca, of the conquering armies.

To these may be added Tibeto-Burman and the minor groups of the Mongoloid and Kolarian language (aboriginal).

The language of the Aryan colonist, whether in India, Persia or the colonies of the West, went on developing as all languages do, in accordance with the needs and the locations of the people. The stereotyping of the cultured Indian form of the Aryan language began when the old religious books and hymns that we know as the *Vedas* were composed, many centuries before Christ. They were not written for many generations but were handed down by memory—always in the past more accurate than the glosses and palimpsests of later copyists—in this case too by the keen and competent Aryan memory of the priests and scholars. We do not quite know when India began to write as well as speak the language of the *Vedas* which from the time it was committed to memory became the cultured language. All over Aryan India, however, the languages went their own way and developed according to needs and climates, into many dialects or *Prakrits*. When writing first came in, texts and religious books were written in dialects, many of which were becoming languages in much the same way that the Romance languages of Europe were being evolved from the Latin basis. As the great Buddhist empire and dominance began to wane as already outlined and the power of Brahmin India to revive, the language of the Aryan scholars and the old tradition became fashionable, and in 300 B.C. Pagani wrote his famous grammar. From that day of stereotyping as has happened elsewhere, the development of a language stops, and we have a correct and classic language. Pagani's was largely the only language of the *Vedas* handed down in those brilliant Aryan memories, and it began to be the language of all literary men in Aryana. It was called the *Sanskrit* or 'built-up' language, as distinct from the *Prakrits*, the developed vernacular tongues. Many of the non-Sanskrit writings, as explained, are written in one of the old *Prakrits* referred to as *Pali*, which merely means 'the old language'. Which of the *Prakrits* it is, however, is not quite certain. The built-up classical language was still used till recent years by Aryan scholars, but is now almost entirely superseded save as a classic, by English, and the analogy of Latin, and the story of Latin fits it fairly closely. The Aryan vernaculars which have become distinct, if allied, languages in the passing of the ages, are Bengali, Guzerati, Mahratti, Uriya, Punjabi and Sindi, as also the more general Hindi and its derivative Urdu. From the fourth to the tenth century the volume of Sanskrit writing was very great, but with the coming of the Musulman conquests, literature largely came to be written in the Urdu aforesaid, which by freely borrowing from the Persian was well suited to literary purposes. Sanskrit writing continued, but it now became the vehicle of Hindu as distinct from Indian thought. The Dravidian languages have entirely different roots and constructions and may have some affinity with Turkish. They are Tamil, Telegu, Canarese and Malayalam. There is an entirely different grouping also, the Tibeto-Burman, which outside Burma is spoken by the Mongoloid hill-tribes in the Himalayas, while there is a Kolarian group of the languages belonging to the aboriginal tribes, Bhils, Sonthals, Gonds and the like.

It will be seen therefore that the statement that there are 222 separate tongues besides dialects and patois, is not a fantastic one. One of the most scientific and valuable publications in ethnology and its kindred sciences is the Linguistic Survey of India.

The Lingua Franca

The Moslem invaders and conquerors with their troops and colonists, consisting of people of many races and many tongues, evolved the *lingua franca*, which is popularly known as Hindustani, but for which the accurate name is *Urdu*, the language of the army. *Urdu* is the Turkish word for an army, or in modern official military language an army corps, and is the same word as our 'horde'. This Urdu is based on the Hindi grammar, but its vocabulary is largely Arabic and Persian, with a few words of French and Portuguese origin. But there is no word of any language which supplies a want that may not perfectly correctly be incorporated into Urdu. For instance, it is perfectly good Urdu to introduce the word 'sausage' for an article made of the pork that obviously a Moslem tongue could not have, while even the vernacular of your *Khansaman*, your 'Lord of things', major-domo or cook, may equally correctly tell you that he has *sausage-wassage* for breakfast for you. Those whose pleasure or pain it has been to study that standard book of correct Urdu, the *Taubat* or '*Repentance*' *of Nussu*, will remember how such words as *chlarodin*, *medical hal* and *kallera pil* have been quite properly used therein as good Urdu.

Urdu is a beautiful and effective language, and the cultured love to introduce a larger number of Persian words than really belong to it, and as the vocabulary of Persian is a very full one, the floweriness of speech is much developed thereby.

Persian was the language of the Moslem Governments, and till 1837, of the British Law Courts. In that year the Company's Government, no doubt wisely, introduced the vernaculars. This had the somewhat disastrous effect of reacting on the education of the Moslem community. Persian being a Moslem language, the establishment connected with the law had for generations provided work and career for the lesser Moslem intelligentsia. It was one of the reasons of Moslem dissatisfaction in 1857, and is mentioned here as one of the difficulties that administration in India meets with, or rather the difficulties of creating that country as one.

Thus Persian since 1837 has waned in India, though it was till very recently the courtly language of Afghanistan. The British officers in India who studied Persian, studied Afghani Persian, which is also very much the language of cultured Persia—though there is a different vowel pronunciation, and a variation in shade of meaning of words.

Because of this ancient tradition of Persian, the police clerks in many parts of India will write up reports in a strangely semi-Persian jargon—of this there is a classical example which I give here for the amusement of the rising generations, who with some knowledge of ordinary Urdu have not run across the perfectly true story. A police officer had occasion to report the riotous behaviour of three young officers, in a state of exhilaration, who broke up the rest-house: *Aj ba tarikh falana, ba waqt-i-shabb. Tin sahiban-i-afsaran tashriff le aye thé. Tannawal farmākar, sa halat-i-nasha, qul asaish-ul-bait, shikast farmaye thé. Main sab-inspector mauqe par rawana hokar, afsaran sahiban maujud paye, ronak afroz hue, etc.*[1]

Persian as well as Urdu has a considerable vocabulary of words of Arabic origin, of which the meaning, however, may have slightly changed, though not outside the idea that the root stands for. A quaint instance of this in the police Urdu referred to above, is one of the derivatives from the Arab root *rkb*, which contains the idea of movement and we have *mărkăb*, something in which you are moved. In Arabic

[1] To-day, such and such a date, in the evening, three high officer gentlemen brought their honoured selves. Having dined and being in a state of exhilaration, they ordered all the furniture of the place to be broken. I the inspector, having sent myself and found them present, their countenances shone, etc.

mărkăb is a boat. The Indian police use the word for a donkey. To those who know the spirit of the Arabic language, this is a typical example thereof.

One of the noticeable changes in Urdu itself has taken place in the last century since Persian ceased to be a language of the streets and courts. The older Indian books use the spelling Mirza Ali Cawn—more properly Khan, also Cawnpore for Khanpur.

The point of interest here is not the more scientific transliteration, but the fact that the older Persian-toned pronunciation of Khan was very deep and the *aw* gives the old deep 'a' of Afghani Persian, which has now passed away in India proper. In Kashmir we still get it, as well as pronunciation of 'a' like 'o'. For instance *lol* for *lal*, 'red'.

The Urdu of the west coast, and the Urdu of the old Turkish and Pathan states of the South, are full of Persian words, and in the latter is very precise. Not being a popular language, it does not develop as time goes on, as does the Urdu of Lucknow and Delhi, where the educated variety is very pure and the popular Urdu progresses to serve the people's needs.

CHAPTER V

THE RELIGIONS OF INDIA

Many Mansions

The many religions of India are a matter of much marvel to those who try to understand the country, without the leisure and the knowledge to study the matter at length. It is known that India is a world of antagonistical and jarring faiths with outlook on the world that nothing can reconcile, and of countless minor cults and beliefs. The religions of India may be indicated briefly enough, under certain names, two main divisions and many lesser ones, but some of those names themselves are ever-expanding portmanteaus. The religions expressed in those general terms are first the two main ones: Hinduism, the religion of the people of Hind; Islam, the faith of 'The Submission', submission to the will of God, which is the true name for what we may call Muhammadanism. Then come lesser divisions: Buddhism, Jainism, Zoroastrianism (the faith of Parsees), Christianity, Sikhism, Judaism, Animism. That in itself is a formidable list, but is nothing to the ramifications that are covered by the word Hinduism. Even mighty Islam, the least contentious of faiths, and the simplest for a thinker to understand, has two great divisions and several lesser ones further from each other in sympathy and doctrine than even the branches and systems of the Christian faith. These different creeds, however, are all easy to explain in outline, with the exception of the complex assembly which exists under the umbrella of what is usually termed inaccurately, but conveniently, Hinduism.

Hinduism through the Ages

The first task in attaining some right perspective of India is to acquire a bowing acquaintance as to what Hinduism means. And the real answer to this, as already suggested, is that Hinduism is the religion of the people of Hind or India, as conceived for them by the priesthood of the Aryan race that overran the land. The Hindus of India do not really use that word for their religion. It has already been explained how the white Aryan race came in from the steppes and the upland plains of Central Asia, from some matrix whence also swept similar waves to Persia and to Europe via the Caucasus. When this wave came down perhaps between two and three thousand years before Christ, such faith as the moving clans held was a simple one, a worship of the being or beings who controlled the great forces of nature. The Aryans were people of active minds as well as bodies, and the original custom where the head of the family was family priest and performed rites of propitiation and thanksgiving, passed in time to one of a priesthood, which in due course became hereditary. Hence derived the holy Brahmin tribe or caste, which as years rolled on became too numerous for priestly work and sent many of its sons to be agriculturists.

Gradually the subtle brains were concerned in the elaboration of a theory of life and religion that fitted with the world and life as they saw it. Just as Christian philosophers evolved the theory of the Trinity as the only one that all the known evidences and happenings of Christ's teaching would fit, so the Brahmins evolved complicated rules and teachings regarding the Godhead in India which would account for the world and its life as they saw it. But they also succeeded in weaving into their life a most complicated social structure, which we know as caste. Now there is little doubt, as explained in Chapter IV., that caste is due to the intense desire and fierce determination of Aryan leaders and lawgivers to keep their white blood pure. The young warriors who spread over the land, conquering tribe after tribe, and principality after principality, consorted freely with the women of the countryside, and a large mixed population was arising. Boys will be boys and soldiers will be soldiers, but it was realized that unless the results of miscegenation could be segregated and insulated, the white blood would be swamped. Thus arose the castes. Half-bloods were to be a race apart. The young men might breed, but their descendants were to be inferior and impure and lower. Only by marriage with their own people would they produce privileges and a status which belonged to the white people.

How fierce and in some ways inhuman is this determination of white races to keep themselves so, is to be seen in the United States with a force every whit as great as that visible in high-caste Hinduism. The most beautiful woman, the most accomplished man, who is known to have any negro blood, can no more cross the rubicon and be considered admissible, than can a sweeper in India eat with a caste man. The rule in both cases is equally ruthless and rigorous. In the United States the 'No Nation' folk are banned for ever. All through the world we have seen the same spirit at work, and often among and between the white folks themselves.

Through the ages the various products of miscegenation took new grades, and with these grades came those of the original inhabitants who accepted the new domination. Each and all were graded. As the great white dominators spread further and conquered more, so their prestige increased, and the conquered wished to belong to the fabric of the rulers, to be in fact a 'Roman Citizen', in some sort.

The priesthood, now hereditary and sacrosanct, took a view that could only be called a liberal one. The conquered and absorbed had some form of worship, recognized a supreme being in some form or other. Such were obviously the best that they could imagine of the great Brahm, the lord of all. All local gods must be emanations and manifestations of one of the recognized *personae* of the Brahmin Godhead, and as this Aryan domination spread, all who were conquered and who would belong to the people of Hind or

An ancient Hindu temple of the Deccan

Rajput India

The entrance to the pass at Ambar

India, and could come under the Hindu umbrella, became a part of this strange warp and weft. The White Folk, the twice-born races of the conquerors and colonizers, Brahmin, Kshattriya or Vaisya, were far above the rest of the groupings formed from the enormous number of conquered and half-bred folk. To this day there are still regions to which Aryanism has never penetrated, and people over whom the Hindu umbrella has never spread. They are largely the aboriginal tribes in the more inaccessible regions. It is they who comprise the eleven million Animists, following some primitive form of spirit and animal worship. Among them it is possible to see some of these folk gradually creeping into the Hindu communion, and receiving some lowly status thereunder. Others are flocking to the Christian Evangel.

How efficacious this age-old system has been in preserving a pure white upper crust in India, is apparent enough to those who know really high-caste folk. There is often nothing so handsome and so pure blooded to be seen as a Brahmin, or a real Rajput. The intellectual Brahmin is a very remarkable personality, and it is to be remembered, as already explained, he is by no means only to be found in the priestly classes, but in many other walks of life both high and humble, since high caste does not necessarily mean this world's wealth.

The Brahminical teaching had evolved a doctrine of compelling force which did seem to explain the phenomena of the world to mankind. It involved the great doctrines of transmigration and of *Karma*. An Almighty, a Supreme Being, caring very little apparently for mankind, sat aloft, to be worshipped and reverenced in various ways. The souls of man after death entered another body or some other living creature of lower status, even to plants. Each life the soul raised itself or debased itself by its actions. That is *Karma*, as a man sows in this life so he shall reap in the next. Gradually the more fortunate soul rises in status till eventually after the last death it is swept up into the great Ishvara, absorbed in the Godhead whence it came. Aeons of time are represented in the happy reabsorption of a soul. It is not hard to realize how this doctrine, the doctrine of *Karma*, does provide some explanation of the evil of the world and all the unevenness in human life. It also makes it clear why the poor and the miserable should be left to 'dree their own weird'; they are but suffering for their misdeeds of a previous life! To attempt to alter that might try and interfere with the will of God. Those who belong to the high castes have souls well on the way to Nirvana, *i.e.* to being absorbed. They may have climbed to that position through many weary aeons.

From the foregoing it will be realized how absolutely important is an orthodox man's caste. It is life. Every low-caste man, and through the ages the multiplications and ramifications have been legion, has someone lower than he, and all the brute creation. Each soul has some place on one of the rungs of the eternal ladder that it must not forfeit.

Now it is not too much to say that no Hindu can think otherwise, unless he is convinced that the whole theory is false, and has broken entirely away from the old tradition. Certain associations of somewhat westernized Indians have done so, such as the small and very emancipated members of the Brahmo Samaj and the wider and more active Arya Samaj.[1] There are some fifteen million Brahmins and about one hundred and thirty million high-caste folk in India; there are sixty millions of the depressed classes, or super-lowly original, at whose tail stand the millions of the 'untouchables'. It might be possible to say that while the depressed classes are non-Aryan, the vast ground between them and the twice-born high-caste folk is filled by the reputable descendants, early colonists, who mingled their blood with earlier comers, and from many other sources that cannot be traced. For it was a feature of this mystical Brahmin *haute direction* that people joining the fold from later colonizations have been given a place in the warp and weft of the

[1] *Samaj* means 'society' or 'association'.

national structure, for national as well as religious in some strange manner it contrives to be.

The Rise and Wane of Buddhism

Before a brief outline of the Hindu tenets can be given we must hark back to the great break that Buddhism wrought.

So complicated had the higher Hinduism become, in the millennium before Christ, that it brought no way of life to the people. Princes and nobles warred under the Hindu umbrella. The poor and lowly were oppressed. Barons were given to war and the chase, for barons thus addicted seem to have been the world's constant feature. Many teachers and reformers arose seeking a Way. Some failed, some flourished and waned, and then in the sixth century B.C. there was born of princely Hindu stock in what is now Nepal, one Gautama Siddartha, who sought truth for years and found it not. Then he developed a charming, compelling teaching of his own which spread widely, and he was known as the *Buddha*, the 'Enlightener'. And about the same time also arose on an entirely eccentric axis, one Mahavira the *Jinna*, or 'Conqueror', who also taught an excellent way of his own expounding. Both 'caught on', the Buddha more especially, and in from three to five hundred years Buddhism had swept Brahminism and Hinduism from the land. Almost the whole of India was Buddhist, the followers of the system of teaching of Prince Gautama, the 'Buddha'.

Brahminism existed but in the pot-holes of the desert and the recesses of the forest, eternal, mystic, proud but trodden under. It would seem that during this period the rules of marriage and caste remained in some sort as clan and tribal customs.

It is no part of this short outline to tell the story of Buddhism. This is far too beautiful, complicated and incomparable, for anything less than a volume. While Buddhism triumphed, the followers of Mahavira, a kindred teacher, remained in unantagonistical quietude. The teaching filled much the same wants in the ground on which it fell as Buddhism.

Buddhism it was that spread, and it mastered for a while the great fierce races of the almond-eye and of Central Asia who had become a terror to the whole world. The Tartars and Huns who flowed into the north of India were swept into its fold, and the teaching of the 'Enlightener' reached to the Oxus through the passes and pockets of Afghanistan.

But power and might and systems are too much for faiths and an immense ecclesiastical framework and authority arose. Great abbots and archbishops, with robes and pomp and ceremony, were evolved. Thinkers began to think and argue. What once was a kindly philosophy proceeded to develop into a religion; there came a great division of thought between the mystical and the simple, between the High and the Low, the Buddhism of the *Mahayana* or High Path, and the *Himayana* or Low Path, and as there was now little to differentiate it in the eyes of the people from the pomp and complications of Brahminism, it lost its grip and faded.

The never-dying leaven of Brahminism must have been patiently, alertly, biding its time through the centuries, and all through the earlier centuries of the Christian era we can watch it without any clear idea of the process, reasserting its influence. Buddhism took five hundred years to spread over India, and it took five hundred years to fade. By the seventh century A.D. it was for the great part dead, save in pockets. It stayed in Burma and Ceylon, it remained up in the Himalaya, and towards the Oxus, but in Hindustan it was dead. How it rolled on and dominated the Far East and the great plateau of Mongolia is another story. Curiously enough the teaching of the *Buddha* vanished, but the lesser cult of Mahavira the *Jinna* has remained. His followers the Jains number over one and a half millions, among certain classes of well-to-do Aryans. Their cult may very roughly be said to be half-way between Brahminism and Buddhism. Its members form a highly respected body. Its temples are among the most beautiful in India, those at Mount Abu in the Aravalli hills being of great beauty and intricacy of ornamentation, and are among the more famous of the sites that tourists are taken to. Especially are they worthy of a pilgrimage to see places of worship to which so much human wealth and skill has been dedicated.

The Hindu Reconstruction

We now come to that part of the story on which the understanding of the position of religion in India rests to-day, and that is the drama or epic of the Hindu Reconstruction. During the waning of Buddhism, there came a time when the Brahminical *haute direction* found itself in the saddle beyond dispute, and it contrived by methods whose detail we know not, to reconstruct the whole fabric on a Hindu basis, and on the traditions of the old white colonization. The old dispensation had recognized three great divisions of the White, priests, soldiers, traders and agriculturists—*Brahmin*, *Kshattriya*, *Vaisya*, and below them in one vast, contemptuous group, the Sudra, the inferior stuff aforesaid. So far as possible these groupings should be perpetuated. All who were princes, leaders and soldiers, who would devote themselves to the preservation of Brahmins and the system, and who would preserve the sacred cow, were classed as Rajputs, 'Sons of Princes', of knightly birth. So many had been the post-Aryan invasions in the recent centuries, that it is to be supposed that the Rajput mesh was not drawn too fine. Tartars and Jăts who had been Buddhists came into the Rajput fold if earnest supporters of the holy Brahmins. The classing of the high-grade exclusive traders was probably easy enough, and 'Peter's pence' no doubt helped the social ambitions of those who were on the fringe. The folk dropped readily enough into the lesser divisions, and increased them among themselves, and the great Hindu umbrella was opened wide, and spread over the land.

There was practically no other faith than the Brahminical in the land, with the countless worships and inventions and gods for the countless outcaste folk, which were admissible as the best conception of higher things they were capable of.

All who belonged to governable India received an acknowledged status, high or low. You came under the umbrella without question. It was only where the umbrella did not reach, as in the aboriginal tracts and countries, that the folk remained outside. It has been said, no doubt with truth, that should Christian folk wish to come under it, a place in the hierarchy awaits them, with Christ but an incarnation of the popular Indian hero and representation, Krishna. *And it is to be remembered in this connection*, that Hindu opinion readily accepts a popular leader as the Deity materializing part of Himself on earth.

By the eighth or ninth century A.D. the old fabric was rewoven, sometimes on lines that were wiser by reason of the centuries that Brahminism had spent in the wilderness.

The Princes, Kings and Barons, and their followers, were now 'Rajput', and all were in their places. Unfortunately dominant Brahminism had not brought the spirit of unity. Great groupings arose under this or that ruler, but never, under the Brahmin rebuilding, showing an effective consolidated Hindu front to the world.

The Hindu Deities and Rulers

This somewhat lengthy presentment of the subject in a book of this nature is to show how Hinduism is a national as well as a religious idea. Now with all this nationalism, which is inherent if not expressed in the conception, it will be found that there is no rule of faith, no creed, no 'church', no central authority. Brahminism, full of great teachings and ideas, strong in this strange subconscious immortality which survived the long years of Buddhist obedience, and brought the structure of the people through the centuries of Moslem domination, has never, at any time, been able to induce political or national success.

To consider the tenets of this religion we must first of all remember how much more developed must be the idea of the Godhead of an earnest Christian theologian than that of the peasant, however devout, at the wayside shrine or chapel. Having admitted this, we may say that Hinduism admits of a great Deity somewhere, Ishvara, or Brahm, and three great *personae* thereof, Brahma the Creator, Vishnu the Preserver, Siva the Destroyer. Whatever great thinkers and mystic believers may evolve and feel, popular high-caste Hinduism, speaking very broadly, divides into two divisions. The first embraces those who turn their daily thoughts to Vishnu, Lord of the kindly, happy, simple side of human life; the second to Siva, more often known as Mahadeo, the Great God, who because he destroys also creates, and who is recognized as that portion of the Godhead who controls all the more active, energetic ways of life. The low-caste Hindus worship a vast pantheon of ancient and local gods, admissible as but a local and lesser conception of the real Gods who are the *personae* of Brahm. To both great divisions the conception of *Karma* already described is common.

In all Hinduism everything to do with birth, creation, procreation and the organs of reproduction of man and beast are revered and symbolic. To every form of the Godhead is also a female side, representing those attributes of the particular *persona* which may be imagined feminine. In certain aspects of Hindu life the emblems of sex symbolism are very prominent, and produce on the temples of Mahadeo those carvings of which Lyall has sung:

> The organs of birth and the circlet of bones,
> And the light loves carved on the temple stones.

These I have tried to describe more completely elsewhere.[1]

But whether a Hindu be a follower of Vishnu or of Siva, there is no rule of belief. If you are a Hindu you do what Hindus do, but you need not be religious, and you are born to your position. Certain laws of life, such as child marriage

[1] *The Religions and Hidden Cults of India.* Sampson, Low and Marston.

and the non-remarriage of widows, are essential to all high-caste ways. Below the high caste you may follow any rule of life that the members of your own circle will accept. But it is to be remembered that there are countless high-caste Hindus who read the ancient writings, observe the ancient rules, sing psalms of praise and content, who do their duty and ponder deeply on their Godhead, and all the works of the Almighty, and further that a good Brahmin is a very righteous, merciful man indeed. He has often other sides to his character as well.

Untouchability and Temple Entry

A great deal has been heard in the last few years of 'untouchability', 'depressed classes', and now since the good Mr. Gandhi has thought well to throw a great apple of discord into a sea already troubled enough, comes to us 'temple entry'.

The depressed classes and their origins have been outlined, and the 'untouchables' are those millions of the former category who are the lowest (not necessarily the poorest) of the latter classes, whose origin is veiled in some obscurity, but who are largely black as distinct from white turned brown by ages of sun. They, condemned from earliest days to the menial offices of society and the unpleasant trades, are outcaste beyond belief. Now many reformers have arisen in Hindu life through the ages, urging the equality before God of the human being, and have founded sects, many of which survive, but orthodox Hinduism would have none of it. The doctrine of *Karma* is too strong, and the high position in spiritual life and prospects of the high caste are so marvellous, that it cannot be abandoned.

Gandhi has urged that the depressed classes must be brought more near the centre of the shade and consideration under the Hindu umbrella. He has urged that they be admitted to the same temples as the high caste. How the Viceroy has refused a bill enabling temple entry to be brought forward in a provincial assembly and make it an all-India matter will be explained.[1]

Temples in India have been built, as elsewhere, by private devotion and munificence, and usually for a specific purpose of worship. They are usually in the hands of trustees, whose duty is regulated by suitable laws and customs, which have been fortified or reiterated by British legislation. The Bill as introduced merely enables trustees to take action with the consent of the community they represent, to admit low-caste folk.

Now the real difficulty is this. In Sivite temples there is no real bar to a congregation or a community so doing if they wish. Sivite temples permit and enjoin the blood sacrifice, and the presence of the blood-sacrificing, flesh-eating untouchables presents no barrier of horror and sacrilege. In Vishnuvite temples the case is far otherwise. Blood and blood sacrifice is there so abhorred that the idea of admission of the untouchables to services is unbelievably abhorrent to the orthodox, and involves the status of each soul in world storms. It could only be passed by some westernized trustees who have recently abandoned all the orthodox ways, and whose decision might condemn their more orthodox *confrères* to become lost souls, who must in the next world slip back the ladder that should lead to heaven. The controversy therefore has already become a bitter one. Nor is it possible to imagine how the matter will end. Mr. Gandhi has coined a charming phrase or expression new in India, viz. *Harijans*, 'God's creatures', for the 'untouchables'. A new phrase has also been introduced for those who prefer the *status quo*, viz. *Sanatanists*, best translated as '*orthodox*'.

Islam

Islam came in the sixth century A.D. to a desert world, which had forgotten much of its old primitive faith in El or Allah. The Prophet Muhammad purported, as did Christ in Judea, to bring a new dispensation and a more

[1] See further remarks on this subject in the next chapter.

intimate knowledge of the God of old, and, as we know, in a very short time his teaching roared like a forest fire over a large part of Asia and Africa, and his hardy warriors, marrying freely with the conquered, produced hosts of warrior children to spread the fierce faith.

It made its first entry into India in the eighth century when the Arabs conquered Sind from the Rajputs. There it stopped till the beginning of the twelfth century, when a stream of proselytizing enthusiasts swept down from the mountains of Afghanistan and the steppes of Central Asia, sword in hand.

This coming of Islam has been outlined in the first chapter, and how for some eight hundred years India was conquered, colonized and ruled by the Moslem conquerors from the Afghan passes. Colonization and proselytization produced a Moslem population which now numbers some seventy millions, of whom the great part are in British India. That seventy million people number some of the bravest and most efficient in the whole land; they also number many who have sunk low in the deterioration of the hotter provinces. The sturdier classes, both peasantry and gentry, have thought more of the plough and the sword than of the class-room, and their general level of education and mental activity is below that of the more facile and, with certain definite exceptions, less manly Hindu. Therefore are they at a disadvantage with the world of education and wordy politics.

It may here be remarked that there are several alternative words for the followers of Islam used indiscriminately and alternatively for general purposes. Muhammadan means the follower of the Prophet Muhammad—whose name is so often spelt in the West 'Mohammed' and 'Mahomet'—but the followers of the Prophet would call themselves Moslem, which is but an Arabic regular derivative of the word Islam, and means one who professes Islam, 'The Submission'. The word is also written 'Muslim'. 'Mussalman' is also in general use for the same thing, and is but another Arabic form derived from 'Islam'.

Now the Muhammadan religion has a test, a belief, and it is described in the short '*Kalima*': 'There is no God but Allah [1] and Muhammad is his Prophet.' There it is, simple and straightforward, *Yahweh* expressed to a modern world not by Christ, but by Muhammad. It is not too much to say that the Muhammadans of India to-day are the most devout of all who follow the Submission. The two main divisions of Islam are represented in India, the *Sunni* or Orthodox who are in the majority, and the *Shiah*, whose name is short for 'Partizans of Ali'. The great schism arose soon after the death of the Prophet as to who was his successor (Caliph) on earth.

To this day the two branches are as far apart as when the Sons of Ali died by the sword. Ali was the Prophet's son-in-law. Another much smaller sect is well known to us because of its head, the Agha Khan, head of the *Khojas* or *Ismaili* sect of Islam.[2] The *Ismailis* are nearer the *Shiahs* than the Orthodox in their beliefs. The *Shiah* and the *Ismaili* sects are said to have a more mystical teaching than the Orthodox Faith, but scholarly theologians are often prepared to read the most mystical teaching into the texts of the Qoran.

The whole tendency of Islam is to be most intensely hostile to what to the outer eye are the polytheisms and inventions of popular Hinduism. The early Moslem invaders destroyed all temples, slew countless priests, and butchered many of those who would not be mustered under the Prophet's banner, and it is to be remembered that with that mustering went the somewhat painful rite of adult circumcision.

There is now no central Moslem authority in the world, nor did the somewhat bogus resurrection of an active caliphate in the person of the Sultan of Turkey a generation or

[1] The ancient desert God, who is but a memory of the God of Abraham, of Isaac and of Jacob.

[2] In the crusader-ing Atkins' slang, the 'old codger' or Khoja, the Old Man of the Mountains.

so ago furnish one. In India it is now the Moslem college at Deoband, near Saharanpur, and within hail of Delhi, that can give a reasonably authoritative ruling on any vexed question of religion. There however is always one difficulty existent in any country where the rule is not Islamic. Islam is an organized force framed with the intention that Church and State must be one, in which the Divine law is always the civil law. To meet this difficulty, as far as possible the '*Shariat*', the Islamic law, is embodied in British statutes to which Moslems are subject, and which control their affairs.

The Moslem community, satisfied with their position under the British Government of India, proud, often arrogantly proud of their past, and the fact that Moslems alone of Indians have ruled all India, busy over their own affairs, and steadily developing their education, have now by political circumstances been forced to a vocative share in the life of India. That is another story, and here we speak of Islam as a religion, and a rule of life. As such it has a grip varying with many circumstances.

Nominally modern Islam for the more western part of the world had a head in the Sultan of Turkey, with the *Sheikh ul Islam* as his religious interpreter. Since his exit the University at Cairo, and the Deoband aforesaid, are prepared to direct in religious difficulties, but Islam now has no head to lead, expound, and direct. There is no such arrangement as holds let us say in the Orthodox Christian Church, where each separate kingdom has its autocephalic religious head, in liaison with all the other heads of branches of the same Church.

In India Islam is a very live power for good, and for order and right living, if properly helped and encouraged. But since the casting of the apple of political discord by Mr. Montague into the comparative quiet of the Indian pools, the Hindu and the Moslem, who under British rule lived happily together, are now gazing fiercely across the table at each other.

Sikhism

Sikhism as a religion, and a religious force, is one of the most interesting subjects in India. It is sometimes described as a form, an offshoot of Hinduism, yet that is only a permissible statement if we look on Hinduism as the national stock of India, from which all springs, and to which all returns. It is true that if you abandon Sikhism, and wish to conform to the Hindu habits of those of your race or clan who are not Sikhs, since Sikhs are only Sikhs by baptism, you may do so. At mature age if you do not get baptized into Sikhism you automatically revert to the briar of Hinduism of sorts. Hindus don't care one way or the other.

About the time of Martin Luther, when religious thoughts and qualms were stirring the world, there arose in the Punjab one Nanak, a Hindu of the Khatri caste, who like many other good folk in India through the ages, pondered much on the evils and miseries and follies of the world. There have been many such, from Gautama, the Enlightener, and Mahavira the Conqueror, to Kabir and Nanak, and many another whose traces are still to be found. Nanak, *Baba* or 'Father' Nanak, as he is affectionately called, taught brotherly love, simplicity, mercy and the worship of that Almighty who is behind all Hinduism. Nothing in his teaching clashes really with Hindu ideas, and so it went on. But Nanak talked of all mankind being one; all *Harijans*, 'God's Creatures', to use the slicker Gandhi phrase already referred to, and all without thought of race, faith or caste, might join the simple brotherhood which followed him. As long as the Nanakis taught and lived their simple ways no one cared. To Brahminism and high-caste Hinduism it was all very well, the world was immutable and men might contemplate and teach what they liked. *Karma* ruled the world, and the twice-born were nearing the end. To Moslem rulers it mattered not at all.

But the Nanakis teaching had come to stay in the north, and he, the first *Guru* or 'Teacher', was followed by a strict succession. Gradually the sect came into the hands of *Gurus* of organizing ability, and from that time Moslem authority seems to have seen a danger, and possibly its disciples were arrogant. Thus began a cruel persecution, which merely gave strength and virility to an otherwise unassuming folk. Then at last there arose Govindh, the famous 'Tenth *Guru*', whose ideas expanded immensely. He took the famous teaching which had now spread to the sturdy Jăt race in the southern and eastern Punjab, and he made of it a great military order, an order of purity, austerity and manly virtue, and he gave to them certain basic signs and symbols known as the 'Five Kakas', or 'K's', all appealing to simplicity and manhood, among which was the injunction of the unshorn locks and hair. Thus arose this military brotherhood, as austere and as righteously simple as the Nanakis, but ready to fight to the death with the now weakening Moguls, their oppressors. In the fierce struggles which followed, the Khalsa, the 'elect', grew in military strength and adhesiveness, and materially contributed to the crash of the Empire. Fiercely cruel were the battles and reprisals, and under the strain the militant Sikhism grew.

To all his followers, Govindh added the Rajput suffix Lion, or *Singh*, and this, the more universal form of Sikhism, is known as 'Singhism' as distinct from the Sikhism of those Nanakis who did not become Singhs.

Singhism made magnificent soldiers, but it also made magnificent men. The teachings of the *Grunth sahib*, the scripture of Baba Nanak, has much of the Christian teaching, and that of the *Japji*, the Law of Govindh, adds the fire and austerity as taught by Duncan Cameron and other Protestants and Puritans.

But Sikhism, especially Singhism, demands a rule of life and self-denial that is always a strain on human nature. The women like the brightness and the variety of popular Hinduism and festivals, and the lesser young men shirk the baptism of the Singhs. Thirty years ago Singhism was on the wane, and the British officers of the Indian Army, knowing what devout, simple soldiers Singhism produced, made the Sikh Corps into homes and nests of Sikh faith and purity. Since then Singhism has gripped itself, and is cognizant of what the British officer did in the days of its faltering.

Yet always exists, as already remarked, the tendency to revert to the briar of Hinduism, and the future of an educated Sikhism with a Western inclination, no one can fathom. Yet in its tenets and ethics Sikhism will remain as a religion worthy of any good and educated man who as yet remains outside the Christian fold. Of its political history an outline has already been given. Its numbers even to-day are less than three million souls.

Christianity

Christianity in India has a very early origin. The traditions of St. Thomas having travelled and preached there may easily be true, while at St. Thomas Mount, close to Madras city, there has been for many hundred years a settlement of Syrian Christians, with many members in the south. The coming of the Portuguese in the fifteenth century brought the dominion and teaching of Rome. The Church of Rome, in addition to the adherence of most of the inhabitants of Portuguese Goa, has adherents all over India, which is covered by dioceses of both the Church of England and the Church of Rome.

Missionary activity has been very active for the last hundred years, while in the south there is in progress the remarkable phenomenon of a mass movement to Christianity among the humbler classes, now numbering millions. The same is in progress in a marked way, but on a much smaller scale, among the depressed classes in the Punjab, where by the nature of life and climate even the depressed have finer physique and more energy to handle the difficulties of life. Those who have even followed a brief outline of Hinduism, will have realized how stimulating is the spiritual position in which the high-caste Hindu finds himself, even when making little of it. It has been explained that through generations of endeavour in earlier lives, his soul, as he believes, has so risen in the social scale that it is now in a white race body, approaching in but a few more lives the wonderful end of absorption in the infinite, in the deity. To such Christianity has no appeal, save by the excellence of its tenets, which is readily admitted, or else by some miraculous and divinely born conviction of its inherent truth, which ordinary teaching cannot produce.

It is just possible that westernization may so reduce Hinduism to nonsense, that the mind and heart of the modern high-caste Hindu may be vacant. If the old gods be gone, there is a house needing a tenant. God send that seven worse devils are not wanting to enter it! Some day in the purpose of the Almighty, Christian conviction may come to the twice-born, the white men of the Indian upper-crust. Until that day there are millions of lesser Hindus and outcastes under the curse of the Sudra for whom Christianity may readily bring better values, until the greater harvest is ready. The haven of the high-caste Hindu is worthy of this reaping.

The Church of Rome, great in its wealth, has a stately edifice throughout India, resting on its European people, its teaching facilities and enterprise, and its historical conversions in Portuguese India. To what extent it may spread the Christian Gospel is also an untold road. The mass of conversions of the south are to a great extent due to the Anglican and Protestant bodies, whose Union is one of the ecclesiastical questions of the day. In the south in Dravidian India, Indian clergy and Indian bishops now lead and control their Church, and will take a larger share in mundane affairs when Provincial autonomy is more pronounced. There may even be some interesting political developments. To the inquirer who would see an Indian Christian people it is to the old Madras Presidency, and especially to the districts of Dornakal and Tinnevelly, that he should turn his steps, and he will find, if of sympathetic mind, a warm welcome.

Other Religions

Among the religions that have no contact with Islam, with Hinduism or with Christian movements, are several held by smaller bodies. There are the Buddhists, of course, of the Himalayas, people of Mongoloid race; there is that most important racial and religious body the Parsees, who maintain the ancient Aryan religion of Zarathustra, whom we usually speak of as Zoroaster. Fleeing from Persia before Islam the Parsees, or Persians (males only it is said), took refuge in western India many centuries ago. A self-contained, perhaps over-clever, trading race, they are amongst the most valued of the population, observe their racial purity strictly, and have no poor. The faith they hold, their temples and observances, are of great purity and dignity, and to students of religion are a remarkable survival of a faith that was old when Islam arose, or even when the Christ was born into the world.

India has few Jews in the sense that the rest of the world has, but she has curious settlements of both 'White' and 'Black' Jews; the former dwell with their white co-religionists in Cochin, and are an interesting relic, presumably of converts, while the 'White' Jews there, and the family of the Ben-i-Israel near Bombay, must come from that home of Jewry, Bagdad. The indigenous and foreign Jews, the latter from Mesopotamia or Aden, have their synagogues in the important towns.

Animism, a portmanteau name for the various non-Hindu cults of the aboriginal tribes aforesaid, is decreasing under attacks from Christianity and Islam, as well as by the social ambition that induces some to aspire to acquire a status, however depressed, under the Hindu umbrella. Indeed among the aboriginals we may see at work some of the world's earliest religious conceptions, and we may also see the process at work under our own eyes, which must have brought Dravidian India into the great Sudra body of Hinduism far away through the ages.

India, while being the home of many religions, is the home of a people who demand instinctively a religious system for their use. Often enough that demand is not in close contact with any moral code, and there are many Christian teachers who deny vehemently that India is a 'spiritual' country. But that may be but a matter of words and meanings. The Indian mind is supremely ready to believe in some supernatural presence, to practise rituals which worship and even aim at union with the Deity, even if they readily entrust the bulk of their religious duties to someone else.

Again let it be said for the visitor and the wayfarer, that the religious ways of this country are well worthy of their attention and their study, whether the austere and stately ways of Islam, the more luscious interpretation of nature's imagery and phenomena of Hinduism, the pure philosophy of the inner Brahminism, or the dignity of the cult of Zoroaster. Wherever he may go are temples, some of very ancient carving, while many are more modern buildings, varying from great simplicity to great ornateness. There will be the *musjids* of Islam, the shrines of Vishnu and Mahadeo, and as a rule, the incumbents and guardians ready to show them, so far as may be, to those who display ordinary deference and courtesy, and will follow whatever conduct is asked of them. The custodians always welcome something for the upkeep of their temples and for the poor-box that all maintain in one form or another!

CHAPTER VI

THE GOVERNMENTS OF INDIA

Concerning Governments

It is no bad thing to understand something of the Government and the system under which we live, and of countries in which we are interested, though it may be admitted that such knowledge is unusual. In the case of India so much has been heard of the matter that it is easy to believe, if one listens to the astounding ineptitudes that are so frequently written, that India is almost wanting in anything worthy of the name. As a matter of simple truth, the facts are far otherwise. India is the most amply, modernly governed country in the world, having due regard to its extraordinary size and conflicting conditions. The machinery of actual Government is entirely separate from Parliaments and how they are formed.

Before describing the Government of India as it is or it will be, it is hardly outside the question to preface this brief outline with a few remarks on Governments, especially in view of the dictatorships of Mussolini, Hitler and Stalin, which control a large part of the Western world.

In the first place, it would be well if we who have lived under a Parliamentary system should entirely disabuse ourselves of the idea that Parliaments govern. It is an attempt by well-meaning amateurs to make Parliament govern that wastes, in these modern days, the time of Parliament, and prevents it doing its work of legislation and influence. Parliaments may call a tune, and should have a watching brief, make the laws, and authorize the taxation. That is about the end of it.

Countries are governed by their ministers and their permanent officials in accordance with the laws that are passed by Parliaments or *ad hoc* bodies, duly confirmed by Crown or President. Parliament has a legislative rôle, and a watching brief and the ministers it wants.

In all times there has been in all countries something equivalent to a body of ministers which we call a Cabinet, and which in India we call the Governor-General's or the Provincial Governors' Councils. Equally good, or even better laws, may be passed for a country by a legislative body that is appointed by Crown or President as by one that is elected. Ministers appointed by the similar authority may be as, or more, efficient for their job as those who are appointed by a leader of a majority in an elected house, or individually elected by such a house. The machinery of Government is the same, through ministers and permanent departments, however the policy-deciding authority may be moved, and the excellence and efficiency of the Government depends on the efficiency and wisdom of the minister and his department, however the minister may be controlled.

Having established in brief this thesis, we can now believe that the Government of India may have been very efficiently, sympathetically and honestly administered for a very long time, evolving steadily in the process. How that has been done will now be shown in its bare outline.

It will be remembered how the three trading areas of the East India Company, after they had become fixed in the centres of Bombay, Madras and Calcutta as distinct from the earlier ones, were treated as three distinct colonies and possessions. The Governors of the three Presidencies, as they were called, were appointed by the Court with the approval of the Crown. From time to time acts and rulings were passed, after much Parliamentary discussion, as to how these Governments should be managed, always be it said with reference to the rights and interests of the Princes and peoples who were coming under our sway. The different Presidencies were separated by the same features which had so entirely controlled not only the early Aryan conquest, but the later Muhammadan ones, viz. the mass of mountains and jungles of Central India, with no navigable rivers to serve as highways. The Bengal, Bombay and Madras Presidencies, almost to the coming of railways after the assumption of control by the Crown, were thus separated. Only in the first half of the nineteenth century did a practicable road connect Delhi with Bombay. It was not till 1784 that Warren Hastings, Governor of Bengal, became as related, the first Governor-General, *i.e.* the first co-ordinating authority, so that he could make the Government of India into a realm of co-ordinated policy and practice.

By the latter days of the eighteenth century, the administration began to take the outward form that it still holds. Each Governor of a Presidency had his Council, of which each member was a minister with a portfolio. Each province had a certain number of groups of sub-provinces or counties with a Commissioner at the head, and each Commissioner's sub-province had its districts and counties presided over by chief magistrates, known in the older provinces as 'collectors', and the younger ones as 'deputy commissioners'.

This system continued and developed as more and more of India came under the Company's rule, and it is to be remembered that the vast Indian Empire of to-day was acquired under the rule of the Honourable East India Company, and not under the Crown.

The Development of the Provinces

When the Governor of Bengal, then the great Warren Hastings, was made *also* and not *separately* Governor-General of India, and when his own Bengal increased in size, we find this province broken up into several lesser sub-provinces in charge of a Lieutenant-Governor or a Chief Commissioner, each with a separate machinery or council, etc. Thus at the time of the coming of the Crown (1858) there were in Bengal several provinces, those of Bengal, the North-West

Provinces, the Punjab and Oudh, and as the years rolled by and we come to the Reforms of 1919, each province became of equal status, with a Governor instead of Lieutenant-Governor or Chief Commissioner, a measure which, however much it may have made for dignity and uniformity, has added very considerably to the overhead charges without increasing the efficiency.

The point of the foregoing is that the system of Provincial Government in India has been complete and elaborate for many years, and that the system of Parliamentary Government introduced in 1920 has not altered the governmental system, though it has given a freedom from more intimate Central control which was overdue when the change came. The provinces as they are, and as they will be, are therefore much the same as they have been for many years. All the framework of cabinets, ministers, etc., has been there almost for generations, appointed by the Governors and the Crown, but doing the same work more efficiently and less expensively than the ministers, responsible to local Parliaments, are ever likely to be able to do.

Nor must it be thought that Indians have had no share in the legislation till the reforms. For long, certainly since the coming of the Crown, both the Central Government and the provinces have had legislative assemblies. In these many eminent Indians have served both by appointment and election, while since 1909, by the Morley-Minto reforms, the elected block exceeded the appointed block in numbers.

It is hardly necessary to dwell on the fact that the vast mass of the officials of India have been Indians even in the days of John Company, *i.e.* some of the highest judges and magistrates, and a great deal of all the departmental machinery. In the whole of India, for instance, the number of officials of the Indian Civil Service concerned in the government of British India, have not exceeded a thousand, of whom a considerable number, though 'covenanted' civilians, are, and have long been, Indians, who have been trained at British universities, and pass the same tests as their British *confrères*.

No amount of 'responsible' Government could improve the system or could want to, except so far as all systems must change as the times change. It is the method of appointment of ministers alone that can be changed by the development of the 'Reforms'. We may be sure, however, that those ministers, as they have been during the last ten years, will be assailed as we are in the House of Commons by those who advocate 'wild-cat' measures, and will probably have more trouble than now in escaping from them. It is safe to say that many an Indian minister will curse the day that he ever involved himself in the mass of intrigue, lobbying, and pressure, that a Western party system in Eastern hands will give birth to!

The unsymmetrical but economical system whereby the Governor-General was nominally Governor of the Presidency of Bengal, working the governments of that swollen area through Lieutenant-Governors and Chief Commissioners of Provinces, lasted till the Reforms of 1920. Even Bengal, the province of over fifty million inhabitants, was controlled till quite recently by a Lieutenant-Governor. The converting of all the provinces into Governors' provinces was a very serious addition to the overhead cost of each,[1] costs which the formation of new provinces under the White Paper of 1933 will still further increase.

These are the provinces of India with their populations as shown in the Census of 1931:

Madras (45,600,000).
Bombay (18,000,000).
Bengal (50,100,000).
United Provinces (48,000,000).
Punjab (23,600,000).
Bihar and Orissa (32,400,000).

[1] See Sir Michael O'Dwyer's evidence before the Joint Committee of both Houses of Parliament on the White Paper, 1933.

Central Provinces (15,500,000).
Assam (8,600,000).
North-West Frontier (2,400,000).

Sind (3,900,000) Orissa (6,700,000)	New provinces to be made under the White Paper, Sind at present being part of Bombay, and Orissa of Bihar and Orissa.

Then there are three little territorial enclaves, remaining outside ordinary provinces for special reasons—Ajmere, Delhi, and Coorg.

Because of its unwieldy size Lord Curzon, in his statesmanlike prescience, broke the province of Bengal into two, the eastern portion, which contained the larger portion of the Moslems of Bengal, becoming a new province. It was hoped that would allow of their developing their cults and aspirations as distinct from Hindu Bengal. A great protest was made by part of Bengal, and a weaker Government gave way and reunited them, after guaranteeing to the new province that it never should be rejoined. Lord Curzon's action was no doubt right in principle, and this province is unwieldy and by no means homogeneous, despite the relief given by the removal of Bihar and Orissa therefrom.

It will be seen that the new proposals make two new and very small provinces, Orissa and Sind. The North-West Frontier province was recently formed into a Governor's province, but cannot afford such a luxury, and has to be subsidized.[1]

The first thing to notice is the size of the provinces, two of them larger in population, and of course in extent, than the whole of Britain. This is worthy of very careful attention, because, as has already been emphasized, no one is really fully informed of the immensity of this building of India.

[1] It may here be stated that evidence before the Joint Parliamentary Committee on the White Paper has shown that the proposed Constitution will cost each province many millions sterling in overhead charges.

The Provinces of the Future

The Government of these provinces will continue under the new conditions with no noticeable difference, and each province should be able to develop its own racial affinities. It is for this end that Orissa has been separated from Bihar. The difficulty of carrying out effectively any scientific racial grouping is that the races overlap and are interwoven as much as in Central Europe, while in and out in a curious network come the territories of the Princes' States, so disposed and dispersed that fiscal custom and control is an extremely difficult matter.

Adjustments of boundaries to make frontiers easier to administer are also difficult, for this reason, that though it is often said that the people are happier in a Prince's State than a British province, yet nevertheless an attempt to transfer any portion of a province to a State is always strongly resisted, and possibly *vice versa.*

It is imaginable that, in the Federated India which the White Paper adumbrates, this impossibility of making the provinces, as a whole, confined to one or other group of races, as some Indians have tried to bring about, will act for the good of the country. A purely Moslem province alongside a Hindu one might mean constant friction. Nor can the boundaries, which have largely come about by chance, separate occupations and modes of life. The provinces differ greatly, but it would be hard to say where those differences begin or end, and to draw a line which separates one people from the other.

As the United Provinces approaches the Punjab there is an atmosphere of the Punjab, while as the Punjab approaches the United Provinces there is an atmosphere of Hindustan. This is more noticeable than in England, where a Sussex man half-a-mile across the border does differ in some subtle way from the Surrey man. In the subdivisions of India it is not possible to have racial sub-provinces, for even in the predominately Sikh districts there are other folk intermingled, while what might be true of to-day might not be so of to-morrow.

The probability is that the provinces of India, as their needs and readiness for development progress, will become more and more concerned in their own affairs, and that the Federal Government will be concerned with matters common to all. There are certain hares started locally which cannot be allowed to run, save as a Federal hare. An instance of this was when the 'temple entry' hare was let loose in 1933 by Mr. Gandhi and others, when legislature was proposed to allow the 'untouchable' classes to enter exclusive Hindu temples. It was proposed to admit a bill in the Madras Legislature, but the Viceroy refused his sanction. Such a bill, he said, could only be introduced in the Central Assembly, since it affected all India, was highly controversial and disturbed religious people very deeply. He would not, he said, admit a bill of the kind in a Local Legislature. The wisdom of his action was soon apparent. The bill, introduced centrally in due course, opened up so many difficult problems that it faded away till times were riper. The enthusiasts who had taken up the matter had the *dhobis* (washermen) to tea and the like, but the matter, for the moment, has faded out of fashion.

The gist of the foregoing is that there will be no outward and visible signs of any change of Government. The well-organized and well-directed administration will go on, gradually losing some of its efficiency—chiefly because only British stamina can drive at the wheel in the long hot months—and possibly gathering other usefulnesses and developments that are not yet contemplated.

The Government of the Princes' States

Reference has already been made to the Princes' States and their origins. The chief point to remember is that though some of them are large, others are not bigger than the estates of a landed proprietor, and they thus vary from the size of half France to that of Battersea Park. Their various origins having been explained we need not do more than glance at their systems of government. These also vary greatly, in accordance with the part of India they are in, and the source from which the ruler's title has sprung. The British Government has long laboured at bringing some slight similarity of system into being, without destroying the many picturesque, distinctive and historical features which exist.

The states themselves are each and all in treaty with His Majesty, through the Viceroy, and have no sort of connection or affiliation with any province or portion of the British India and its peoples, except that in the case of the lesser states they have till recently been dealt with by the local Governors and their representatives. This has been so from the earliest days of 'The Raj', partly because the original Presidencies were so far apart from each other and the Government of Bengal, which also became the Central Government. Also the interests of the smaller states and the fact that their actual boundaries are often curiously indented, and even have islands within British India, made handling by local authority, in the name of the Viceroy, a much greater convenience. The coming of the 'Reforms', however, clearly indicated that the interests of the states were now best in central hands.

It would be idle to pretend that all the several hundred Princes govern their states well. The necessity for occasionally removing a chief has shown that. There have been those who deprecate interference by the Central Government with the ruling Princes. A little reflection will show that it is impossible to avoid doing so. Indeed it has been felt that the policy of letting the chiefs more alone, as introduced twenty years or so ago, has been in certain cases disastrous. It is to be remembered that from time immemorial there are only two ways of getting rid of an intolerable Eastern ruler, viz. revolution or palace murder. British protection or support has removed the fear of the one, and made the other a dangerous amusement. But since we support and protect the Princes against both outside and inside enemies, we as the Paramount Power have thereby made ourselves responsible that their government be reasonably good. There are disturbances in one or two states in progress at present that would never have taken place had not we, in process of some hot-air principle, shirked our responsibility for using the guiding and restraining hand too long. Interference and advice when necessary, and not too late, is a very different matter from the tactless, meddling which now and again some Resident may have practised in the past.

Some of the larger states are admirably governed, and have also of the ruler's own initiative introduced forms of popular government. Almost all have availed themselves at one time or other of the service of British officers or British-trained Indian officials to put their revenues and public services in order, and to-day especially so.

Some of them are still intensely old-fashioned and patriarchal in their systems, and it would not be too much to add that in many cases it is these old-world oases, where the patriarch is amiable and capable, that the people are the happiest.

The Princes, as has been said, are each and all in touch with the Central Government, but this does not mean that normally the Foreign Department must deal with each. The lesser are grouped for the purposes of reference and general liaison under a senior 'Agent' of the Governor-General, in various parts of the country. The 'Montford' Reforms introduced an informal body, constituted as the 'Chamber of Princes', which aimed at giving the various Princes an opportunity to meet and discuss their own special problems. Some of them have had boots so big that they have always held aloof from the Chamber, but the majority have taken considerable trouble to attend and carry out work useful to them all. The question of federation and discussion thereon is one for which the Chamber

By courtesy of Indian Railways Bureau

A wall in the palace at Udaipur

has provided a machine of which full use has been made. Those who have perused the articles of the White Paper will be aware that there is an interesting anomaly, which has been put into words. Neither the Princes' States themselves nor even the great provinces of India are competent to enter a federation. They have to be made so. His Majesty in Council will wave a fairy wand, if the time should come, declare each and all independent sovereign states and provinces. Half an hour later they will surrender their wand-granted status and sign instruments of accession. But the very fact that this is necessary is a striking illustration of the complications and vast machinery which an attempt to federalize a continent so peculiarly constituted must involve.

In the systems of government, some still intensely Oriental, it is possible not only to trace survivals of great antiquity, but to see them at work much as Megasthenes, the Greek ambassador to the Court of Chandra-Gupta, saw them several generations before the Christian era. In those states, and they are many, which were carved by modern adventurers in perhaps Georgian times, this would not be the case so completely; but in the Rajputana states, habits and tradition reach back into the mists of time, and are pregnant with history and custom that are still worth further study by the ethnological expert, as well as the historian.

Since the Moslem states are few, and even where the rulers are Moslem the people are Hindu, the working of the old Moslem way of government is not seen so freely and completely as is the Hindu law in the old Hindu states. It is not till you get to the frontier state of Kelat that you see the Qoran and the *Shariat* in any sort of operation with a Moslem ruler, ruling a Moslem people. Even there the *jiziah*, the poll tax on the non-Moslem, that Aurungzebe tried to impose, nay did by force impose, on India, will not be seen.

The Touch with the People and the Government of the Districts

Ever since the British first took over the Diwani, that is to say the Departments of Revenue and Justice, of Bengal at the behest of the Mogul Emperor who could not manage it himself, and thus began to come into touch with the daily wants and needs of the people, the system adopted has remained the same. It was indeed inherited, in a decadent state too often, from the Moguls. It consisted of a series of counties each governed by an official, a *Hakim Ala,* a *Wazir Wizarat* or what not, who managed the affairs of the county—so many counties to the province. In India under British jurisdiction, as already explained, this county official is known as 'collector' in the old Presidencies, and 'deputy commissioner' in the younger provinces, such as the Punjab, Central Provinces, etc., and he corresponds to the higher-sounding 'Governor' used in Egypt and Palestine or the Soudan. In India the term Governor, as we know, is used for the heads of the vast provinces.

The head of a county or 'district', to use the Indian phrase, is the important person, and on his assiduity and competence prosperity and happiness depend. He is chief revenue officer, chief magistrate and chief administrator. The incumbents are generally of the Indian Civil Service, British or Indians in race as may be, while in the younger provinces some of them are drawn from other sources. As the Indianization of the personnel advances to the statutory limit, more and more of the personnel are, or will be, of India. Some such there have been for many many years.

For some considerable time, municipalities, district boards, etc., have been composed of elected Indians, and since the Montford Reforms they have been empowered to elect their own chairman. Prior to that, in a controlling and educational capacity as chairman, was the collector.[1] In

[1] This term is used to embrace also the other term in use—deputy commissioner.

most provinces this privilege has been used, the Punjab, however, long preferring to avoid the communal jars among members by having as before the independent British or Indian chairman of the Civil Service. It cannot be said that this municipal devolution has been successful, for almost every municipality is now bankrupt where it was solvent, and in the Punjab its budgets are fraudulent and balanced only by faking, its employees are unpaid, its elections are fudged and nominations are sold (*vide* Punjab Government reports of 1931 and 1932).

However, the complacent higher governments think that knowledge comes by making mistakes, though hardly by calculated fraud. Nevertheless this must not be taken as poking fun at India, but only a light allusion to what it reports of itself.

The old traditional village system of self-government and self-sufficiency, long defunct, which has been believed to have been so admirable, and of which traces have remained, has been referred to, and for many years efforts to revive it have been made with varying and sometimes noteworthy success, though also with marked failures. In some parts of India the ancient system had still seeds that would germinate, in others the revival had nothing indigenous left in memory or instinct. The institution of the long past had, by some process that we did not know, settled in each village sufficient of the depressed and untouchable classes to make them the hereditary servants of the community—water-carriers, scavengers, watchmen, messengers, barbers, midwives—everything that a community needed, and all confined within the strange rule and custom that Hinduism had established. The headman of a village, termed in more northern India the *Lambardar*, principally a revenue agent of Government, had long crystallized into an hereditary position to which prestige attached, and we constantly see resemblances in India to dead or dying Western land and feudal systems. Just as the Black Death in England upset entirely the village villeinage, so has the World War with its call for labour upset much of the village life and labour system in the Indian countryside. So many thousands of men broke as it were their hereditary indentures, to see and learn something of the wide world, to be fed and clothed as they had never been fed before, and to demand a new life on their return. The ancient structure of village life was rudely stirred thereby, and *pace* reformers, the stirring by abrupt means of ancient structures is apt to bring new troubles in return for new good, and often are the new troubles worse than the old.

However that may be, as has been explained, the village system has to some extent been restored for several years past, and village public opinion has some check on the great curse of India, the dishonest and oppressive instincts of the minor Government myrmidon.

From the earliest days of British control, the cold weather touring of the 'district officer', the collector or deputy commissioner aforesaid, has been the great source of our administration and rebuilding. By a practice perfected through the generations, the officer has had two camps, one of which was always ahead of him, so that he has ridden from camp to camp to find his accommodation waiting, and has held meetings and interviews of all kinds, *en route* and at each halt. Various durbars, that is to say representative assemblies in which every man might have his say, were waiting for him along his route. Problems, troubles, the Governmental policy and benevolences, were all discussed and explained. The district officer in light and informal guise was carrying out the 'shirt-sleeve' Government, the direct personal touch, without which the great reconstruction could never have taken place, and during which the most implicit faith in the impartiality of the European amid inter-racial and communal jealousies was, and is, much appreciated.

To anyone, to any visitor to India who would study the real India and the real Indian life, a month's tour with a collector will give him an insight into the people, and the charm of the Indian countryside which he will get no other way. He will see the yeoman peasantry, the hereditary landowner, their just and their unjust struggles, the veteran with his medals, who comes to make obeisance to receive his due meed of welcome, the good and the bad of the moneylender and his strangle-hold, the importance that the coming of the rains has on daily life, the difficulties of the land revenue in bad years, the methods of allowing rebate, the troubles over women, the jinking of anklets, and the eyes behind the veil, the searching questions of the district officer, the wise advice, the judgment of Solomon that heals a quarrel or prevents ruinous legislation; the killing once and for all, by a sharp and firm order, of some evil-winded move . . . these were and indeed are the daily sights of the touring district officer.

Every Committee-man from England should thus undergo his preliminary month in the countryside where 90 per cent of India live in the villages. His pleasure and his edification would be equally developed.

This system, both in British and Princes' India, is the one on which the administration is based, and it is essential as the method whereby the people understand the Government and its aims, for all Governments must have aims and should explain them efficiently.

It is the decay of this system that is the universal complaint of the countryside . . . decay because the amount of work and correspondence that modern methods have demanded have tied the district officer greatly to his office. Not only have the legitimate demands and needs of expanding services, of irrigation, of education and sanitation immensely increased the indoor work, but every benevolent crank has been allowed to try and foster the little activities of the West among the peoples of the East. Many hours have been spent in trying to obey the behest for fal-lal committees to try this and that measure, to get up local committees for this and that society, till the unfortunate man cannot turn for the 'kag' that flows in on him. Shirt-sleeve government, on which India's happiness and content and the British Raj depended, has been slowly dying, killed by redundant attempts at efficiency.

Still the relics survive, and the touring of a district officer, especially a really good one, is still the thing to see and take part in, and how few there be who do so! Added to the modern complications, has been the failure to suppress the unnecessary sedition when it began. With that sedition at work, attempts are made to undermine the district magistrates' psychological authority, on which all government depends, and to instigate school children to take their lives, as in the Bengal tragedy. The murder of Mr. Holmes,[1] the kindly magistrate who was trying to find out what two girl students wanted, what their trouble was and how he could help them, only to be pistoled at their hands, is about the most bitter comment on the feebleness of rulers to listen to warning, that the world could imagine.

This pressure of work that removes the district officer from contact—and it will apply equally to any form of government—gives the feet of clay, the dishonest Eastern subordinate, opportunity, which he is the quickest, probably of any race, to avail himself of. The only remedy is his murder at regular intervals as a warning to his class: for the East has its own ways. With the deterioration of good government in the districts, which has been increasing since 1920, possibly a very short way with such will be taken by the public. If so it will be a set-off against the other drawbacks of which the country now so complains.

Under the district officers, apart from the subdivisional magistrates, who may or may not be Indian, is a large class of Indian officials known as *Tahsildars* in charge of a revenue sub-district; their positions are important, carrying prestige, and it is with them that most of the daily life of the districts is concerned under the district officers and his assistants. They are usually second-class magistrates. The same general system more or less efficiently but sometimes in travesty exists in the Princes' States.

[1] And later the horror of the murder of Mr. Burge at Midnapore, as a culminating point in the long series of outrages by the sinister organizations we have allowed to grow up.

It is the fashion to say, or perhaps it used to be, that the people were happier in the States than in British India, appreciating the pomp, the occasional personal touch of one with supreme power, who could raise the lowest to the highest at his caprice, who could reward forthwith, and who could also depose and debase. At one time those who advocated Indian reform wished to recreate more Princes' States. A commentary on this, however, is the fact already referred to, that any proposal to transfer Crown territory to a state usually produces the keenest protest from the inhabitants.

Criminal law is administered in the first case, after some minor authority in civil and criminal law that has been left with the village headman or *punchayat*, by the subdivisional magistrates, who may be salaried or honorary. The more serious cases go to the subdivisional judges for criminal work, to the *munsiffs* for civil cases. Over all, appellate and supervisory, is the district and sessions judge, and over him again the High Court of the province. On the efficiency and human-mindedness of the district officer, and the effectiveness and probity of the judiciary, the whole prosperity and content of India, as indeed of similar institutions all the world over, depends.

It is over this very question of the appointment of the judiciary as proposed in the White Paper changes—there is no need to use the unsuitable phrase 'reforms'—that public opinion both in Britain and in India is so apprehensive, lest an inadequate but specious method of appointment shall be introduced. The air is always full of charges of corruption, unfounded no doubt, but there is always in the background the old Oriental custom of the judge taking a consideration from both parties, not to do an unfair thing, but to take the trouble to do a fair one; and the East is still a strange *mélange* of memories.

One of the problems of India is that the system of higher education that we have allowed to overgrow, turns out thousands of lawyers. Lawyers like anyone else must live, and the inherent tendency to litigation of the East, which has turned out to be even more fun than lotteries, and more exciting than blood-feuds and Borgian poisonings, is being artificially fostered to an evil degree. It is much more fun to see your adversary hauled to a prison, that he does not on this occasion at least, deserve, or heavily mulcted in unjust damages, due to well-arranged and cozened false evidence, than to see him to his grave with a knife in his back.

CHAPTER VII

THE STORY OF INDIAN EDUCATION

India and Education

Three hundred and fifty-three million people to be educated! What a problem! What fun for educationalists and theorists! What disagreements and quarrellings and criticisms! Even if we give the professional educationalist the go-by, we can easily see that the basic problems are immense, when we think of the 222 Indian languages, and of wretched little children in Ireland being made to learn dormouse-dead Irse. In how many languages shall young India be taught? Which nationality and raciality shall be suppressed? In how many languages and for what purpose? Again what fun for the education-monger and faddist and super-patriot, what a course for hares to gallop on, and how difficult for the wisest and most human folk to come to a decision. The criss-cross row in 222 languages, staggers the imagination. Then can there be a *lingua franca*?

What has the continent of India planned and done for herself in the matter? Sentimentalists who revel in the unpractical, are very prone to criticize the Government for taking the lead, to abuse Lord William Bentinck for having accepted Macaulay's famous memorandum and prescribed, with the wish of most Indians of the time, over a century ago, that English shall be the language of higher education. They speak of the British stifling the national spirit, of clogging the racial aspirations and psychology, and generally of all the crimes that that type of hot-air after-thinkers will attribute to a bewildered Government, working at a period when the world was a far more sealed book than now, and public education, and education with a big 'E', almost a forgotten subject.

Lest we too should be in a hurry to heave half a brick at the great and wise East India Company and their anxious successors let us remember a fact or two. The so-called South African Dutch settlers were very largely Huguenot French;[1] yet there is not a French word left in the *Taal*, which men now like to call *Africaans*; the Dutch Government stamped it out. It is only in the good manners that the French traits remain. Then again, in French Canada, in the province of Quebec, in which the British allowed and gave every facility for the French tongue to remain—despite the grumbles of the British settlers—Great Britain to-day is openly accused of perfidy therefor, of deliberately handicapping the prospects of the *habitant* in the world's race! It is a hard world to please, my masters!

Now in ancient times India was a land of education, philosophy and learning, as well as of quaint and queer mythologies long handed on by that word of mouth. The charm of such learning has often induced both Indians and super-sentimental English to lament British failure to revive them. But it must be remembered that for perhaps close on a thousand years, the Aryan and his faith and his philosophy, though they had, as already explained, survived Buddhism, were actually downed, crushed, and depressed, by the Muhammadan invaders and conquerors. The Hindu faith was ruthlessly suppressed, priests slaughtered, conversions made at the sword's point, and temples reduced to ruins in large numbers. Even the Moslem culture which supervened in Moslem circles, as full of charm as was the old Hindu one in quite a different way, was falling when the Empire fell, and was like to be strangled when Mahratta and Sikh were thinking of dominion.

It is therefore not out of place to ask what had the

[1] Cf. Delarey, Joubert, Fouchée, De Celliers, De Villiers, Terblanche, hardly a Dutchman in the whole of the galley.

shattered continent been able to do or what had it cared to do for itself in all these broken years. How did such Governments as India has had deal with the question or did they touch it at all, those Governments of the sword and the spear?

Seeing how ancient is Indian philosophic teaching, literature and artistic learning, and how deep in many directions in the past her scholarship, what lead has Britain given in helping a revival, and how does the result now stand in the Condominium?

If we glance again at the recent past, we at once see how all the energies of the British were expended in bringing peace to the shattered land, giving security to traders, ensuring that a modicum of personal safety and prosperity should exist in a land which had been withered to the last blade of grass by the devastation of Mahratta and Pindari hordes. The last had but followed the ruthless extirpations and slaughters of the Duranis, and the equally domineering Gurkha conquests of the Duns. Order, peace, security for trade, sufficient income for men to live, and the extirpating of such foul horrors as the widespread semi-religious murder and robbery of the secret Thug community, widow-burning, female infanticide and human sacrifice were the first needs. With such to handle, was the Company's Government likely to be more advanced in the matter of education than Merry England whence it derived?

When the British came to India there were no printed books in Indian tongues, and no Western education had been introduced, while since local Governments at first could but keep the peace and develop the national essential of agriculture, there was little to be done but let the indigenous process alone for a while.

The Position at the Beginning of the Nineteenth Century

But that was little enough, save for the rather tattered survivals of earlier religious endowments, and such private schools and colleges as had managed to maintain themselves during the centuries of upheaval.

Nevertheless with all the vicissitudes that the continent had experienced, the old network of indigenous schools, patched and tattered though it was, remained. There were the *tols*, the Brahmin schools in which Brahmin teachers taught Brahmin children—the folk of the white super-crust —the sacred faith of their forefathers, their science, their philosophy and their literature, much of which had come down through the mists of time by word of mouth alone, that word of mouth often so much safer than the productions of the careless copyist, the interpositionist and the glossifier of the ages.

There were also the *Pathsalas*, elementary schools of the lower castes of Hindus, maintained by the pious from ancient endowments and the like. The conquests, and proseletyzing of the Moslems had also left their schools, the higher called *madrassahs*, the lower *maktabs*. These Moslem schools were open to all grades, there being in theory no social inequality in Islam. All Moslem schools taught the Qoran in Arabic and the simple outline of the Islamic creed.

Old as was the network, the numbers of scholars were few, the elementary teachers ill-paid, and owing little allegiance to anyone. In fact it may be said that so submerged was political India, that education of any kind survived in spite of, rather than by, the help of Governments or lack of Governments.

The great, wise, though personally illiterate, Akbar (time of our Elizabeth) laid down plenty of rules for education, as he did other things, mostly by intention.

When the somewhat surprised British found that power and might and dominion were to be theirs, almost the first constructive act was to pay attention to the revival of Indian learning, a tendency in which the hand of some of the earlier missionary bodies was always evident. So far back as 1781 Warren Hastings, always the instigator and encourager of what was good and great, founded the Calcutta Madrassah.

Like all other orderly Governments the Government of Bengal wanted educated men for the offices of state, for the administration and the judiciary. In 1792 Resident Duncan, with the approval of the Governor-General, founded the Sanskrit College at Benares, the home of Brahmin tradition with scholars only asking for encouragement, and vast stores of knowledge and literature behind them to be revised and exploited.

When the new East India Company Act of 1813 was introduced, at a time when State aids to education were few and far between, the Company made provision for devoting a sum of money, a lakh as a beginning, towards education—this at a time when in England education as a State responsibility was as yet undreamt of.

The two new colleges referred to, but dealt with higher education in the cultured languages of India, Sanskrit, Persian and Arabic. There was too much foundation work needed in the securing of law and order and personal safety for mass education to be thought of.

The early demand for a Western education so far as Bengal was concerned came from the people themselves. So far back as 1823 Ram Mohun Roy, a famous Indian reformer and teacher, wrote somewhat bitterly to the Governor-General at the proposal to open a Sanskrit College in Calcutta as a step calculated to keep the people back rather than bring them forward. From that time onward controversy was bitter as to whether higher education should be encouraged in Eastern or Western guise. The great administrators in early India were very strongly imbued with the principles of keeping India Eastern, and only holding the gates as it were to prevent disturbers of peace and trade from upsetting the people. The British-made laws then as now, did, to a great extent, but codify the existing laws, customs and general tone of the country. It was only where custom was distinctly inimical to humanity and civilization, as in the case of the burning alive of widows, that Government tried to ride counter to Indian habits and customs.

It has already been mentioned that the early missionaries took an active part in stimulating education especially in Bengal, and to this day some of the colleges most popular among Indians as introducing character-building and high-grade education, are those of the missionary-controlled non-Christian colleges. By 1826 there was a Council of Public Instruction set up in each of the Presidencies. The controversy as to the vehicle of higher education already referred to now ran hot. Lord William Bentinck, the Governor-General who had first been Governor in Madras and therefore had a wider purview than most Governor-Generals, came down with Lord Macaulay on the side of English. The Oriental Colleges whose founding has been referred to, remained as centres of learning in those tongues, but not as part of the scheme of general education.

The decision taken in 1837, already referred to, to abandon the old Mogul Persian had an adverse effect on Moslem education. This was now abandoned in favour of the vernacular of the province, as was entirely right and wise. But the Moslems had been the chief teachers and exponents of what was in reality their *lingua franca*, found their usefulness largely gone, and many were deprived of their livelihood. It is this very decision which to some extent threw back the whole Moslem community in the race for educated intelligence.

There had long been a tradition of female education in India, but it was now little more than a tradition, and indeed the purdah or veil system that was the Moslem custom, had largely spread among Hindus, partly, it is believed, as a protection against Moslem military licence, and it operated very effectively against female education.[1]

[1] So deep-rooted is the old Moslem prejudice in favour of absolute purdah that we read in 1930 of an operation to the head of a woman that would alone save her life being forbidden because of the unveiling involved, and of the surgeon at last only being permitted to operate by cutting a small hole in the veil.

The Modern Development and the People

It is not necessary to follow here the story of the development of education in India, or to discuss how far the expansion may or may not have followed sane lines. There are countless views, and there are certain facts that result therefrom. We need not be critical, knowing how impractical much of our own mass education is declared on all sides to be. Indeed the Simon Commission who were very specially charged with investigation of the subject, had nothing but admiration of how difficulties had been overcome. The turn where energies had taken the wrong road, it also pointed out, as have many others before them.

After passing through varying stages of policy as a branch of the Home Department's activities at the centre, in 1910 Education became a Department of Government with its own Minister, and at the Durbar of 1911–12 His Majesty announced a substantial grant for popular education. Replying to an address from the Calcutta University in January 1912, His Majesty said: 'It is my wish that there be spread over land a network of schools and colleges from which will go forth loyal and manly and useful citizens, able to hold their own in industries and agriculture and all the vocations of life. And it is my wish, too, that the home of the Indian subject may be brightened and their labour sweetened by the spread of knowledge, with all that follows in its train, a higher level of thought, of comfort and of health. It is through Education that my wish will be fulfilled and the cause of Education in India will ever be very close to my heart.'

In extension of the policy thus enunciated, vast efforts have been made to extend primary education, happily perhaps, without very wide success—happily because education in excess of the standard of living attainable breeds fierce discontent, of which it is no remedy. The cultivation of a goobar patch, with a book of Milton or Saadi in the pockets, does not result in the happy issue that educational enthusiasts of the past have envisaged.

The clamour for more schools and more education in India is often but the voicing of the desires of the educated intelligentsia who want employment as teachers. How great the progress is, at any rate on paper, is to be noted from the number of primary schools, as instanced by the following figures for British India. Recognized educational establishments rose from 154,952 in 1917 to 211,048 in 1928, and of these under instruction from seven and a quarter to ten and a half millions. There were also 37,803 recognized and 35,216 unrecognized institutions as well. The number of females compared with males in school is put at one to eighteen. Since the figures given further progress has been steady enough.

The Universities

The first universities as distinct from individual colleges were opened in India so far back as 1857, the year of the Mutiny of the Bengal Army, which did not disturb the capitals of the three Presidencies, Calcutta being preserved by an effective disarming of the adjacent garrison. The first universities then were those of Calcutta, Madras, and Bombay. It was not till 1882 that a university of the North was formed at Lahore, to be followed in 1887 by the first unitary university at Allahabad. The rush for higher education almost entirely English, meant that as the years rolled on these five were intolerably over-burdened, dealing with something like 60,000 students in 184 affiliated Arts colleges. In 1920 Aligarh, the famous Moslem college, became a university, Rangoon and Lucknow followed, Aligarh and Lucknow being unitary.

After this the rate of growth was astounding: Dacca, Delhi, Nagpur, Andra, The Scindiah, Chindabaram, Benares, with its old Sanskrit College, a solely Hindu university, Patna, at the Moslem centre, followed, there being 232 affiliated Arts colleges by 1927 and 16 universities. Since then Osmania and Mysore have also been declared universities—a total of 18.

It is not too much to say that as far as the principles of organization are concerned these universities are as modern as any in the world. In their practice, efficiency and detail of course, many are not fully developed. Nevertheless there is no branch of education and science that cannot be followed and studied.

The pity is that in the unavoidable economic conditions of India the existence of 18 universities is a tragedy and a folly. The desire of young India for education, the clamour for degrees of some kind, the entirely admirable self-sacrifice of parents to give their children a university education, is far in excess of openings and opportunities. Just as for many years B.A.'s have clamoured for minor clerkships in the lowest divisions of the Civil Service, so now are young Indian engineers with even British degrees thankful to take up the humblest job, that needs none of the scientific acquirements that are theirs.

Medicine and science on Western lines, are only necessary to a limited degree in a country with little purchasing and earning power. The filling of every post in India with young Indians would give no relief. Just as in the Western countries the collapse of the inflated world is leaving countless young men with no outlook in life, and is filling the colleges with gloom,[1] so in India is the trouble accentuated a hundredfold. In the West it is depression, in India it is unlimited educational inflation in a market which never existed, save to a very limited extent, that caused the trouble. The conditions of life due to soil and climate have been outlined. Who wants or can afford a panel doctor, architects and surveyors, in a country which can but support mud-houses and few public buildings, not from want of Government or a lead, but because the conditions of the country can never afford such in the sense that Europe can? Only one educated class grows and grows, that is lawyers, and lawyers' clerks, an evil of which many of high authority have written warning—

[1] *Vide* articles in *The Times.*

law for the sake of law, litigation for the sake of litigation—as the new wine goes more freely into the old bottles.

Save therefore that there is far too much of them, those ways and learnings of universities attract and offer much to charm visitors in search of such if they find their way to the more dignified and stately of the institutions.

A new phase that seemingly needs more attention with less feeble hand than it is getting, is that of those universities in which a cell of the bomb-cult is allowed to flourish. They should get the shortest shrift. It has been proposed that a sharp cut in the state grants should be the temporary fate of such, though how far that may be practical is another matter. Nevertheless guilt of this sort can only be purged at the expense of the innocent.

The bomb-cult and the over-manufacturing of graduates for the country's needs are the two evils in what in other ways is the most monumental testimony to the Eastern desire for learning and the British lead and stimulant in the matter.

The truly pathetic point that must not be missed—as obvious now in the West as it should be in the East—is the existence aforesaid of a soured and disappointed intelligentsia educated for a state of affairs that never did exist or exists no longer as a source of danger. It must in the very nature of things give communism and revolutionary movements an entirely unmerited stimulant or at least place crime on a more organized and more intelligent level; for, as Falstaff said at Gadshill, young men must live, and gorbellied knaves with fat purses are fair game.

Technical Education

The more recent educational developments in university scope had gone far in the direction of technical and scientific education, and in angle and intent the technical colleges affiliated to the universities are advanced and modern. How far again they may be in advance of the country's needs is another matter. Indian parents who have sent their boys to the more expensive English colleges to find that that is no royal road to life, will not think better of the home-grown article. But technical education is obviously the need in a country where an Arts education for culture's sake is not an advantage to nine-tenths of the graduates. The real problem for India in the educational line is on what lines will higher or lower education help the country to prosperity, or what is more important, happiness? Mr. Gandhi has always been right in saying that India had a peaceful way of life of her own. Unfortunately the history of the last thousand years, the story of conquering Turks, has much disturbed the old Hindu way, which is not to be recaptured by Mr. Gandhi and his spinning-wheel however much we may wish it were feasible. It is the great peace of the last hundred years, the Pax Britannica, that has made the return to the old simple life to some extent possible, when every man might go his way free from the terror of the sword and spear of raiders and conquerors—Gandhi papers please copy.

What particular form of education is best for the village folk or for the choice young men and goodly of the universities probably needs a good deal harder thinking than it has yet received. It would be so easy to set up Soviet misery and starvation if education were to go wrong, and the half-starved Bolshie schoolmaster aforesaid were loosed on the land. In this connection be it remembered that Russia will turn bitter attention to every incipient cesspool. And then my masters! if John Bull may speak as a friend to Brahminy Bull it would be well to discourage that attempt of undergraduates to get their degrees and qualifications by the fraudulent means that college dons in India sometimes tell us of, means that are something quite different from merely time-honoured cribbing at examinations. If the medical colleges would dwell on character and responsibility, the shame of bogus operations, which does so much to smirch the fair fame of Indian graduates in medicine and surgery, would not be set against even an individual. Indeed universities and schools should put character-building and honest resolve in the very forefront of all their platforms, happy in the assurance that the Vedas, El Qoran, and the teachings of Zoroaster, are all one with them in their high endeavour.

In this matter of technical education and facilities for scientific research, an inquirer will be surprised to see how far on the modern road some of the universities have gone, and if they follow some of the work, they will see how Indian students and scientists have already made notable contributions to the world's knowledge. This in the minds of the less prejudiced might even reflect some credit on the British lead which has put them on this road, which outside the Gandhi mentality is not so 'satanic' as it appears to that particular form of jaundice.

It is of course in the universities that the Indian cricket and lawn tennis spoken of further on are engendered.

CHAPTER VIII

SOME PROBLEMS OF THE PEOPLE

The Country People

To have a bowing acquaintance with the daily life of these 353 millions, is an essential for any intelligent visitor and student. It must be realized, as already remarked, that India is primarily a country of agriculturists and in many parts of peasant proprietors, 90 per cent live in the villages and over 70 per cent are actual cultivators. The general rule of India is that land belongs to the Crown, and that rent is payable to the Crown, and is the basic source of public revenue. In British India alone there are over half a million villages. In many cases the villagers, the land-owners and their labourers, live in villages rather than on farms, since centuries of rapine, invaders and marauding bands have compelled them to do so for protection. It has been related how the constant decay of rule after rule, and the constant come-and-go of invaders or the armies of quarrelling kings, was the routine of centuries. To this day in Khandeish, in the Deccan and any great area within the come-and-go of armies, the villages have bastioned walls of mud and stone, while the lofty fortresses, whether governmental or the adulterine castles of the barons, crown every hill which could boast a spring or support a tank.

India being unfortunately a land as a whole of little or only seasonal moisture, the yeoman peasant and the small-holder gets even less from the soil for his year's work than elsewhere. It has already been explained that the races and classes are many, and how they came to be so has also been outlined, and how important these matters are, far more, inconceivably more, than in the blended West. That, however, is only an introduction to the people as they are to-day, the people of the sun-baked fields, the cramped cities and mud-walled villages. As in every other country, the life of the villager is a very different thing from the life of the town, and India is a country of villages, and of mud villages at that. Mud, unbaked sun-dried mud brick, is the material of which most villages are made. Not that mud, that is to say, unbaked or *kuchcha* bricks, are a bad material. Some of the most comfortable of the better-class houses and English bungalows in India are made thereof. These houses are infinitely cooler than houses made of burnt brick. Others in stony country are made of rough stones set in mud. A *pukkha* house is made of baked brick or of stone set in mortar, and this style is called '*pukkha*', 'cooked' or 'baked', as distinct from '*kuchcha*', 'uncooked', and for this reason the first word is used for 'genuine' or 'thorough'. The phrase '*pukkha sahib*' means the most thorough and true-hearted gentleman who would never do a dirty trick or let anyone down. The little half-baked English writer with an inferiority complex who writes about India thinks it means an overbearing '*bahaduring*' Briton of swashbuckling type, but it is never used except in true knightly sense. It is not the word for what in grammar-school eyes is a typical 'public school' man. The villages themselves in the North will use the phrase in this sense of those Britons they love and trust, which perhaps is a digression that may be excused therefore in conjunction with this chance *rencontre* with the word in its building sense. To resume—

The secret of maintaining *kuchcha* houses is their constant repair, especially after rain, the repair consisting of an application of a plaster of mud, chopped straw and cow-dung. Unfortunately for their appearance the mud huts and cottages of the villages do not always get repair, at any rate on the outside, and Indian villages are often forlorn affairs. Roofs in the South are made of tiles, often a bright and cheerful red, of flat stones or of thatch, and the ubiquitous corrugated iron has long been in evidence also. On the other hand, where some special type of agriculture is possible and has been developed, villages present a better appearance, and the pensioned army officer, usually a small yeoman farmer, will perhaps have built himself a '*pukkha*' house. There are, of course, villages and villages, and some will be found grouped round brick houses of a local landowner which stand high on the piled debris of centuries. In most cases pigs' and cows' manure and rubbish will lie about in happy confusion and filth. The tragedy of most mud villages is that they have been built from mud excavated at their doors, and the excavations, filled with rain water for many months, pour forth the mosquito that fills the countryside with malaria. It is perhaps not too much to say that the miserable physique of the ordinary cultivators of the South may be due to centuries of destruction of red corpuscles by the malarial parasite. Reference has been made herein to the temporarily successful village uplift with which an enthusiastic English magistrate and his wife inoculated a district and its contented relapse therefrom when the uplifters' backs were turned. One of the most interesting things in India is the ancient village system already referred to, with its contingent of hereditary outcaste menials and servants. These, while existing in servility as members of the strange untouchables whose origin is so wrapped in mystery, do the village work admirably, and are reasonably treated and maintained, so long as they do not upset matters by presumption or contumacy. The scavengers, water-carriers, midwives, and night watchmen, all have their place as related, while the village headman and the village council or *panchayat* rule the villages, and are equipped with certain lesser powers as magistrates and quarrel-menders. This system has come to us through the ages, and the wiser British magistrates and governors have done much to revive and foster it, and to use it for the development of co-operative banking and the like. It is the fashion now to say that it is breaking down, though if that be so it is worth many efforts to maintain. The wisdom of a *panchayat* settling some village dispute is like unto the wisdom of Solomon.

The Revenue System

As has just been said, in India most land belongs to the Crown, and from time immemorial the revenue of the state is derived from the rent thereof, which is fixed on a portion of the produce and revised from time to time. The people generally are hereditary tenants, who cannot be deprived so long as they pay their revenue. In some parts the system is one of peasant proprietorship, when the peasants own the land and pay revenue themselves, which is called *ryotwari*—*ryot* being a peasant—or else the system is *zemindari*, where the land is in the hands of larger landowners who either farm themselves or allow tenants to do so on the half-profits system, and whose position has become hereditary. As a rule the *zemindar* pays the revenue to the Crown. Some lands have been granted in the past for services to the Crown, which are entirely or partially revenue-free. Such grants are usually known as *jaghirs*, and are from titles as a rule previous to British occupation.

Whenever a province has come under British rule in the past a Domesday Book was at once compiled, known as the 'Settlement'. 'Settlement' consists of a complete record of all land rights and the revenues to accrue therefrom, which are duly recorded and against the terms of which rights of appeal were permissible.[1] When it is realized that the bulk of the Indian revenue is involved, it will be seen how important both to the state and the individual the accurate and just compiling of this Domesday Book was. But the difference will be noted, that whereas William the Norman had given his land away, and was compiling the titles of those to whom it had been granted, newly in the case of his

[1] It was extremely unpopular among those who had 'jumped' land by force or fraud.

Norman and French, reaffirmed in the case of his Saxons and Danes, the rent was not for the Crown. Rent was taken in feudal service and when that was abandoned, a cash liability should have taken its place. Those who ponder on such matters will realize how much better a source of basic revenue is Crown rent for land rather than income-tax, which, as our Treasury ruefully finds, fades when people's income fades and dividends are not forthcoming. But even under the land rental system of India, a period of bad times involves remissions of revenue to the embarrassment of the state.

Hard times in India come under two quite different categories; *first*, failure of rains with the consequent scantiness of crops for markets, obviated now in areas on which canalized rivers and storage lakes bring water, and the *second* due to times of depression. Thus at the present juncture, the Indian cannot market his cash crops, and even if he has plenty of food, cash for revenue is sadly short.

Irrigation

Among Britain's greater claims to the admiration of the world and the gratitude of India, lies the Irrigation System with which an arid and parched country has been supplied.

The nature of the rivers has been referred to, those that are perennial from the Himalayas, and those that merely drain off the heavy downpour of the rainy season. Every drop of water that runs into the sea in a parched country like India is a loss to food production and wealth. For centuries the country has developed its own system of storage of rain-water, usually weak and trivial, with here or there some ambitious Royal dam. The taking-off of the flood water in the snow-fed rivers, by inundation canals that acted when the waters rose, has long been practised, but the rise of Western engineering and modern engineering science alone, has introduced the distributary system of ancient Babylonia magnified a thousand-fold.

The Five Rivers of the Punjab ran through a desert

country, with some catch-crops grown in the winter rain, largely inhabited by graziers and camel-breeders and masterless men. Save near the river cultivation was in a poor state, but now each of these great rivers has head-works comparable with Assouan, sending gigantic trunk canals across arid tracks, with countless branches, even has the surplus water from one river been taken overland to help the demands on another. The result has been that for the last thirty years colony after colony, thoughtfully planted by race and by homogeneous clan, has been settled on the new lands on a town-planned basis, and a vast number of people have thus been transported from congested areas. As the railway from Karachi or Lahore bears you up and down the land in April, trying perhaps to escape from the coming summer, you will pass through millions of acres of golden corn land, of wheat and barley. Alas! for the moment it is a criminal act to grow wheat in an over-corned world, and whereas a few years ago the yeomen of the Punjab colonies were coining money and several hundred ships carried wheat and barley to Europe, now unwanted it is all thrown back on their hands. The great sturdy yeomen who throng the railway sidings in the canal country have but one cry: 'Our bellies are full, but our pockets are empty. Why? Why? Why?' And the answer no man can give them. Some put it down to Mr. Gandhi. On the other hand, with good wheat-meal flour at a knock-down price, all the poor and the lowly who lived on millets are taking to wheat-meal, and they will grow the stronger thereby, and all the while the railways of the Satanic British Government and British Shareholder carry the cheap wheat south to lands that never saw it.

Now the mighty Indus itself has been harnessed at Sukkur, where it cuts through a conglomerate ridge, and is being spread over dusty Sind. The Sukkur barrage is perhaps the most famous in the world, but what is to be the result in view of the *bouleversement* of all production, remains to be seen. Comfort and prosperity to the people certainly, while the Indian Agricultural Department and the Civil Administration are trying to turn the farmers' thoughts to crops that are wanted. Java sends too much sugar, so sugar-cane that will stand varied climates is being fostered, oil-bearing crops, etc.

Further south-east the Ganges and Jumna have long been spread on the land, the great Ganges Canal having been made and opened by the East India Company.

In the south and west, a huge storage scheme for rain-water has been carried out, and more remains to be done, and from such storage lakes made in the southern and western hills, canal systems lay out the store of water as required.

The visitor to India who would see the truer wonders of the East should arrange a motor drive along the great avenues that grow along the canals; he will be astounded at what has been done. The glory of the Punjab Canal System, the beauty of the ways, say in March when the young *shisham* leaves are coming out, far transcends the glory and interest of any of the relics of the past.

There are 75,000 miles of canals and nearly thirty-two million acres[1] of canal-watered land. Lest irrigation engineers, however, raise their brows, let it be mentioned that over-irrigation and a careless peasantry have brought their own diseases. Seepage means mosquitoes and malaria, and irrigation is bringing salts to the surface, as it did in Babylonia, and new remedies are required for new troubles. Yet arid land cannot be turned to gardens and fields without some set-backs for science to handle.

Agriculture Generally

It has been said that 95 per cent of the population are rural and over 70 per cent actual agriculturalists. There are over 1166 million acres in the whole land; of this about 18 per cent is unculturable, but in British India the uncultur-

[1] Figures of 1930 (British India only). It will when existing schemes are finished, be 40,000,000, and eventually 50,000,000; which is about equal to the rest of the world.

able percentage is double that of Princes' India. Taking the figures for British India, which will at any rate give a conception of the immensity of the subject: of the culturable balance 30 millions must lie fallow, and 154 millions is culturable waste, leaving 228 million acres under crops of which 210 millions were food crops and 51[1] millions other produce.

In case a few more figures can still be digested, the live-stock figures may be given. They stand at over 218 millions, of which 154 millions are bovine, some 62 million sheep and goats and nearly 4 million equines and camels.

What are the crops? The food crops are rice, wheat, barley, in the North, *gram* which is a pulse, many lentils, the millets in the South and more rice: some maize and cotton everywhere; buckwheat in the terraced hills; sugar-cane, and then many cash crops; oil, castor, mustard, etc., jute, opium, and so forth. The farming is, for the most part, simple enough; two bullocks and a wooden plough with an iron-shod toe does the business, though there is a considerable trade in American ploughs. The method of carriage is the bullock-cart, usually drawn by a pair. As you travel through the plains of the Deccan you will pass millions of acres of unfenced open fields, just as you still see them near Ewell and a few other parts of England, lightly ploughed, for the land is light. The Indian farmer is lucky, for he can, at any rate on irrigated land, get a spring and an autumn crop—the *rabbi* and the *kharif*. The women will be working in the fields; in fact all agricultural families work the day long, and the folk are tired by evening.

As you go up north you will find what is known as the *abadi*, the little homestead with a well; usually the well is worked by a Persian wheel, with a long ring of earthenware pots tied to a rope chain. Lazily, drowsily, drones the wheel as the bullock goes round and round, the sound of the warm season coming on, and the ripening of the spring crop that lies emerald-green around, brightened by a patch of *tili*, the yellow mustard. It is only in districts where law and order

[1] These figures include certain lands cropped twice in the year.

have long prevailed that you find the homestead. In many parts of India folk lived in villages because they needed protection in the bad old times, while up in the north they live so because it is still a land of dacoity or robbery under arms. In a country where *pace* all the efforts of a good police the gangs now and again round up even a village, decapitate while alive a policeman (a quite recent occurrence) to create terror, let off guns, torture old ladies and shopkeepers, one cannot be surprised that farmers shun homesteads and prefer to walk out to their fields. The homestead country is always full of quiet charm, a mango tree, a group of mimosa round the well, the little canals for the well water, and a few Persian rose bushes.

But while simple village farming with ancient tools is the normal order, the larger men farm now with plenty of enterprise. The experimental agricultural farms attached to the various agricultural institutes, the improved seed, the methods taught there, and the number of young men now trying to go through the agricultural colleges, all mean to some extent better farming. Wheats are being bred that can be grown further south, so that people hitherto fed on the millets may, in time, come to the good wheat whole-meal and increase their miserable physique thereby.

In the irrigated tracts there will be the new villages of the colonies set in the rich crops that never fail. Here till the world depression came the people were earning big money and curiously enough becoming more extravagant and more indebted than their poorer brethren, like beggars set on horseback.

The Cattle, Milk and Beef Problems

The want of principle on which cattle are grown is very hard for the West to realize, and the difference will be evident when it is said that no cattle are grown at all for the food market, whereas the breeding of store cattle, of cattle for the meat market, is as much or more the object of cattle-farming in the West and in the New World. In India, with its millions of Hindus, the cow is sacred. To kill it is an abomination which sends the killer to the nethermost hell and ensures his reincarnation as the soul of one of the lowest of the beasts. So no cattle are grown for meat. The Muhammadan will eat beef and does so, it is true; the British soldier and the European must have it, save that if he lives in the territory of a Hindu Prince he will have to go without. Cattle are bred for traction and for milk. Some of the draught cattle are magnificent beasts, and in the days of the Mogul and earlier British artillery, when bullocks were used for draught and for army transport purposes, they were specially so. Whence then comes the beef that the soldier and the European resident have for their rations? The answer is that it *comes from the waste products sub rosa.* No Hindu farmer dare kill his useless barren cow or his bullock too lame and too intractable to plough or draw a wagon. He must pension such and help to feed them. But there is a subterfuge. There is no reason why he should not sell them, and he sells to a Muhammadan grazier and no questions are asked. The grazier drives the miserable half-starved beasts that he has purchased for an old song to some spot where grazing is lush, and there he leaves them till they are in marketable state, and then do they come to the beef market. They are cheap beasts and are sold for a penny or twopence a pound. A very few are fattened on grain for such markets as Calcutta or Simla. Even then, since cow-killing may easily give occasion for a riot, the butcheries are put by order of Government far from Hindu residences. Another interesting point regarding butcher's meat is the question of humane killing. When the author was Quartermaster-General of the Army in India and concerned with Army housekeeping, a very strong representation as to methods of killing and the use of the humane killer came to Army headquarters in India from England. But it was pointed out that all Muhammadan flesh must have the blood run out, like *kosher* meat, that the Army only took the best and bigger joints, that the contractors sold the rest of the carcase to the Muhammadan population who would only buy meat made *hallal* or 'lawful' by throat-cutting. To use a humane killer would at least double the price of Army beef. Happily the cutting of throats by an Eastern butcher is usually a quick procedure, and there is no such thing as unskilled stunning which is or was the scandal of Europe.

It will be seen that it is only by the subterfuge of selling to Moslems that an Indian farmer can get even a hide price, unless he waits for natural death. Sheep and goats are grown for wool and also as meat, and both, but specially the latter, are milked. The milking value of the cattle is often far too small, owing to the entirely promiscuous breeding that takes place and the fact that holy bulls, good and bad, roam about at will, propagating freely. There are one or two indigenous breeds of splendid milkers, such as the Saiwal, but only in the Army dairies, in the Government instructional farms and in a few of the Princes' studs is the improvement of breed and yield thought of. Fortunately much of the milk and butter yield comes from the huge old black mud-caked water buffalo, who is often to be seen lying in a muddy pond to defeat his adversary the fly. Buffalo milk is very heavy in cream content, especially if well fed. Cotton seed is the main food that makes for heavy cream yield. Despite the millions of bovines, many are so inferior that the available milk supply is far too small for the population, while *ghee*, the melted butter that is a food staple, is greatly deficient and is adulterated with vegetable oils, and it is to be feared often with animal fat sufficient to lose every Hindu his place in heaven. The Royal Commission on Indian Agriculture stated that there are millions of cows and bulls quite unfit for any purpose, that are impoverishing the land and giving no yield, the cows quite unfit for breeding. And yet deeply ingrained religious prejudice forbids their destruction. Not, unless we destroy Hinduism, does it seem possible to remedy this evil. Hinduism is a very ancient belief, and ancient beliefs based on revelation do not readily go down before either reason or Western apparent carelessness. To this day it is very easy to get up an agitation and violent riots on the matter of cow-killing; in fact anti-cow-killing is very much a platform at times in modern politics. Lord Linlithgow's Royal Commission on Agriculture reported that fifteen million entirely useless and workless cattle were on the land.

As regards the improvement in the cow life of the country it is probable that it will never be arrived at save by Government providing bulls, letting farmers keep them and charge a trivial fee, receiving themselves a grant for their upkeep. The whole village and agricultural life is so simple that private enterprise is outside the picture.

A strange feature in village and cantonment bazaars is the cakes of cow-dung, drying for fuel. All the little girls and half the women walk in the wake of the cows, to collect the droppings, often running out with their hands together to catch the excreta before it falls, not as in the roads of England for the garden, but for the kitchen fire. A well-known cause of the low yield of village land is the fact that dung that should be on the land is used for the fire. Fuel is scarce, trees are not sufficient to provide firewood, goats destroy scrub that might grow to fuel. Nevertheless the fact remains that manure is thus diverted from the land, and the kneading of the flat dung-cakes, and setting them to dry, is the popular morning's amusement of the housewife. Cow-dung being one of the holy things of Hindu India, the occupation cannot be other than pleasing.

That the people should prefer dung to wood as fuel will be appreciated by those veterans of the Boer War, who know how much better the turfs of dried sheep-dung cut from the *kraal* that has held stalled sheep for donkey's years are for boiling a billy, even than the lid of the harmonium.

It is the fashion to think that education will improve the people, make them lose their more irrational prejudices, and slowly take to more profitable ways. To a certain extent that may be so, but the educationalist who thinks there is nothing like education is responsible for much of the unhappiness of the world. The idea that culture makes a man happier when his work is done, and makes his mind turn to delightful thoughts, is fairly exploded, unless a man's standard of living can be raised too. If it were possible to get more from the Indian soil, then folk might live better. And it is to this end that the British Government have laboured only to have their results thrown on their hands by depression. Where millions are small-holders the small-holding troubles can readily be seen. The want of any capital has put the whole population of rural India into the hands of the moneylender. In every village the *bunniah*, the man of the trading class, is a moneylender. Because the land, unless matured and irrigated, gives a poor and uncertain crop, the small-holder must always borrow, even if his harvest will eventually pay, of necessity in arrears, the cost of its production and of its farmer's keep. The moneylender, for a handsome consideration, will finance him, and the cultivator is always in debt. Most moneylenders are rapacious, but undue rapacity will often end in the moneylender being murdered with boiling oil. Between that and the benefits of co-operative land banks, at which Government have been working for years, there are various possible stages. It may be said that the moneylender has been, and indeed is, until land banks can be made universal, a necessity for the whole small-holder system, unless that small-holder can make each year more than 'wash and wear'. But even the good moneylender expects rates of interest which in ordinary life are exorbitant. On the other hand the moneylender cannot now by law foreclose on the land except under special specified circumstances. We are therefore to some extent up against, in justification of high interest, the old moneylender's query, 'At what rate of interest would you lend a mutton chop to a starving dog?'

Indebtedness and Co-operative Societies

But far away above all other causes of the indebtedness of the people, that is to say, of the poor, is the money spent at family feasts, especially marriage feasts. Marriage as it should be is the great feast and sacrament of life. In a moral community it is the loosing of the day-spring that makes the world. It is in India, as in Christian countries, woman's great expression of herself, as the real business portion of a world that must continue. So for ages past, all and sundry make merry on the auspicious occasion of their children's marriage, regardless of their purses, and the moneylender makes it so. Nothing pleases him more than to have the people deeply in his debt. It is true he could not realize all his securities; they lie in the life and work of the people. If they do not practically hand over to him their earnings, which do not liquidate as a rule the debt, then they will starve. The moneylender is far better in some ways as an institution than the dole or any State insurance. The out-of-work poor who can work, he will keep on a subsistence ration till they are in work again. The mere fact that they owe him money, will compel him to keep them, and it will compel them to work when work is obtainable.

It is a strange system and has manifest advantages if understood, and it is inextricably woven into the life of the people. Only very foolish people would seek to upset it save gradually and by improved conditions, since so far as the cultivator goes, it is an essential part of the system, until replaced by co-operative land banks. Here again, the co-operative bank will only lend on the reasonable security of an average worker's crop. It does not finance marriages when it knows it can never be repaid, but the *bunniah* does so—at a price. The watching of the small-holder, stimulating and helping him, and keeping the moneylender within bounds has long been an important part of the work of the Indian civilian who is a district officer.

It is indeed in this matter of co-operative banks and co-operative societies that the best prospects of Indian rural life lie. It also appeals to the old *punchayat* customs of the people. Some of the ablest officers of this Civil Service have been deeply concerned in its development.

A potter at his wheel

A Peshawur fruit stall; Indian oranges, Kashmir apples, Kabul grapes

Improvements in Agriculture

For many years the attention of the Central and Provincial Government has been directed to the improvement of agriculture under the following main headings, several of which have just been referred to:

Training of Indians in scientific agriculture to work in experimental farms, to teach and lecture, and to conduct research.

Institution of agricultural laboratories, and experimental farms in which improvements in seed, breeds of cattle and prevention of disease are studied.

The establishment of centres where the indigenous breeds of cattle sheep and goats are studied from the view of Indian needs and climate.

The success that has been met with has been remarkable, so far as it goes, and the Indian farmer has been brought to realize the importance of good seed grain. Immense amount of work has been done with wheat and barley, sugar, cotton, fruit, jute, etc. In fact no branch of Indian agriculture has come under study that has not resulted in better produce, and better resistance to disease. Among interesting and important matters would be the production of wheat that will grow further south. As the wealth of the people has improved, more and more wheat is being eaten, eaten always in its whole-meal form, but if it can be grown further south by a seed that will stand the heat, more and more will it be taken into use as a food.

Although sugar is widely grown in India, a large amount is still imported, and there is room for a better cane that gives a better yield for all the trouble taken. But sugar is an expensive crop to grow, requiring both manure and irrigation, and assistance in getting manures is now one of the objects of the agricultural co-operative societies, with which the land has been honeycombed in the last few years.

How to describe all that has been and is being done to help

the peasantry is outside of the province of this scamper over the 350 million course. But the whole story of India really lies in the poorness of the land, the harshness of the climate and the difficulties in making improvement. Many a young commercial traveller dreams of the day when this apparently countless field for the gramophone and the safety razor can be opened up, failing to see that never never, can this barren soil and this prolific people ever rise to the standards of life that will serve his purpose.

There is one element of truth in the fraudulent Gandhi propaganda, and the story is so old that even the Civil Service who love the people have forgotten. A century ago the coming of the world trade to India and the importance of bright machine-made clothes killed the village weaving industries. In those days villages spun their own clothes. Steadily since then has local effort been ousted. The scenes in the ditches of forts and city walls where the long cloths were woven by hand in the open by men, women and children out in the sunlight, with hand shuttles, are gone, and gone, as has been said, many a long year. It is deplorably sad, but an inevitable result of machinery and the modern ways of life.

Industry

With 90 per cent of the people living in villages, industry, as we know it, is almost unknown outside the great ports. The amount of machinery in use in India is very small. In Bombay and Ahmedabad and a few other places there are, it is true, many huge cotton mills. A very considerable increase in factories and machinery has it is also true taken place in the last few years, but in the aggregate it is comparatively trivial. Even here but little of the labour is stabilized and continuous, it all comes in from distant villages, the villager coming to spin when work on the land is slack. The same applies to the workers in the coal-mines, and only perhaps in the railway workshops are the hands at all permanent. It will be readily observed that this has its good side; but the fact is that India is not an industrialized country.

Its manufactured wants are so few. It largely goes barefoot and the huge leather sabots are made by hand in the shops in the towns; its clothes are rarely tailored. The *dhoti*, a cloth round the body, tucked into the waist by being brought up between the legs, does for both sexes. The little brassière of the women, the jackets of the men, if such be worn, are easily made by hand, and give no demand for mass production. No one wants furniture. More than half the population probably sleep on platted grass mats on the ground, folk eat with their fingers. There is neither scope for the manufactured article nor money with which to buy it. Even now there are no car works, and outside the Army shops few heavy repair shops for motor vehicles exist. Motors there are by the thousand, and the most recent importation, and one of great usefulness, the cheap American motor bus that careers over the fairweather mud roads from railway station to village, is driven to a standstill and then cast by the wayside. Distances are so great that heavy shops, even if they existed, would hardly be worth the cost of getting stuff to them. Now and again a camel and its rat-trap carriage will lie dead and broken by the way, a tribute to the light-hearted Lizzie driver.

The sight of the ports will of course belie this statement regarding manufactures, but once you have left those scenes of busy factory, there is nothing. Handicrafts yes! factories no! For oil and sugar-crushing hardly come under the name of industry. Because there is little industry, there are again few of the openings for the black-coated worker and office functionary in which the young intelligentsia will find a career.

To a limited extent industry does increase, but think! No one wants hats, clothes, furniture, fancy goods or anything else at all. It is a country of the handicraftsman who caters for a simple life and a poor people. The streets of a European town, a residential district such as Bayswater are unthinkable in the East. At most you might get a Hampstead for a few of your westernized or very wealthy folk.

Works on small boats, on iron barges, on country carts are not Industry in the Western sense. There is one article, however, in which the trade is immense, the one article that everyone needs, and that is cotton. It is in cotton knitting-thread that there exists a really industrial India. It is here that Industry has really increased and developed enormously in the last fifty years, and as said, the great ports especially are busy scenes and have busy mill areas.

The fact, however, that the labour even here is largely village labour brings its own difficulties. Comparatively few women come with their husbands into residence from the villages, with the results that are inevitable where such conditions exist. Because the conditions are so unstable, trades-unionism introduced by Europeans, from tiresomeness rather than from any idea of improving conditions, flourishes in an ineffective and exotic way. Because the labour comes from far and wide it is made up of many different creeds and antagonistic races living cheek by jowl in industrial dwellings known as *chawls*. The union officials are almost always intelligentsia, and are doing the work for a living, sometimes to make political trouble, but usually pretty well out of touch at heart with the folk they represent. Indian mill-owners varying greatly in their excellence or otherwise, as employers of labour, would, from the very nature of things Indian, have a different outlook from employers in a Christian country, who must always be accessible and sympathetic to welfare and uplift movements in modern times.

In India many Government acts for labour regulation and welfare have been passed, but difficulties peculiar to the country also exist in fair control. There are, of course, many thousands of women at work, especially in the coal-mines, and their presence produces also problems that are not easy to handle wisely or successfully. It is also to be imagined that in India where every Western importation may suddenly assume an unexpected exotic modification, trades-unionism and strikes assume strange proportions. Underground combination is, of course, an Eastern faculty that knows no limit, and the local governments, as time rolls by, are likely to find some ill-winded pirns to unravel.

An interesting feature of any great work requiring large amounts of unskilled or coolie labour, such as heavy railway and dam embankments, is the labour that works in the shape of the gypsy and criminal tribes who arrive to undertake earth work. It is a matter of baskets and somewhere to dig the spoil from. The tribes and clans will camp under thorn bushes, with the family matting and battered tin sheet as shelter, and then will proceed, father, mother and children, to carry baskets of earth on their heads, like a stream of countless ants all day, till the work be built, and far cheaper than all the steam shovels in the world. A few grain merchants open booths, the contractors produce medical assistant and dispensary, the great embankments grow, and all are pleased.

While we may deplore the small outlook for Industry that the poverty of the land postulates, we may equally recognize that the climate of a large portion of the land is tempered to its poverty. Life is very easily sustained in three parts of India.

CHAPTER IX

THE LIGHTER SIDE OF THE PEOPLE

Amusements

How do the people of India amuse themselves? It is a very interesting question. In towns, for the moment, the cinema has come with a rush. They have even invaded the villages, for in India, for half the year and more, the open-air evening cinema is always a possibility, nay they will be found in the most unlikely places. What the unsophisticated people think of them, or whether plucking up kisses by the roots has any meaning, would be worth knowing.

What else? First it should be observed that the Indian dearly loves all sights and spectacles. We will leave out horse-racing, and the westernized sports and games. The townsman loves wrestling and huge sums change hands; cock, quail and partridge fighting are all popular, and many a young blood keeps his own fighting partridge.

The villagers do not see many of the organized sights, but the travelling gypsies often act little plays, and have performing animals. It is marriages and religious festivals, with the lesser satisfaction of burials and burnings, that are perhaps their only real amusement, save for resting in the evening when work is done. But there are many *melas* or fairs where the fun can get quite fast and furious. 'Crown and Anchor', that gambling game with the odds heavily on the side of the bank, that the police are always after in England, is one of the most popular forms of gambling. The Eastern loves a gamble of every kind. There will be merry-go-rounds, and a rough wood 'great wheel', and if you are in the hills, the hill girls in their green and crimson velvet trousers and embroidered waistcoats, will smoke and giggle and make bright eyes. If you are in the plains the women will be there too, but grave and outwardly decorous, unless they are upbraiding their men-kind. Most of the fancy things that are on sale at the fairs come from Central Europe specially made for the Indian fair market. Often the so-called Indian flash jewelry comes from the same source.

The conjurer and the three-card-trick man is there as in the West; the eater of fire, the *atash-khor*, and the man with the monkeys, the snake and the mango trick, and the poor old bear that gets poked to make him dance. *Nautcho Balu!* Dance away bear, dear! that all the children may see, and the great *cobra di capello* or Hooded Snake that does want to sleep, to sleep so terribly, is also poked and made to hiss, while the mongoose on a string frantically tries to escape from the snake, and from being made to tackle him.

Love-making

Somewhat ribaldly I have ventured to include love-making among the amusements of the people, as Hyde Park on a summer afternoon justifies my doing. But you will remember that Alice when she got to the little hill through the looking-glass and proceeded to enumerate in the Victorian manner the principal mountains, said, 'why there are none'. So in India love-making as an amusement of the people, that is to say courting seriously or otherwise *coram publico*, does not take place. In Britain it is *par excellence* the amusement of the people. You see marriages in India are made up by families, betrothals are a family business, and in all but the humblest circles pre-nuptial friendships of young people do not exist. That is why in the reference to the cinemas I venture to wonder what impression on the village mind is made by the kisses of the cinema that are so vigorously picked up by the roots. The experts tell one that even kissing is an unusual sex practice in Hindustan, but of that in privacy I 'hae ma doots'; if so, what a pity! but in any case a large nose ring, such as the best beauties wear, would be *incommode*.

Except among the nomads and the impudent if luscious baggages of the gypsy and criminal tribes where pre-nuptial licence is the rule, courting, as understood in the West, does not go. That there is fierce love-making between those who shouldn't is another story, when marriages are *mariages de convenance*, and when widows are drearily neglected, the little devil Cupid can be busy enough. Woman is fire and man is tow all the world over if it comes to that, and the East within its carved verandahs and its secluded portals, knows all about passion, and even no doubt, the 'Thirst of the soul', but honest village love-makings, the kiss in the ring, and 'I see you, Rooney', games exist not at all. But if you look at the picture of the young lady caught stealing mulberries,[1] you will agree that some day there may be some stealing of kisses to be done, or perhaps no need to steal 'em.

But when we come to merry-making the marriage festival is another matter.

Marriage in the Countryside

The economic troubles that marriage brings to the folk of India, in their deep-seated desire to do justice to this greatest of all the world's festivals, has been referred to; how the poorest ruin themselves, and get deep in the clutches of the moneylender, and how the rich and the royalty dip unduly deep into the family purse.

But when we set such thoughts aside we can rejoice with the spectacles that even the humbler marriages bring to town and village. Since all high-caste Hindus aim at the first marriage in childhood, like the old formal family marriage of the West—marriage, which is quite distinct from the *mukhlawa*, the coming together of adults—and since Islam is apt to follow suit and low-caste India that does have any pretence at all does the same, the wedding scenes are generally of the young. Much of the ceremony involves some tradition

[1] *Vide* p. 154.

of the day when brides were carried off by force of arms, indeed in some cases the scene of the rape is still enacted. We see the youthful bridegroom riding in tinsel state to fetch his bride to his parents' house, and the little bride being carried, also super-tinselled in a curtain litter or bullock-cart. Friends and attendants will be in the procession, and swordsmen and mace-bearers, pipe and tabor, flowers and garlands, the village singing-women, the barber, and the family priest.

Wedding ceremonies are long, and it is a very tired little bride and bridegroom who sit solemnly through them, and whose parents eventually pop them to bed, while the village chatters their criticisms of the day's *tamasha*.[1]

If you, a stranger from the West, would see an Indian wedding, your servant or your courier could probably arrange for you to see the procession—nay, it is possible that an invitation might be arranged for you. Indians sympathize greatly with the would-be *tamasha-bin*, the sightseer.

Pilgrimages

If you would see the simple people of India in their most interesting and human conditions, you must try and go with them to one of the great religious gatherings or fairs—to the great festival at Holy Praag or Allahabad, to celebrate the mystic commingling of Ganges and Jumna. In that Indian complex which makes all unions and minglings the mystical signs of rebirth, that rebirth which takes another life one more stage up on the ascending scale—always supposing a man has not earned for himself a downward one—this particular confluence is super-holy. Or let us try the great fair at Hardwar, or most dramatic, pathetic and human of all, one of those thousand-mile-long walks to the sacred lakes among the snows of Haramukh in Kashmir, or somewhere in the more eastern Himalaya to where Ganges and Jumna have their birth amid the eternal snows below the great twin peaks of Gangotri and Jamnotri.

[1] *Tamasha*—spectacle.

It is an astounding business this pilgrimage of thousands of Hindus seeking 'The Way', seeking remission of sins, and peace on a road untold, anything that will lead a man to sense another world, to feel another existence.

Far is the road and hard the journey for the old and the weak, and there are people who crowd and jostle, and many would be trampled down, drowned in the tarn and the tank in their eagerness. But the good British will be there, the magistrates and the policemen to check, to warn and to help, the doctor and the sanitary expert, that the cholera may not gain its footing, nor the smallpox take heavy toll. Fools there be by the hundred who must jostle for a sight of the tarn, jostle by side of precipice, or rush and press for the holy river, running so swift perhaps that he who falls will rise no more. To such, a British magistrate or an Indian police sergeant will call 'Steady, brothers! Have patience, mother! Wait for the word, the river is always there. Stop pushing behind, or I strike,' for they had been given charge over them.[1]

Faqirs

There are in India five million folk who live on their neighbours, the so-called 'religious mendicants'.

Faqir, though the popular term, is inaccurate, as it is the Arabic for a Muhammadan devotee. The mendicants of India are ninety-nine times out of a hundred Hindu.

I have even classed them somewhat heedlessly with the lighter side of the people, when they really belong to the serious side, because you will always see them *en évidence* on pilgrimages and at fairs, whether the fair be holy and religious, or secular and commercial. You will see them wherever you go, these, to European eyes, revolting individuals, naked, smeared in mud and ashes, matted of hair and beard, blear-eyed, sometimes resigned, sometimes scornful, sometimes humble, far-away, and mystical.

What do they mean, whence do they come, what is the good or evil that they do? They are but another aspect of

[1] A pilgrimage to the snows in Kashmir is shown in Chapter XXI.

that desire, which we see equally in the West, to get away from the world, to be free of trammels and conventions, to find where man ends and God begins. Some of them endure great tortures. Some live with one or both arms so held overhead that the muscles have stiffened and the arm must stay so for ever. Some live on beds of close-packed iron nail-points, in memory of a hero of legend through whose body countless enemy arrow-points penetrated; some are swung head downwards over smouldering wood fires at fairs; some used to swing by hooks let into strips cut into the back. The people tolerate them good-naturedly, feed them with grumblings, knowing those that are worth, and those that are worthless, knowing some for—as the good old mediaeval English has it —mere abbey-lubbers, others for genuine seekers.

What do they stand for? They stand as an outward and visible sign before the people, that there is something else that moves men, besides the love of ease, of comfort and of wealth, and that is a reminder that may well stand in all lands.

They belong to many orders, orders formed by teachers, by ascetic leaders and hermits of the past; they come from certain schools, temples or centres to which each particular order is affiliated, and to which from time to time they circulate. Some orders take only Brahmin and other high-caste folk, others are open to all. Some of them are always naked, known as the *Digambaras*, the 'sky-clad'. To the general public they are spoken of confusingly as *gosains*, *sannyasins*, *bhairagis*, *saddhus*, *jogis*, *swamis* and the like. *Gosain* means 'Lord' or 'master'. *Swami* also means 'Lord'. *Saddhu* means 'good'. *Jogis* are those who preach *yoga*, the strange austere philosophy and rule of life. The austerities referred to are called *tapas*, and Siva the Great God practised *tapas* on earth for many years.

The sects follow one or other of the great divisions and dispensations of Hinduism, that of Vishnu or of Siva, so like and yet so unlike in their trend and teaching. There are seven principal Sivite orders, while the Vishnuvite ascetics are more often wandering monks than members of different fraternities. The *Dandins*, so called from their *dandas* or 'staves', also known as the Dasnamahs, or 'ten names', are exclusively Brahmin.

One sect, now almost extinct, but capable like everything else in the East, of revival, are the *Aghorins*, or *Aghorapanths*, whose members have acquired a strange and repulsive taste for the flesh of corpses, only explicable as one of the ways of inflicting intense mortification on the human body, and its likes and dislikes.

The ascetics are often kindly and simple folk despite their horrifying make-up, with many a Friar Tuck among them, and those who are rogues are well enough known of the people.

Let us, before leaving this interesting fraternity watch some of them coming through the bazaar of a town. They are wearing, jingling the emblems of their fraternity, the great necklaces of the *rudraksha* berry, the brown nobbly beads of our childhood, of which the Latin name is *Elaeocarpus Ganitrus*; if Sivites, or, if Vishnuvites, of the holy Basil (*Ocimum sanctum*), they will have chains and brass belts that rattle and shake, a tiger-skin perhaps over their shoulders, the only cover for the *ensemble*, a staff with loose metal ends to jingle, so that all the world may know that 'the beggars are coming to town'. Each and all have the beggar's bowl, the bowl for food and the bowl for pence. Now India is both generous and frugal. Generous in that it cannot pass a beggar, frugal because it has not much to give. The smallest known copper coin is a *pie*, a twelfth of a penny. Below that you come to the sacred cowrie shell, sacred because it represents the male and the female elements and forms the old Celtic *coq* and *cwym*, the hump and the hollow. Thirty-two of these go to the *pie*, and every stall-keeper will have a basket of these, so that one or two or three go to the importunate holy one—less he mutter curses on the grudging.

They share the streets in Hindu cities with the Holy Bull of Siva, who walks where he likes, poking his nose into sweetmeats-sellers' baskets and into greengrocers' stalls. He covers his neighbours' cows at will, however inferior as a progeny-begetter he may be. His urine dribbles and splashes on the cobbles and on the dirty roads traces a Persian-like straggle that the unco' wise profess to read—bulls and faqirs are perhaps a bore in the bazaars.

There is one aspect of the mendicants that the village knows and reverences. The barren women, the family who have not the son who must help the soul to heaven, the husband who has got past hope, turn to such to cure the ill and fill the cradle, in one despairing change of bowler.

Somewhat akin to such fraternities are the associations of beggars, who adopt for a consideration deformed children, who are thus trained and provided for not unhappily. Charitable people actually subscribe to such and apprentice them, the children thus provided for being known as 'Shah Doulat's rats', though who Shah Doulat was, tradition does not say; but it is a quaint and pathetic example of the, to Western eyes, topsy-turvydom of Eastern train of thought.

Dacoity

To include dacoity, which means robbery under arms, in a chapter that is meant to deal with merriment and brightness, is of course wrong, but it balances the chapter, and has one faint claim to be here, and that is that the young men, the more virile young men of the countryside, do rejoice therein. It is however a dangerous menace to the countryside, always increasing when law and order is defied, and has always been so. It demands the greatest activity and courage from the police, both in British India and still more so in Princes' India. So often has India of the past been swept by wars and invasions that never has any part of the countryside enjoyed peace for long.

When stout young men have a difficulty in living according to their fancy, a proposal to live at someone else's expense is welcome enough. Certain desperate leaders are able to raise gangs who follow them devotedly, sometimes permanent gangs in action and consequent hiding, but more frequently gangs that only assemble like the Thugs of old for a raid. Dacoity consists in surrounding some village or house, letting off firearms to intimidate neighbours and constable, killing one or two if need be—quite recently a village constable was decapitated while alive to create a sensation—and then the fun begins. Merchants are tortured to deliver up their hoards, old ladies are slippered and peppered to dig up their buried savings or jewelry, and a helpless village cowers in its hovels. The dacoits will often put up a fierce fight with police, and are often well armed and reckless, and it is only very determined and well-led police that can cope with them. This sport of dacoity easily gains way, and it is for this reason that those behind the scenes dread the handing over of the police control to an Indian minister entirely, in the proposals for Provincial autonomy. They know the difficult time the police have in the Princes' States to keep the evil under.

Indeed, to this day no one often knows who may be in the know and share the swag. In the earlier days in India irregular military forces were formed locally, not only to keep the evildoers down, but to give the young men something better to do than join the gangs. Perhaps therefore, in some sense, dacoity may be included among the amusements of the people! In all cases terrorism is the dacoit's stock-in-trade, and sufficient ruthless murders and maimings are perpetrated for the purpose. In Burma it would be not out of place to crucify the village headman and set the cross up at the village entrance, and in the recent risings and disorders this sort of tragedy occurred, as in days gone by.

BOOK II

THE SERVICES AND EUROPEAN LIFE

CHAPTER X

THE ARMY

The Army Generally

The Army in India, since the middle of the eighteenth century, has consisted of a varying number of European and Indian soldiers and it has existed for progressively varying purposes. Since, until 1858, India was administered by the Crown in Commission, viz. by the East India Company, the armies in India were, to a great extent, the affair of that great Company. European troops, not always of British origin, were maintained to serve alongside their Indian soldiers who began from the humble origin of armed night-watchmen and caravan guards. But the ambitions of Imperial France produced a situation which was more than the trading Company, however powerful, could tackle, and in 1739 the first unit of the British Army, to be followed by many others, went to India. From those days till the assumption of direct authority by the Crown, the growing armies of India, needed by the astounding series of happenings outlined in Chapter II., consisted of the Forces of the Crown, and the European and Indian Forces of the Company, whose officers indeed were also commissioned by the Crown, and who were then indirectly as 'Royal' an Army as to-day.

The armies of India in those days developed in three quite separate bodies; for the purpose of maintaining the

Company's territories against the external aggression of the French, against the threats of Napoleon and the Tsar, and against those independent states of India who were always combining to drive the English into the sea and who trained their armies on European model.

Of later years, as greater responsibilities fell to the British, the saving of India from her external enemies became her first care, such as the rescuing of the submontane Himalayas from the ruthless conquest by Gurkha invaders of Mogul provinces, and especially against the cruel Afghan invasions which so devastated the Punjab in the latter days of the eighteenth century. This fear of the Afghan invasions which, till about the second decade of the next century, was a very real dread, tinged British military policy very greatly.

As Britain more and more succeeded to the derelict authority left by the crash of the Mogul Empire, she was the more concerned with seeing that those great states in which at one time French influence was so powerful, slipped into their place as an agreeing part of a peaceful India rather than a disturbing factor. More especially had she to destroy the marauding side of the Mahratta States and to smash that terrible scourge of masterless men, the vast pirate settlements in Central India, known as Pindaris, which leagued with the Mahrattas to pillage half India. It is but illustrative of the transience of human memory and gratitude that the service of the paramount power to India's everyday existence by the extermination of these universal pests shall be forgotten, as well as the gruesome horror which flourished most in times of disorder, that secret brotherhood of robbery and murder known to history as the Thugs.

The Army of the East India Company

The Army in India until 1860 consisted, as already said, principally of the armies of the East India Company, both European and Native, supplemented by a small force of the Army of the Crown, numbering about 25,000 men. The whole of the Artillery in India, European as well as Native, was of the Company's service. The East India Company and the India Office, or in those days the Court of Directors, controlled a far larger military force than did ever the Horse Guards, and their Military Department in Leadenhall Street was equally important, though most of the staff work was done in India. Nevertheless the Company had a big depot at Warley where it trained its recruits, an important and highly efficient Cadet College at Addiscombe where it trained its officers for Artillery and Engineers, and a large bureau where the appointment and retirement of its European military officers was controlled.

Because of the conditions aforesaid, under which the separate Presidencies arose, the East India Company had three separate armies existing under quite distinct conditions, each consisting of complete departments, artillery and engineers, a large line of infantry and cavalry, and everything appertaining thereto. It was only as these provinces came closer together that the armies were amalgamated in the nineties of the nineteenth century and put on one list. Indeed until the Crown took over the forces of the Company, the three were extraordinarily separate, only meeting occasionally in the theatres of the greater wars, or, curiously enough, its officers on those selected fields of the Punjab Irregular Force which kept watch and ward so long on the frontiers of Afghanistan.

Each of those three armies of the Company were highly organized and extremely efficient for their purpose, and though the Coast Army, as that of Madras was affectionately known, suffered from a dying fire in the material from which it recruited, each has a place in our military annals which should never be forgotten. The Madras Army, for instance, besides its European infantry and artillery, had fifty-two battalions and eight regular cavalry regiments at the time of amalgamation, as well as irregulars, artillery, etc. Although the largest, the Bengal Army, blew up in that strange hysteria of 1857, that should not dim the memories of a century of fighting. In addition to the struggle of the great campaigns to rescue India from lawlessness, the bayonets of all three armies, but especially of Bengal, had carried the Union Jack to China, and had fought the French in Java, in Bourbon, in the Mauritius and in Egypt, when George III. was king, showing that service overseas by Indian soldiers was no new thing.

It will be remembered that the artillery and the European regiments of the Company were incorporated with the Forces of the Crown in 1860.

The Army of the Crown and the World War

Since the taking-over by the Crown, the re-raising of a Northern Army in place of the one that had mutinied, and the preparation to meet, not as heretofore disturbers of the peace within India but fiercer or more highly armed enemies without our gates, the Indian Army has gone through a long series of developments and selections. Happily this period of growth had brought it to the stage that made it so famous an auxiliary in the World War, and sent the great forest of masts and smoke-stacks bringing it into Marseilles harbour to the wild rejoicing of the sore-tried French.

That regeneration, apart from its military trainings, grouping and equipment, had largely taken the form of the careful selection of the martial races and the elimination of all who had lost their military aptitude by reasons of generations of the *Pax Britannica*. Even at the best of times the most careful examination of all the sources of recruitment during the World War had shown that, of the 323 million inhabitants (of the then Census) not more than 35 million men, women and children could, by any stretch of imagination, be considered by physique or any attribute of courage, fit to bear arms or produce those who could, the which alone is an illuminating light on the Indian problem.

The story of the Indian Army both before and since the coming of the Crown is a matter of well-known history, illustrated in the annals of countless families whose sons have served India and led the Indian soldier, in the cause of India

Sir George MacMunn and veterans of the Indian artillery, Ambala, 1933

(The two officers in front marched to Kandahar with Lord Roberts in 1880)

Choice young men and goodly

and of civilization, from the China Wall to the Flanders Flats—they proud to lead, the Indian soldier eager to follow. Whenever the British Empire comes to make up its jewels—the long tallies of those who do it service—the Indian soldier will always be numbered there among.

As we who visit India go among them, we shall see the trains of the North crowded with those who serve, crowded with those who would and might serve, the choice young men and goodly of the Punjab or the territories of the Jāt below Delhi. Save only the mountain rats of Sivaji, the lean and active Mahrattas from the hills of Western India and a few of the descendants of Turkish and Afghan colonists of the Deccan, there are no men south of Delhi into whose hands a rifle and a sword can be put, vapour the intelligentsia never so vaingloriously. The red corpuscles that make for courage dwell not for many reasons, possibly climatic and malarial, in the physical weaklings of the bulk of India. There, curiously to English ideas, the cricket-bat and the football do not make men even if they make skilled players, the which is also an enigma.

So necessary is it if we would know our India to see something of the Indian soldier, that visitors should tarry awhile in some cantonment and make love to some soldier at their hotel to show them the thousand who march like one. In a later chapter it is explained that perhaps Rawalpindi is the most convenient for this purpose. There too, you will see the British battalions at their best, close on a thousand strong—riflemen, fusiliers, linesmen, barbarians, guns and more guns and all those whose special charge is the *Pax Britannica* as aforesaid.

The Army of the Future

It will not be out of place to say a few words here about the Indian Army of the future. Most of those who travel Indiawards will have heard something of the 'Indianization' of the Indian Army that is in progress. Till the days of the World War, too long perhaps unfortunately, the superior officers of the Indian Army have all been British. An Indian regiment of say 900 rank and file has had all its personnel Indian, both men and officers except about a dozen who were British. The Indian officers, largely of the small land-owning or yeoman farmer type, could never rise into the British grade except by courtesy at the end of their service. This has been in the main due to two causes, first that the martial classes, the men of thews and courage, were backward in the education that could make a modern officer; secondly, that the experience of the later wars against Afghan and frontier tribesmen had shown that only with more British leading could even the most martial classes do well against a worthy foe.

Nevertheless, partly owing to a sense of the incongruity of the situation, partly to political representation, for some years young Indians have been sent home to be trained at Sandhurst, and have been given the positions of British officers in Indian corps. The Indian Army has coined the useful phrase 'Brindian', the Indian with a British position, to describe these gentlemen, and very usefully so, since every new science and condition needs its own terminology.

To meet two conditions, firstly political agitation, singularly unnecessary in this case, and secondly because at one time it seemed that young English officers would not enter the Indian Army if there was any chance of their being commanded by Indians, it was decided to keep the Briton and the Indian separate. It was felt that we are a Christian people with Christian codes however much it may please us for a while to pretend otherwise, that life in a regimental mess is an extremely intimate affair, and men of one way and outlook on life cannot live so intimately as mess life postulates with men of other ways. Other heads, wiser heads probably, thought otherwise. Nevertheless the fiat went forth that certain of the Indian Army units were entirely to be Indianized by the simple process of filling them from the bottom with young Indians from Sandhurst and elsewhere and the new Indian Military Academy. Yes, that is now the next stage of what some call the '*Descensus Averno*', the getting on to the slippery plank so that the slide may some day be rapid.

The making of the Indianized regiments came as a great blow to the Indian young men themselves, who, treated with great kindness by their British confrères, only wished to stay among them and serve their lives free of the racial aversions, intrigues and enmities that they envisaged and are beginning to experience in the Indianized regiments.

The young men from Sandhurst are very charming young men, very lovable boys. The new Indian Sandhurst is an admirably and sympathetically run college, and a really first-class imitation—I use the word advisedly—of a high-grade Public School with 10 per cent of a good College superadded. The British staff excel in training and bringing the lads on.

What then of the future? What is to be the fighting value of these Indianized corps, and the Brindian? No one knows, but one thing is certain that after about twelve years' experience it is found that the wastage of Brindians in the regiments is close on 60 per cent. Some by weariness of regimental work, some by increasing girth, some by the inevitable desire for indoor work, drift away to the lesser departments where perhaps the Indians' less energetic day's work may be possible.

Regimental life is a disappointment to many. Army pay is small for any luxuries, the daily routine of regimental life in some hole on the frontier is hard and grim; it is hard enough even in the pleasant places. Just as there is more in marriage as the Spanish say than four bare legs, so is there more in regimental life than dining before regimental plate in a pretty coat; and half of them did not know it! Regimental life is hard. For us the lads of Britain, it only appeals to the old hereditary warriors; the sleek lad who makes for city life and the Stock Exchange and some day the fleshpots of life, can rarely find the hard life of the Services bearable. That is why we go on father and son, father and son, and our women too. The mud loopholes of a frontier post to us are romance, as the bugles ring out sundown and the trumpets watch-setting, because our father and our grandfathers, among whose miniatures and swords on the wall we have been brought up, have done so. It is foreign service that makes the quiet home villa wistful and that is why we like it. Turning out in grey dawn in khaki shorts has its glamour, the hard cheap sport, unobtainable save at great price in Merry England, the pig in his *beyla*, the wild fowl and the goat on his mountains, take us round the world to our satisfaction. These advantages are not so appealing to the young Indian, unless indeed we are allowed to choose from that salt of the earth that here and there we know of.

But the Indian politicians imagine that their nice boys will enjoy life and prosper in the red and blue coat and the scarlet and gold, and little realize that to anyone who loves ease it is a whited sepulchre indeed. Most Indians love ease at far too early a period in their life. We are trying as experiments these nice little brown intelligentsia lads, and if the experiment is successful, then indeed shall we have worked such a miracle as the world of India has not yet seen. It won't be for the want of trying.

At present it is the almost universal experience that after five years the Indian subaltern falls off, loses the efficiency with which he was first equipped, and there are not very many who wish to be alongside an Indianized regiment in time of danger. The English lead Indian soldiers by some temperamental and psychological means, and Indian soldiers not so led have never yet been able to stand up to us.

On the other hand, *there is going to be a residue of fine gold*, of Indian officers like old Pertab Singh of Idak, not only the first gentleman in the British Empire, but one of the best of soldiers so far as courage and bearing went. When we find these, as of course we shall, if the politicians will let us, then we shall have men whom any British officer will *gladly serve under*.

We must remember the long course of character-building that the British lad of the well-to-do classes goes through before he can become a leader, and think too how India lacks it. The Indian Military Academy starts under the best auspices, and if it is successful in turning out leaders no one will rejoice thereat more than the British officers who are making the experiment.

However successful the young Indian may be as an officer, there is no doubt that the Indian Army will remain as a career for British officers in the future, even if for a lesser number. It will need able men, men of character and sympathy, and men to whom India and its peoples are acceptable. If the ultimate British predominance in leading and helping as envisaged in the White Paper of 1933 is not to be thrown away, only the best among our more virile young men will be good enough for the job. Happily an Army career does appeal to the best of our lads still, and numbers there be who still inherit the Indian sympathy and the Indian tradition. The confidence that exists between Indian soldiers and their officers should grow equally between comrades in the commissioned ranks, if only the makers of bad blood will let them alone.

The Indian Army and Citizenship

One of the most interesting phenomena in the Indian Army, as has so long been the case in Great Britain, is its excellence as a school of citizenship and character-building, far ahead of the machinery of civil life. The Simon Commission was most struck at what they saw, and were very gratified at the way the Army education and its various evolutionary schools had succeeded in bringing on and developing the men of the martial races. Perhaps with the others the real problem is to develop the red blood corpuscles so that they too shall have sufficient of physique and courage to enable them to acquire some at least of the qualities that endear the Indian soldier to those who know him. Indeed it is this character-building in which, as will be seen, the

Indian education from time immemorial has been so deficient. Another point, while we are on the subject of soldiers. An old Bengali judge who served on the Indian Army Esher Committee in 1920, told the writer that what struck him most was this; the Committee had heard the evidence of many British officers on Indian Army matters and future; 'not once had anyone spoken of their own affairs, conditions or prospects. Always had it been of their men; prospects, pay, land, village troubles, their rights, their efficiency, their well-being'. He had had a glimpse of a world, unknown in the Law Courts of Bengal, where honour and *camaraderie* are prized before wealth and rank, and he was left wondering.

CHAPTER XI

THE SERVICES THAT HAVE REBUILT INDIA

The Indian Civil Service

The Civil Service of India, known almost to the whole civilized world as the 'Indian Civil Service', is perhaps one of the most remarkable bodies of men who have ever served a crown and a people. Because the life and the prospects have been alluring, and the emoluments and pension adequate it has commanded for several generations the pick of the English professional classes and their schools and colleges. During its existence in organized form, from let us say the beginning of the nineteenth century, it has been through two phases. One was that of appointment through the influence of the directors of the old East India Company, the other following on the assumption of direct responsibility by the Crown, by open candidature and examination. The second method may have produced a higher general level in attainments, but the former men were equally, and perhaps better, calculated to succeed in their special rôle, and much of the greatest work of these earlier days of building came from those who had been nominated by the Directors to the Company's College at Haileybury. That College was then the route to the Indian Service, and is now among the open public schools of the country. The term 'Civil Service', for those who don't know India, may be explained as covering the whole scope of Government, and is far wider in its meaning than the same word as used in England. The Secretariats of the Government Departments in India would be analogous to the more usual run of the work in London, while the Indian Civil Service provides secretarial personnel, as well as all the higher magistracy and administration, and some of the judges. The analogy lies more with the 'Civil Service' of the Crown Colonies. Mr. Lloyd George has described this Indian Service, which comprises many Indians who have graduated in England and gone through the same entrance mill as the European member, as the 'steel frame' on which the whole structure of India rests, and he is indubitably right. How to blend it with a politician's India is one of the problems. In the past this service has been one of assured position and status, hard work, long hours, exile and good prospects. In fact a man's job in the best sense of the word.

However much the platitude-mongers may talk, India cannot get on without this Civil Service in the future. This strange age-old Hind, with its jungles and its struggling peoples, can never entirely manage itself, or rather find its own service of local officials unsupported. And we may be sure that, unless Great Britain, having messed up a working proposition, then wrings her hands clear of the stew, the steel frame must remain. Whether there will in future be any Indians imperially appointed, or whether there will be a fixed number of Europeans only of this class, mingled with the locally appointed Civil Service remains to be seen. The proposals of the White Paper are not yet concrete.

We may take it as certain that the Civil Services of the provinces will contain a fixed number of British officers, as the vivifying stiffening of the frame-work, and that being so, their life in India will not differ materially from that to-day. The British and Indian Governments if any sense of proportion remains, will see to it that the standard of civil servants shall not deteriorate for want of scope and want of prospects. The modernized India will need the very best stuff it can borrow to help it carry its burdens.

The Political Service

One of the mysterious terms in India is that of 'political officer', and to the world outside, we know its significance is baffling. Countries that are peculiar, unusual and illogical

By courtesy of Indian Railways Bureau

The lake palaces at Udaipur

in their structure, require unusual organization and services. The Political Department of the Government of India is really the Diplomatic Department, and its members may be divided into two main groups, those who deal, somewhat as diplomats, somewhat as advisers, with the several hundred ruling Princes, and those who deal with the independent tribes on our borders. The men who deal with the Princes live to a great extent interesting, if secluded lives, in and near the states in which they act as go-between to the chief and his government, and the Imperial Government. Often much good sport is theirs, and the affairs of most interesting people, but for years on end it may be a lonely life. On the other hand, those who deal with the tribes, especially on the North-West Frontier, need to be men of a special kidney, both as to the influence they can wield and their own disregard of danger. All day long are they at work to keep the tribes content, to counteract lawless tendencies and movements, and to lead their thoughts into the more peaceful amenities of life, which the British Government brings to their coasts and offers to them, from work on roads, to new noses for unfaithful wives. In Baluchistan and in the North-West Frontier Province, the ordinary work of civil administration within the border is coupled with supping with a long spoon with the wild men without. The Political Service draws its recruits both from the Civil Service and from the Army. Under the changing conditions the 'Frontier' political will remain, and work as now, since independent tribes are reserved subjects. Quite what the status of the diplomatic side will be under federation is a matter for consideration and the full implications of the White Paper are not clear. In the case of the 'States' it is to be remembered that the Princes only resign to the Federal Government such of their prerogative as they wish. In 80 per cent of their activities they will live as now, in the exercise of their authority as enacted by their treaties. The political officers in some form will be just as necessary both for liaison work, for advice and intercommunication as before.

The great States have many troubles before them, as we see in the case of Alwar, where a Hindu chief's measures added perhaps to a Moslem problem, have resulted in the chief's withdrawal. In states with Moslem rulers and Hindu subjects and *vice versa* mischief is brewing, and the mischief-makers whom British prestige kept within bounds, are now on the prowl having been made *be-dur*, 'without fear'. Until fear re-enters into their make-up, troubles endless and unnecessary there will be. Many of the chiefs are men of modern ideas and energy, and in giving rein to their modernity the help of a political officer is no mean asset.

The Political Service in India, even if it be camouflaged, according to modern custom, by a new name, must remain and be more important and useful than ever.

The Police Service

The Police Service of India with its prow of hammered steel, is one of the great pillars on which the happiness and prosperity of India stand and must stand. It has at its head a small number of British officers, and a few British inspectors, and for use in the great seaports, a small force of British gendarmes. The total number of British among close on 200,000 constables and Indian police officers, and a population of 353 millions of whom two-thirds are actually in British India, is 700 officers and 600 others. This small prow of steel has brought law and order in most adverse conditions to all India, it has taught the Indian constable by instinct—the old official instinct of the East—a bully, and a profiteer, to be a trusted friend of the people. The mere maintenance of law and order by fear was alone an immense task, but to bring the Indian constable, even a short way along the road towards holding the position *vis-à-vis* the people, that the constable holds in Britain, has been a monumental work. Even in England we know how many forces there are at work tending to demoralize the constable. In India they are a hundredfold more. Yet in the last quarter of a century the

Indian Police Service has been brought to a remarkable state of honesty and efficiency.

The first Indian Constabulary, as distinct from the village wardens supported by soldiers, was raised by General Sir Charles Napier in Sind on a model which was to be copied throughout India. The Indian constable undergoes many dangers. He is shot by robbers under arms, he is beheaded alive to create a 'funk', he is burnt alive by the dozen when Mr. Gandhi is on the move, and yet he has preserved a phenomenal loyalty to his Government under the most hideous conditions, even while wondering if his Government will be loyal to him. He comes from the honest peasantry happily, not from the town rubbish. Even the worst of the 'yes-men' till recently have kept their hands off the police, and Indianization of the Police Service has a limit of 50/50 in the positions hitherto held by Europeans. That limit, 50/50, can possibly be maintained without *débâcle*. The standard of right and wrong, of honesty and dishonesty, will be that of the West. If you reduce that proportion, the standard will slip down to the dishonest one inherent in the East. In all countries the integrity of the police is the most vital matter, and the most difficult to attain. In all Eastern countries an inferior police is a scourge and a thorn-bit unimaginable to us who live under better conditions.

The Simon Commission, reporting *before* the extraordinary outbreak of what is curiously enough termed 'civil disobedience', recommended that the police in each province should be transferred to the control of an Indian minister, as part of provincial autonomy. In making this recommendation the Commission specially added that they did so after very grave consideration, and some misgiving, holding this responsibility an essential part of local government. But since then we have seen the form of rebellion instigated by Gandhi and Congress, countenanced too for a while by the Viceroy. This civil disobedience was no more nor less than revolution *cum* hysteria. It lost many good British and Indian lives for no reason. And the conditions thus revealed differed very considerably from those apparent when the Commission made its recommendation. The White Paper, forgetful of all that transpired, has made the same proposals, deplored by all the police of all ranks and races. Were we dealing with a straightforward question of devolution and democracy, it might well be right, but we are dealing with a continent that answers to no understood rules and codes of ethics. We know something of what a country which has a streak in its population that has bile for its wet nurse and venom for its sacrament can do, across the Irish Channel, and we know the police of the Free State get 'De Valera-ed' badly. How much more it can be so, is horribly evident to most who know the instincts and difficulties that beset India. But it is felt that if the theorist statesmen do still hold that compromise is not possible on this matter, although it is perfectly easy to make the police a subject reserved to the Governor, then there is still one method which may steady the police ship. That is, always postulating that the next batch of 'yes-men' won't give away such strength as remains in the Federal Government—the appointment of a Federal Inspector-General of Police. His duties would be, after inspecting or studying the Provincial police in their general efficiency, and thus hearing of any evil which may be budding, to see from time to time the minister concerned and talk over the subject and very possibly provide a prop that the minister will gladly have. He would warn the minister if things were tending to go wrong, would have access to the Governor and tell him the same, if need be, and would also, of course, tell the Federal Government. So long as ministers were doing their duty the occasional visits and advice of the Inspector-General would be invaluable, and no sort of hamper.

This seems to be the only possible method in which British public sense of the fitness of things would consent to the Simon Commission's recommendation—made, as said, before the Civil Disobedience Movement—being embodied in the Provincial autonomy provisions. Such an arrangement would be very joyful news to the honest policeman who fears local venom more than anything else, especially for his family. In this connection the bystander will be interested to know that in one province there were twelve police heads, of whom one was an Indian. Their opinions were recently asked on this matter of handing over police control to an Indian minister. The eleven Europeans said 'madness', the Indian said 'That it appeared unavoidable but that it was most deplorable'. However, we may safely hope that before the step is taken the traditional wisdom and instinct of the British will insist on their leaders coming to some wiser policy of compromise before the matter is settled. It is in the interest of many millions of helpless people that the control of the police is so jealously regarded.

In April 1932 a Hindu widow was burnt alive not far from Lucknow, on her husband's funeral pyre in the presence of 200 people. The police arrived too late. In the same province in the same month seven singing women finding their throats hoarse, cut up a girl of nine with a sharp mattock and offered her to the Goddess Kali to cure their complaint.

In countries where such crimes can happen, it is only because a really prompt and efficient police exists that they are not more prevalent.

The Other Services

Under the heading of 'The Other Services' I group the remainder, each and all well worthy of separate treatment. Those who have criticized the Indian Civil Service of the past may say that it is their d——d exclusiveness that has brought them to their present unworthy plight. The reason for this allegation is that they have succeeded in the face of enough advice in keeping the other important services in a less privileged position. A good many years ago it was recommended by a Royal Commission that all the imperially recruited Government services should be considered 'covenanted' and put on one level, urging that the trend of the world's development placed technical services equally high up in the world's estimation as administration. This recommendation was never given effect to, though, no doubt, the status and prospects of the other services were raised in proportion to their increasing importance.

The greatest of all the services, the Public Works, otherwise the various engineering branches, whether general or irrigation, was at one time the proud product of the famous College at Cooper's Hill.[1] They are the men who have built the great roads and State edifices of India, and, with the railway engineers, those enormous bridges over the Indian rivers that are world famous, to which reference has already been made. Under the new proposals many of the branches of this service have had to, or will, drop from their Imperial status, viz. from the position of an Empire service appointed by the Secretary of State, to that appointed by the Government of India, or the Provincial Governments. The trouble of this is the intense wire-pulling often engendered in the eager desire of numerous fairly qualified young Indians to attain to one of the scanty openings available. Up till lately the superior services, whether the openings were for Europeans or Indians, were filled by the Secretary of State. Now all save those specially reserved will be filled in India. Certain essential and super-important services such as irrigation, will still be 'Federal' to use the new name, and at any rate for the present, the number of British Europeans in certain services is fixed. If India is to be kept on the straight path by certain judicious excisions and improvements of the White Paper, then service in such departments as still employ Europeans, the Civil Service, the Police, the Irrigation, etc., will still be worth having and India will still be worth serving. There is no reason whatever, if the situation is handled with a little ultimate decision, why the British and Indian shall not continue to serve India as happily as heretofore. The best type of young Briton should have as useful and interesting a career in India in the future as in the past. On the other hand if a De Valera-esque position is to be

[1] When Cooper's Hill was abolished, now many years ago, the Indian services were recruiting from the ordinary sources of the Empire.

allowed, and all power of control and balance is to be removed by too much application of hot-air, then the situation in India may easily become unbearable, and it would take all the King's horses and men to put it right, even if we ourselves are men enough to do so.

There is every right to hope that this situation will not arise, but it is unfair to the people of this country who have been thrown into such a state of astonishment at proposals which may lead to a loss of India, that this should not be mentioned here, especially as so many wonder whether or no to encourage their sons to serve India as their forbears have done so long.

When we come to the consideration of each of the services and what has been done, say since the Crown took over, an event which largely corresponded with the commencement of modern world development, those who know the conditions may well be lost in admiration. The great roads and bridges, the railways, the gorges and rifts that are spanned, are some of the world's feats, made too with an expenditure and economy that perhaps no other country can show. Roads, railways and irrigation will stand for ever as monuments of their work, but unless there is a due proportion of the thorough-minded European to stimulate the Indian engineers, they are not likely to remain so. Engineering work in India, however, should be a fine enough career for a European in the future, and there will be plenty to do, though the conditions of the country so frequently referred to, will not produce the engineering requirements of a Western country of its size.

The Irrigation Service has been one that the whole world is cognisant of. What Egypt has done once or twice India has done a dozen times, and the great canal head-works on the big rivers and the latest of all, the Sukkur Barrage on the Indus, are all monumental, and their Chief Engineers' names should remain famous for all time. Their work is so big that if one went beyond a brief mention, one must go on to the whole volume that their undertakings merit.

The Indian Forest Service, once also the proud child of Cooper's Hill, is now Provincial. It is perhaps fair to say that there is no service which can more suitably be so, were it not for the fact that most Indians dislike the true forest work. Forest conservancy is a lonely life, with a loneliness more than compensated for those so inclined, by the glory of the jungle and the forest, the flora and the fauna. The Indian is likely to shirk the real district work, without which the forests cannot thrive, and glory in the office of his centre and on paper reports. Further since Forest conservancy—the State against villager and squatter who would squander—is unpopular with the folk, many will be the perfectly innocent pleas for remission of rule, for exceptions and the like, and much the indirect pressure. To anyone except the independent Briton, these are hard nuts to crack and hard propositions to withstand. The Forest Service too has big need of large ideas, and perhaps a bigger share of expenditure—expenditure that is productive—than it usually gets. Good forests mean good revenue and large exports, as well as material to meet the growing timber requirements of India herself.

Post Offices and Telegraphs are big services with records of efficiency and progress. In all these services the Indian help has been always considerable, but India alone would be hard put to it to maintain the reputation of the past.

The Education Service of the Government of India has, for the last thirty years, held considerable pride of place, and the results recorded are due to much enterprise and the overcoming of many difficulties. In this department British and Indian officials find more in common perhaps than in any other, and cordial co-operation should continue whatever the future of the European personnel. Education is a subject that perhaps more than any other in India makes one wish to jump into the time machine and look at what the future contains. Incidentally it may again be remarked that in education more than in any other direction, it is possible to travel along the wrong road. In India it is far harder to gauge the people's needs than in any of the more civilized portions of the globe.

No outline of the great services of India would be complete without references to the builders and managers of those forty odd thousand miles of railways, whether State or Company owned. A very unworthy pressure has been put on the Companies to take more Indians than they thought advisable in the last ten years or so, and there is no subject in which the peace, prosperity and good order of India is more involved. To place the whole control of the traffic side of the railways into Indian hands is to put the public within reach of a strike organization which has taken on an exotic form in the East and which can be far more hysterical and unreasonable than its British parent. In times of rebellion it may paralyse the whole executive and jeopardize the movements of the Army for both internal and external crises. It is typical of the slide into which the central mentality of the Indian Government has got, that this matter of safety has not been recognized from the first.

The Indian Railway Service is one of convenience and efficiency so far as ordinary passenger traffic is concerned, and it is due to seventy years of devoted service in the subordinate levels by a large number of Anglo-Indians [1] that the Indian public have been so well and safely carried. In goods traffic there is unfortunately an opening for the inherent chicanery of the East, and many a merchant will tell you stories of trucks side-tracked, and even unloaded by the way, for want of a *douceur* to station officialdom. Also is there a merry little dishonesty often afoot in such matters as cash-on-delivery railway vouchers, whose telling might cause dismay. The intricacies of the modern West have introduced countless new opportunities of defrauding the simple and helpless.

That, however, is by the way. The engineering and traffic services of the Indian railways have been honourable openings for many devoted Europeans and it is not imagin-

[1] Viz. men of mixed blood.

able that either the Indian public or the British holders of shares in railways, almost all built by British capital, on the Secretary of State's guarantee, will accept an Indianization below the margin of safety. To protect such interest the White Paper proposes the creation of a Railway Board free from political domination, and if this is fairly done the future of service in the Indian railways should be safe, and employment therein still desirable. It is for the protection of such interests, if need be, that the Viceroy has been given far-reaching ultimate powers in the hope that their mere existence will obviate their ever being called into use.

CHAPTER XII

THE NON-OFFICIAL EUROPEANS AND ANGLO-INDIANS

The Great Merchants

From the earliest days of the coming of the merchant adventurers, and the chartered companies to India, Trade with a very big T has been the object of non-official Britons. England is a nation of venturous travellers, venturous traders and venturous shopkeepers. The English are not folk who bury the talent that is given them, but expect to turn one talent into two by their own energy and venture. Therefore our Government and our statesmen exist to that end more than any other—the making of *milieus* for our trade. It is a trite saying yet one that should be believed. Hence it is that there grew up in India, but especially in Calcutta, and to a lesser degree in Bombay, Madras and Karachi, big wealthy importing and exporting firms whose activities, in addition to their own important profits, have opened up Indian trades and industries innumerable with exports and imports for generations, to the great advantage of all concerned. In Calcutta specially have the European firms predominated, forming an aristocracy and tradition of commerce that was old when Warren Hastings was appointed the first Governor-General. The ways and the habits of these Indian houses have been stately and distinguished; round them stock exchanges and all the activities of a big commercial capital have grown up. Before the War, however, the American hustler came on the scene, and during the War, while many of this community went a-soldiering and gave their lives, Calcutta and indeed the rest of trading

India dipped its hand freely into the profit bag, that so widespread a speeding-up of demand offered to all who could supply.

In Bombay the predominant trading-houses have been largely Indian and Parsee, in contradistinction to Calcutta; but at all the great ports, wealthy houses, great merchants, large demand for labour, and especially for clerical labour, European and Indian prevailed. Immediately after the War, the world's rush to refill was intensified in India, and a boom that could not last, rose and failed. It was followed by normal return to prosperity, before the world's depression involved not only the great houses British and Indian, of the ports, but of the whole of India.

The falsehood and venom which Congress and Gandhi succeeded in engendering have disturbed harmonious business relations, and have brought out trade and racial animosities against the British firms, that are often entirely unreasonable. They have been guided by a blind attempt to harm, rather than to share, an attempt based on some racial chimera that has fizzled and bubbled in minds gone sour. It is to tackle such trouble that the White Paper proposes to give the Governor-General power to prevent all legislation based on unfair or one-sided discrimination, the blocking of European, Moslem and Hindu trade, for racial reasons. In the blind hysteria which can sometimes be called forth in India, this is an essential reserve power to be kept in the hands of authority.

Far more however, than hostility, Congress venom, and the like, it is the great collapse of world trade and prosperity that has wrought havoc with the big European business firms as it has with Indian ones. It is doubtful if ever again the commercial aristocracy of Calcutta can rise in its old stately form. The advantageous opening for the fortunate young men who entered the cadet services of the firms may not exist again on similar lines, and the number of European partners, managers and assistants will probably be less. That question, however, is generally outside the scope of this book save to state the situation, and to draw attention to the interest which attaches to the story of the firms. Also to remind those who have but heard it cursorily, that there is a story of affluence and dignity behind them, which we may hope is not to disappear among the stately edifices of the past. But trades demand business, and business is what the world is finding so hard to produce in proportion to the organization waiting to handle it.

Nevertheless, whatever the future holds, there will always be a large European business community and it must always, according to the English organization of society, be divided into two classes, viz. the management in all its grades, and the employés in all their varying grades. The dividing line between the two is distinct but always crossable. When, however, we come to the social life, the amusements and interests which are so essential to life in India, the arrangements for Europeans in the great ports are always a matter for concern. The 'gazetted' classes to use an Indian official phrase, in business 'the management' and those who will eventually rise thereto, have the social clubs of all kinds at their disposal according to their means. Games of all kinds, golf courses, cricket clubs and meeting-places are available. At Bombay the coterie who sail have a most attractive change from the heat of the shore at their disposal. The horse-racing, which is in many ways better organized in India than anywhere else, attracts all and sundry. But business hours are long, and the release which the Army gets for afternoon recreation, by reason of their early morning start, is often denied to business men on working days, unless they are energetic enough to get it before the hours of office commence.

Failing commerce, world depression and competition however, have done much to injure and to change the old firms' prosperity, and the pleasant and dignified lives of the members and cadets of the great houses, and less money is available for the amenities of the employer. The post-War boom referred to when the returning rush of commerce to fill empty warehouses seemed to promise an expansion that reason should have curbed, saw an immense temporary increase in the European mercantile community and the absorption of the demobilized, only to be followed by the greatest distress, as the bottom fell out of the boom and the inevitable contraction took place. Then were the organizations existing for the relief of stranded Europeans heavily strained by the great efforts to mitigate conditions which were as bad as those the present world contraction has again brought forth. As the world re-emerges the old British mercantile prosperity will have to take on a different aspect, and will have to face fresh conditions and competitors. But it is devoutly to be hoped that the old stateliness of Calcutta referred to will remain.

The Missionaries

India is a country of many missions, many mission clergy and workers, and, as already said, the harvest in the South is very great, and in the Punjab is showing above the ground. Elsewhere it is, with a few special exceptions, little more than sowing the seed. But this missionary community is a very numerous and important one. It is largely Anglican, but all the Free Churches have keen and successful bodies, many of whom are combining with the Church of England to form the new Evangelical and Episcopal Church of India, a readjusting of extreme difficulty and of great importance. Indian Christians resent the multitude of bodies which, attempting evangelization must, in a country where dissension is deep-seated, but add to confusion and hamper Christianity. The Indian, Christian and non-Christian, can understand such distinct bodies as the Church of Rome, and some other large division, as Islam understands Sunni and Shiah, but not a hundred.

Some of the best education in India is obtained in the mission colleges and in this connection the Church of Rome is among the first. Stations in some of the southern hills are almost entirely devoted to mission settlements' schools and rest-houses, and there is no doubt that mission work will slowly play a greater part in India, and may even be called to put up a fight with the interference from older religions that Gandhi is vowed to effect. To prevent this the White Paper gives the Governor-General special authority.

Unless you seek it out, this community, large and important though it is, is not *en evidence.* Because this is so, some of the lesser vehicles develop an inferiority complex and inveigh against the official class that they rarely see and do not understand, and even let themselves be nobbled by, and slobber over, Gandhi. That happily is not the usual attitude, for most understand better than that. It is indeed only mentioned here because one or two egregious members have tried to mislead folk at home in pulpit and by the printed word. Perhaps the American missionary has the less clean record in this respect.

The institutions of the Church of Rome, owing to its antiquity, its convents and convent schools, are very rightly much in evidence and held in esteem. The official Anglican hierarchy as well as that of Rome is largely concerned with the care and education of the Anglo-Indian and Domiciled Community, rather than with the troops who are in a special category. Indeed it is with the former that the interesting and 'parish' type of work occurs.

The missionary body is one that should be suitably represented in the new constitution, and it should be remembered that its members during the last hundred years have contributed greatly to the scientific, historical and linguistical knowledge of India.

The Anglo-Indian Community

The future of the Anglo-Indian Community is inseparably mixed up with that of India, and is the one indissoluble link in the chain that binds Britain to India.

'Anglo-Indian' is the official term originally selected by the community itself for what was formerly known as Eurasian, an obviously unsuitable term except in a far wider Asiatic sense. It includes all those persons of mixed European and Indian parentage, whether as the result of direct union of persons of the two races or by the union of those already of mixed descent. Its source is a wide one, and may descend from the union, regular or irregular, of members of the official class, civil and military, with Indian women of high or lowly birth, or may have its origin in the marriage of retired European soldiers with the women of the country. In the last few generations, the community principally marries within itself or with those of pure European origin, in place of augmentation by the direct union of persons of European or Indian races.

The union of officials and officers of the Royal and Company's forces with Indian women was common enough in the earlier days when English ladies and the ways of organized society had hardly penetrated beyond the Presidency Ports. In the older Indian cantonments are to be seen to this day, as will be described hereafter, the separate arrangements for the zenana. The types from which the Indian wives were drawn varied from formal unions with ladies of good family contracted in state, to simpler unions with girls of the peasantry. Sometimes as in the case of the Gardners and Hearseys, it was the highest in the land, and their union with the Begums of Cambay, the wards of the Mogul Emperor, was by no means the only instance of such romances. In more than one case has the English peerage been so mingled. Then again the British soldiers' progeny is to be found all over the land. In the South where at the time of Srinagapatam the regiments were largely Scottish, Scottish names abound. Only a few years ago in a schoolyard in the South half a dozen brown lads were marching to the pipes played by a still browner playfellow, who on being questioned by the author said that his name was Ian MacLeod. Two or three generations ago a good many of the attractive girls of mixed parentage married into the services, but this seldom occurs to-day, and the direct reinforcement of new European blood comes by marriage with the retired non-commissioned officer who has stayed in India

The humbler Anglo-Indian children, one of the problems of India

The girl who was caught stealing mulberries

or with the railway employé from Home. The community thus represents mingling and counter-mingling to the *n*th degree, though no statistical study has been made of the working of the Mendelian Law, to tell us how the strains mix and how they survive in the succeeding generations.

Many an Anglo-Indian family cherishes somewhat pathetically its distinct connection with some dead and gone civil or military worthy and his descendants at Home.

Some of the great romances of India lie within the history of the community. The Mutiny and its massacres took heavy toll of many, as that remarkable tablet referred to hereafter on the north door of old James Skinner's Church at Delhi tells us, recording how men, women and children of one family, old and young to the third and fourth generation, fell in one holocaust, for the Glory of God and His Prophet. James Skinner himself, so affectionately known in the Army as 'Old Sekunder', was the son of a British officer and a Rajputni mother of birth and station. The family that he founded still own large estates round Delhi and are typical of the wealthier members of the community. General Sir Hugh Wheeler of Cawnpore tragedy was married to an Indian lady [1] and the Wheelers who escaped the massacre are in the same category. Incidental to the same legend is that charming romance of a Resident at Hyderabad who married a Mussalmani of high degree and strict purdah. For her he built within her enclosed garden a model of his official residence in which she could trace for herself the routine of his daily life as he passed from hall of audience to office and to his meals, so that she should not be entirely alienated from the life she could not share. And the model is still in the enclosed garden, and has still some atmosphere of the romance about it.

It is, of course, hard to say where the Anglo-Indian ends and the native Christian of English name and English clothes begins. It is one of the practical difficulties of the com-

[1] *Vide* Trevelyan's *Cawnpore.*

munity in fitting itself into modern life and conditions. Though in many ways linked with each other's destiny, their problems are only allied on the grounds of religion. The domiciled European community consists principally of those Europeans who have settled down in India and for many reasons, chiefly those of income, educate and start their children there. This community in a generation or so tends to join the Anglo-Indian one, for Anglo-Indian girls are attractive enough, and Cupid will overcome any prejudice of the domiciled against a strain of colour. Further, it is by no means easy, as the Abbé Mendel will tell you, to say where colour begins and ends. So that the two communities wisely link their future together to some extent, for both live European lives and have European aspirations. It is with these communities as just said, that the Anglican and other Churches and educational life are largely concerned in India, rather than with the official class and the Army. Lack of educational facilities is one of the difficulties which the community feel, especially if their children are to compete in life with their Indian neighbours.

During the Great War, as Colonel Sir Henry Gidney, the spokesman of their deputation, told the Joint Committee, nearly a half of the community served in some capacity, the men largely in the technical services and in the artillery, the girls in the hospitals. In the Mutiny a special corps of artillery drivers was raised from them and continued for several years. It is one of those typical Anglo-Saxon failures to understand, that has been responsible for the Army in India failing to make use of them. Pure utilitarian views no doubt say that the Anglo-Indian costs as much and is not as generally useful as the European, but vision says that Great Britain is wedded to the people of this mixed race for ever, chained as they are to her interests by the facts of their existence, and it must not be left uncherished and unhelped. They would long ago have made good artillerymen for some of the compulsory garrisons of India, and they would also have been most useful in some of the technical corps. Sir

Henry Gidney now demands some opening in the Army,[1] but the time when such was an easy matter to arrange may have passed. For the last sixty years the rank and file of the railway running staff all over India, guards, ticket collectors and drivers, have come from this community, and at the great railway centres are railway settlements, highly organized and self-supporting, that are almost unknown to the ordinary European world of India. Without their leaven, the Army may find the railways gone west at a crisis. The old Volunteers, the 'Defence Force' of the Great War, and since the War the 'Auxiliary Force', were and are largely furnished by the Anglo-Indian and domiciled communities. As they are Indian-born they must not be shouldered out when Indianization is the order of the day. Gidney pleads for a recognition and an enforcement of this. He pleads for a measure of Army service, he asks for educational facilities and assistance, and he instances the severe phase of unemployment among them, which is quite new and is largely a result of a policy that is crowding them off the railways and from Government offices. He has obtained some assurance and some concession, but the community is in a parlous state.

It must be remembered that this community, by the very nature of its origin, is not wealthy. Those who have come to wealth and fame are not many, and such as are successful in life are prone to settle in Europe and hide their origins. Thus at the top the community loses its leaders, and at the bottom merges with those native Christians who take baptismal names and surnames from the cemetery. Nevertheless it has been the lot of these people to bear much of the heat and burden of British India in the subordinate walks of life. Millions of Indians have travelled in safety in their charge, and a sense of responsibility and also a political vision demands that we should not leave them by the wayside. In the reconstruction of India that we are trying to make, it is not possible to leave a community as large as theirs, but with none of that wealth to help it, on an insecure

[1] Other than as officer.

footing. It is a community, too, that has had to endure a good deal from heedless Anglo-Saxondom, and being both of East and West it has something both of the good and bad of each hemisphere in its constitution. It was Rudyard Kipling who said that until the mixed race throws up its poet we, the unthinking overdogs, shall not know of its sorrows and its aspirations.

Sufficient provision for their education, and a reasonable reservation of opportunity is their just need. If Britain is still Britain, we should see that they get both. There are War Memorial tablets in the hill schools, as numerous and as pathetic as those in the Cloisters of Eton.

Marriage to India: a New Problem

There is a new Anglo-Indian problem arising under our very noses that is going to have some strange and almost unpredictable consequences, consequences that are by no means all bad. That is, the tendency of the present day for English and American women, especially English, to marry Indians, both Hindu and Moslem. In the past forty or fifty years, one has known one or two cases—cases quite exceptional—that have not been at all disastrous, but now we are seeing what might almost be described as a mass movement. In two cities in India lately I inquired into the matter. In Lahore I was told there were about a hundred European women married to Indians, in Hyderabad Deccan perhaps fifty. In the latter I asked, 'Are they happy?' The answer came, 'Very few'. In the North I gathered that, despite certain intimate difficulties, domestic prospects were better, but it in itself is an astoundingly difficult problem. Nor is there any sign yet of the opposite. Young Britons do not at present seem to be marrying the beautiful young Indian women who are leaving purdah. The normal familiar problem of the mixed race was due to European men marrying Indian women, as already discussed. The mixed marriages and irregular unions ran the whole gamut of the social scale. But for many generations, the process has stopped. The older mixed community as stated, reproduced itself, and Europeans fuse with girls of mixed descent, but the fresh mixed article is now rarely fathered.

The European women who are to-day marrying Indians by no means all come from the less educated, typist, landlady's daughter class, though no doubt several do. That is inevitable in the conditions of Indian student life in England, and I make bold to say that such girls under average suitable conditions may make a success of their venture. But many young English women of higher education and status are thus taking fate by the hand. You meet them at such occasions as receptions at India House, *saris* over their pretty heads, rejoicing in their pride of loyalty, in the bogus, for them, caste-marks on their foreheads. I met lately a charming educated English woman happily married to a middle-aged Sikh. There was a bonny daughter of raven-black lock and very olive skin. Where is it all to end? Will the result be a new mixed race? Which way will the blend go? Sometimes when on occasion I have been speaking of the mixed race, in *very* liberal circles, I have referred to it as joining the strong points of both races (cheers), and let us trust that in the new mingling it may be so. One thing I am quite sure of is, these ladies will need the help and support of other white women and not the cold shoulder. The old instinct, which is the instinct of ancient caste India, is to abhor mixed unions and miscegenation. The instinct so bitterly strong in the United States must go. Let Aryan join with Aryan uncriticized. It is curious that while reason has disliked miscegenation, sexual sense finds some curious unholy attractions especially on the female side. Nature's ways in such matters are none too fathomable.

The mixed marriage, whether it be good or whether it be evil, has come. The pretty little London or Edinburgh girl who marries the douce—and this old Scoto-French word exactly describes him—the quiet, well-behaved, biddable young Indian student, should ascertain something of where she is going. Let her read *Marriage to India*. As to home life, even the kindliest Indian 'in-laws', who live in Indian style and who have pinched for years to send Ram Dass to England and buy him plum-coloured dittos, have no home to offer. A grass mat on the floor, and a *pillau* in a brass dish, is not a *milieu* in which the most genuine hospitality can make an English girl at home, nor is maternity in a *chaul*, or India mass-dwelling, possible. If the young man does not come of a westernized family, and has no prospects which guarantee a Western mode of living, the marriage is impossible. Once more, read, my attractive English girl who loves an Indian lad, *Marriage to India*, the pathetic life-story of a girl student in an American University, who married a charming brown Indian lad, with the tan body that did not fade.

A great and a grave subject for all who reflect, with, like everything else, both good and evil in its womb.

CHAPTER XIII

THE DAILY LIFE OF THE EUROPEAN IN INDIA

THE GRIM STEPMOTHER

IT is Kipling, as already mentioned, who has described India as 'The grim Stepmother of our kind', and that description still has a stern significance, as the countless Christian cemeteries—those cemeteries which are the best claim that Britain has to be dominant in the land, *primus inter pares*—denote.

For two hundred years and more our young men, merchants, traders, soldiers, writers, have gone to India, where service was at one time almost a life exile. Slow to learn the ways of the land, they lived and drank as in the temperate West, and died of fever and the bloody flux. Wise in our living and diet, temperate in our liquor as most men are to-day, frequent our return to the breezes of the West, ample our hospitals and nurses, mostly new the last thirty years—still nevertheless, it is a land of sudden death and of quick sepulture. It is a land where, until the motor and flying accidents brought unnecessary death to our doors everywhere, the young man might be cut off in his prime by disease inadequately tended, by disease unnecessarily acquired, and by the accidents of field and chase which he would not run the risk of at Home. And his wife and his children have paid the same toll.

Outside the great cities of the coast and outside the great cantonments, the same story still holds. The boys in the districts, the engineer, the prospector, the employee of business firms has the odds still against him, save that telegraph and motor do fight on his side. The microbe and the insanitary East are against him.

Despite all these drawbacks, despite the rows of children's graves in the dusty cemetery, the young men and women of Britain have gone and go freely to the East. Before the women took to going, there was plenty of 'black velvet', and the very beautiful brown velvet of the high-caste races who did not disdain to marry the *sahib log* by bell, book and candle and every honourable status.

So we still go East, by steamer and aeroplane and by car, who for 180 years went by sailing ship round the Cape.

So what is the life we lead to-day, and what is our work, we who now and in the future hasten by comfortable quick speed liners, whose ancestors for generations spent four to six months in the equally comfortable Green's liners? There are folk still living who went that way.

The British who go to the East, go in many capacities. Of them a very large number are in the Indian Services, or married thereto, but there are as many or even more in the great trade and business of the country, the exports and the imports, the planting and the like. Our Eastern lives may thus be divided into two categories, those in the great seaports, where are 90 per cent of the mercantile Europeans, and those in what is roughly known as 'up country', and in old Indian parlance the *moffussil*, the 'countryside'.

The Government servants, the soldiers, 'civilians', which by common consent means the 'covenanted civil service', or otherwise the administration, engineers, forest officers, doctors, etc., are largely in the *moffussil*, except the comparative few, who for the time are in the seaports, Calcutta, Bombay, Karachi, Madras. Here let it be explained, that while the whole of the inferior posts have been held by Indians, for many years they have also borne a share of the higher ones, being trained for the purpose in England, and for several years have held even a further share. That is only by the way, to prevent misconception at this stage.

Modern educational life with its residential facilities is rather in a category by itself.

An Up-country Station

As most of those in India live in an up-country station, it is to an up-country station we will go first. Here let it be remarked that in spite of the fact that for generations tens of thousands have gone and go to live in India, yet nevertheless that life seems a sealed book in the imaginations of those who are not connected with the country.

Up-country stations vary, apart from the intense climatic variation, from the large cantonments, in which also dwell the civil official population—where the presence of, to use an odious word, 'the Military', provide numbers, society and amusements—down to the tiny civil station, where a magistrate, doctor and policeman may mean the only society. That may nowadays be even more restricted than formerly for the European, when one or two of his sole neighbours may be Indian. British and Indian, however friendly they may be and almost always are, have not except on the tennis-court many tastes in common, though perhaps these are increasing. The coming of the many beautiful and charming Indian women from their ancient seclusion to everyday social life has and is changing greatly and naturally the old insulated social life.

In this connection it should be recorded, what perhaps is hard to realize in the West, that outside the great seaports and larger capitals, where westernized merchants and lawyers have adopted the British type of bungalow, residential conditions are entirely different from the West. Well-to-do Indians, traders for the most part, and to some extent land-owners with town houses, dwell in a strange narrow medley of secluded courts, to which even the relics of the middle ages in Europe give no parallel. No modern ways of life are expected or possible. The people go their way, their ancient way, on their own, content that the great continent shall be managed in peace and good order. Hardly in the whole of India is there wealth sufficient to produce and build a Bayswater.

This does not mean that municipal progress has not been possible. Piped water, sanitation on the removal system, schools, police, hospitals, are all organized, but Indian cities and ways of living are as they have always been. They are what the people like and want and know; all over India there are of course Indian gentlemen of means who have set up European types of houses with electric light machines; but their total would be trivial.

The small civil stations, where most of the good work of India is done, consist of perhaps half a dozen bungalows, a small club with a couple of mud tennis-courts, and a small dust and mud golf-links. In such places in the cold and rainy season, life in quiet and lonely ways has its charm. For the man, work, books and a little odd shooting. For the wife, if such there be, house, horse, and garden are the chief attractions. Some women can make their district home and life very attractive indeed. There is a daily paper by post, news twenty-four hours old at least, but that is of no real matter. If the station is not too small there will be a library, but without sufficient income to have much that is new. Folk are apt to buy books and magazines and have a circulation circle of their own.

But the officials in these small stations often spend the cold season in camp. Camping for the man means inspection of treasuries, small magisterial courts, revenue offices, meeting local magnates, hearing petitions, inspecting canal systems, police *thanas* [1] or what-not. For women who like out-door life, to whom the morning ride, the scampering terrier and the charms of tent life appeal, it is a delightful period. Children can be taken, for all Indian servants enjoy camp life and excel in it. The coming of the motor car has made it all the easier. But district life is a simple, uneventful existence, the sort of life that those who do the world's work lead. Holiday visits to the hills and the leave Home every

[1] Station-houses.

four or five years make it bearable. Now and again comes a change to the big station, where social life hums in comparison.

Life in Large Stations

A large station means cantonments, *i.e.* a place where troops are quartered. The days when single corps were scattered about the country are gone. Troops are more concentrated than formerly, for many reasons, principally, however, for facility for modern training.

A military cantonment will therefore as a rule have four or five units at least, cavalry, artillery and infantry. Where there are British, viz. European units, there are shops of sorts, and such extras as a joint of beef, quite unknown in the small stations, may be had. British blood is the better for beef, shudder the Hindu mind never so terribly.

In a military station there are that blessed desideratum to life and merriment, young people, young men, colonels' daughters—in modern naval and military parlance *bints*, *bint* being perfectly honourable Arabic for daughter. Compare the well-known Palestinian name for the bridge across Jordan into Syria—*Jisr-ul-banat*(plural of *bint*)*-ul-yakub*: 'The bridge of the daughters of Jacob'.

Cantonments have desirable clubs, that is to say 'assembly rooms', where folk play tennis and cards, dance and read the 'Europe' papers. There is a library with some pretension to new books. *On y danse* and social life with dinners, and amusements of all sorts are rife. There are polo and cricket to watch, military bands to listen to, and there is the come-and-go of horse and foot and gun, tramp, clatter, dash and glamour. The men are hard-bitten and athletic, choice young men and goodly.

The Army is not idle, far from it, but as it begins work at 6 A.M. it may look to being free to play games by 4 P.M. Civilian office hours begin at 9 and last till 5 and 6. You cannot have life both ways. Therefore the soldier is freer to relax than the office-tied civilian, and the women are more amused thereby.

The cold weathers in the cantonments are however interrupted enough, for the garrisons are often away in camp, and now and again feminine hearts run cold as troop trains run into the siding and husbands are mysteriously swept off to trouble on the frontier, the troops a-cheering. It means hurried cancelling of passages home, summer plans thrown into the air, *mais, c'est la vie d'un soldat.*

During the Boer War an Irish Militia battalion was marching through Dublin on its way to embark, when discipline was horrified to hear a man in the ranks shout, 'Three cheers for ould Kruger!' but as he explained to his commanding officer, 'Sure, your honour, if it was not for the ould divil we wouldn't be here a-tall'.

So if there were no bad men and no wars there would not be pretty soldiers in scarlet and gold to make merry with.

Concerning Bungalows

Since this part of the book deals with life with our grim stepmother, the question of housing is not out of order. Here in India, 'where we pray for the Viceroy', as the Anglican prayer has it, the world lives in bungalows, and bungalows are very varied items, the word itself being derived from a Portuguese word. Bungalows may be old or new, mostly old, and may be good, bad or indifferent, rarely the first. Most of the cantonments and many of the civil stations were built in the days of John Company, in fact many of the best bungalows, despite their age, date from those more spacious days. While civilian bungalows have usually been built under Government auspices, those in military cantonments have been built willy-nilly in the past by officers for themselves. When officers moved elsewhere, they were let, sold to Indian merchants, taken over by banks on foreclosed mortgages and the like. Army officers, owing to the frequent change of stations due to war, to the too hasty laying-out and abandonment of cantonments, etc., often had two or three houses on their hands, and were very hard put to it and rightfully aggrieved. The Government's view was that an officer's emoluments included an item for tentage or housing, and that he must shift for himself.

For many years now the bungalows have been in the hands of Indian merchants and shopkeepers who rent them to officers. Under new conditions, however, the Army Department is rebuying them, which is wise but often inconvenient. Some are good and some are bad landlords, while equally all tenants are not reasonably considerate or prompt payers. In days that are passing, Muhammadans thought house property a form of investment that did not transgress the laws of usury, which ordinary investing was believed to do. House-owning was also a pleasant way of making the acquaintance of European tenants.

The bungalows vary from large, thick-walled, often double-storeyed houses fit to resist the heat of the summer, to the little three-roomed shacks that a couple of subalterns would erect. Some stand in bare deserts, some in good gardens, well planted with flowering shrubs, for in India as in England the too much neglected flowering shrub is a thing of almost perennial joy. Some, and the coolest, are heavily thatched, some are tiled, and in the North the roofs are flat and plastered in mud, and good to sleep on. The thatched bungalows are picturesque, but always liable to fire. In 1857 the discontent of the Sepoys took the form of mysterious house fires. Many regiments had served in the Sonthal rebellion of 1856 and had learnt from the aboriginal tribe the trick of firing arrows with burning paper attached and thus firing ricks or roofs from a distance.

The old bungalows are often very complete, and at times romantic. To this day many of them in the old stations have the *bibi-garh*, the 'lady's quarters', with covered way attached—a memory of the days lying so far back as the 'forties, when 'black velvet' was the companion of most officers; sometimes velvet of high degree, more often humble enough, if comely and helpful. Because it was so, comes that Anglo-Indian population which is our inheritance and our problem, and has just been dwelt on.

Bungalows consist usually of drawing-room, dining-room and two or more bedrooms. To each bedroom is a dressing-room and bathroom, the latter with a masonry recess for the good enamelled iron bath, a grating over the overflow opening to keep snakes away. Hot water laid-on? there ain't no such thing, but excellent hot baths are heated outside in empty kerosene tins. Electricity has appeared in the larger places, but anywhere else oil-lamps must of necessity prevail. Floors are mud or stone, and beneath your rug is usually some matting. The sweet scent of the grass, which half a dozen women plait for you as you are moving in, is one of the smells of India that remain.

Most bungalows have verandahs all or half-way round, many stand on plinths three or four feet high.

Across the compounds, as the garden or desert of your premises is called—another Portuguese word—are the stables. If the bungalow is one frequented by cavalry or artillery officers, there will be a dozen stalls and a coach-house, all of mud bricks, in the corner and near it the line of servants' houses.

Horses I have known

The mention of stables in the compound brings one to that most charming side of Indian life, one's horses and the horse's life. In spite of the vogue of the tin-lizzie, most people still keep horses, for pleasure and for their duty. Most men and women ride, and riding is *par excellence* the exercise that keeps both sexes fit, especially in the hotter season. Women in India, as elsewhere, ride astride, a great advantage, since it avoids the provision of the costly and unportable side-saddle. You can thus use your husband's or your admirer's saddles and also his long brown boots, which simplifies your equestrian outfit.

There is no pleasanter hour than that spent in the stable on Sunday morning—the saddles and bridles laid out, the horses with an extra grooming and ready to accept eagerly the sugar and green lucerne you bring them. The good

Indian groom, the *sais*, is an estimable creature, fond of his charges and within limits eminently trustworthy, and like other servants, at his best in camp and on the march. Indeed the writer has a very lively remembrance of a very tight corner in the Burma hills, and an empty revolver and ammunition pouch, when his *sais*, engaged in bandaging a wounded charger, suddenly ran up with a forgotten packet of ammunition from a holster. Your *sais* may be Hindu or Moslem, but belongs to a horse-keeping caste that has done the job for generations.

But now what of the horses? Ah! what of them? That will depend on your rôle in life, your corps or your husband's corps. If he is a cavalryman, or a gunner, there may be one of the 16-hand Australian horses of imperfect manners. If he is a polo player there will be a couple or so of polo ponies, who in these spacious days must be Waler, *i.e.* Australian (for Waler, as the world should know, is but short for New South Wales). The reason for this is that now there are no height rules, the Country-bred, the Kabuli, and the Arab, are not big enough, the which in many ways is a folly and a loss.

The horses of India of the few indigenous breeds that are worthy of the name, are not many. There are myriads of little by-blows that carry yeomen to town, but the others are few and must be talked of later. Here we deal with your friend the horse of your stables. *Par excellence* the horse for a lady's hack is still the Arab. The Arab, the true Arab, as apart from the fatter, commoner Gulf Arab, as the Persian horse is often called, is the greatest gentleman in the world. He comes usually from far-away Mosul, three hundred miles north of Bagdad, from the dark underground stable of Ali Bin Talib and his friends, who buy him from the Anizah and other horse-breeding tribes. The finest horses come for Arab racing, which still flourishes in Western India, but not to the extent of days gone by, for the English horse and the Australian now have pride of place. But even the lesser and cheaper Arab, the horse that won't win a race, is the purest of thoroughbreds, and a charming friend. Did I say a *good* hack? That is not quite right, for as a hack *qua* hack he is not at his best. In his walk he will take too much interest in all and sundry; in his desert, sand-bred trot he is apt to trip on stones. His pace, and for this reason in open country he is undoubtedly a lady's horse, is a hand canter and a gallop. He is the ideal horse for the dweller in the smaller station, where there is the daily ride across open country, the coursing of hare and fox with long dogs and terrier pack. The Waler polo pony, now a horse of over 15 hands, may be an equally good hack as a polo pony, and the modern country-bred of the North is equally desirable.

All look happily at home in the mud stalls, with the lump of red rock-salt to give them iodine, and all will appreciate the *gaja*, which is carrot, or the handful of green lucerne, the *alfalfa* of the States, which the groom will always have handy for the master's visit. At the end will probably be the coach-house, which is now the garage, for the days of the dog-cart are unfortunately gone—unfortunately for the married officer, who drove his charger or his polo pony, but now must often keep a car as well, or be hopelessly out of life, as all but the very wise think.

Happily the riding horse must still be in the stable of many, and the hack ride in India is one of the good things that the East can give you, and a pleasant courting medium too if need be. I like to look back on my own vista from *Youth*, the bucking well-bred Waler ex-racehorse that was my first charger and a gentleman's horse for all his ways, and was staunch as steel at a pig; to *Gentle Jane* the *yabu* bred of a Deccani mare and an Arab sire, that is to say of gentle blood on both sides, who carried a lady, taught in a Sunday School, and was the handiest thing with a polo ball that you can imagine. I sold her for many rupees when I left India in my younger days. There was *Abdulla* too, a chestnut Arab polo pony, not up to my weight, but a charming irresponsible hack, whose only decent pace was the gallop. If you're desert-bred, stones to stumble on are outside your ken. With his handsome pace, if he had a mind to, with his interest in *minas* and other cockioly birds, his heartiness to small dogs, and his good manner inherited from a long line of blood ancestors among the Anizah west of Mosul, he was more a friend than a horse. He would come to tea, walk up the steps through the drawing-room out at the back like one gentleman in another gentleman's house. Alas, he broke a leg hog-hunting and no doubt went where good Arabs go.

They are a pleasant memory, one's horses and one's women, as an old Rajah friend once said, and he knew the points of both.

Behind the Bungalow

Close on fifty years ago there appeared from the pen of E. H. A. a delightful book, *Behind the Bungalow*, about life and the inhabitants of that line of servants' quarters behind the house, where shrill-voiced women argue the point, and swarms of little swollen-tummied brats play knuckle-bones. And it is well that one should know and think something of that willing useful body, the *amla* or the *naukar-chakar*. This is important to all, visitors or residents, and it is not too much to say that a European's life in India depends on good servants. But good masters get good servants all the world over. India has many good servants, plenty of average ones, and not a few bad ones. The story of the number of servants necessary in India is often told. The customs of the country do require several, but others are due to the condition of housing. For instance the sweeper, the night soil removalist, exists partly because there is no water-borne drainage, partly because no man of other caste dare wield a broom. The house-man may dust, he *must not sweep*, or his soul in the next incarnation will have slipped down many pegs in its weary climb towards the Source and the Goal.

The married man with a smallish household will need—and it is to be remembered that servants have different names in different parts of the country—an establishment as follows:

A cook, known as the *khansaman*, the 'lord of things'. If

you have a biggish house and entertain, a good and important cook wants a 'mate', equivalent to a kitchenmaid. Your cook goes marketing every day, a job he likes and makes his little profit off. The bigger the dinner the greater the profit, and he will like a dinner party six days a week. An Indian cook with a mistress who knows a little can be very good indeed. But unless the mistress knows how many eggs—Indian eggs are small—cakes require, she will be done. Every day she must, if wise, take the *hissab*, the account of the day before. The cook will spend his money each day and give account. There will be no tradesmen's books. If you are in camp, you may expect a six-course dinner cooked admirably in a hole in the ground and may ask guests at short notice, even if they must bring their own plates. The bachelor who lives in his own house will do well to contract for his food with his cook—so much a day—and take an intelligent interest. He won't do too badly.

The *bearer*. He is the head servant of the house and looks after the table and master's clothes. Sahibs should have high-caste Hindu bearers, or else Muhammadans. The low-caste convenient bearers who will do anything, do not redound to their master's prestige with Indians. A clever sweeper servant will save you much trouble, but in all Indian eyes you would be terribly debased by his presence. If you have a high-caste Hindu bearer, you must have a separate table-servant known as *khitmutgar*. But if you have Muhammadan servants, the staff of a small house need only be: cook, bearer, *khit* and general assistant houseman, the last two Muhammadans. The *sweeper* you must have and the *bhisti*, or water-carrier, the 'man of paradise', if you have no piped water. A lady needs a maid, but many find a house-boy less trouble, and very good with clothes.

You have your own *dhobi* or washerman, and he is part lady's-maid, since he will iron dresses at any hour of the day or night. He is necessary because there are no laundries. If you have not a shirt fit to wear out to dinner, he will lend you one from some other client's or neighbouring *dhobi's* master's wardrobe. This is the kindly way of the East! Similarly you must have a gardener, a *mali*, because civilization demands that you contribute thereto, and if you have a gardener you need not worry about flowers, he will see that you always have them, of your own or from someone else's garden.

Grooms there must be at one per horse, good, faithful servants and fond of their horses, and where you do not buy hay, you must have a *grass-cut*, male or female, often the latter, who will slither from off the land enough of the succulent *doub* grass each day for your horse.

I have not spoken of *ayahs*, the ladies'-maids. If you have one you marry trouble. But as they are often indispensable, you should have a high-caste one. The convenience of a low-caste woman is very great, but the lady whose husband has any sort of position, especially if in touch with Indian life, will avoid one. The high-caste ayah will employ the sweeper's wife for lesser duties, and she will be trustworthy and perhaps moral.

So that is in some sort a tally of the folk 'Behind the Bungalow'. Simple, kindly, helpful and vexatious folk at times. Don't, kind lady! take too much notice of the brown babies with eyes like sloes, because of the mystery of the evil-eye, that sudden withering of child life that may come on, and will surely be attributed to you. Give them sweetmeats and penny toys *en masse* if you like, the head bearer assisting, but to take too much notice of some lollipop in a pink woollen hood in its mother's arms may mean disaster. The mother will be half gratified, half apprehensive of your strange overlooking.

The rage for rushing to England destroys the servant class. The old faithful retainer is being to some extent replaced by the dearer schemer who knows too much. There was, nay, there still is the wonderful bearer who keeps your keys and runs you entirely. Would you and your household move to the hills, all is arranged in the twinkling of an eye. Nothing is forgotten. Run away and play marbles; he will do everything and forget nothing. Nor shall anyone rob Master, save he himself and then only to the minor extent limited by Master's salary. Supremely honest within this trivial limit prescribed by centuries, a treasure of treasures!

The Christian servants from Madras too are eminently satisfactory. There is an old Virginian flavour about the Madras household, where each servant in turn comes in about nine o'clock, and the chorus begins: 'Good night, *Sahib*! Good night, *Mem-sahib*! Good night, Miss *Sahib*! Good night, *chota Sahib*!' It still goes on and you should always be pleased and say, 'Good night, *Anthony*! Good night, *José*! Good night, *Mari-anne*!' and so forth. They will usually be of the Church of Rome, and if you are wise you will let them have time off for Church and encourage the visits of the priest. He will chasten them for you if need be.

Your good-class Indian servant, Hindu, Moslem and Christian, will like you to keep Bible and Prayer Book by your bedside. He will have them ready on Sunday and think better of you if you go to Church. Non-church-going ways pain them. In the days when I read the Service at Parade Service in the absence of the chaplain, my old Muhammadan bearer bristled with pride and said how he too read the Qoran in the mosque. If you can satisfy your servants' ideas of what a European should be, you will do well in India, and plenty of quinine and aspirin tablets in your drawer, will acclaim you as the friend of man.

It was early in 1933 that I returned to India on a visit. My old Anthony, grown fat and portly, but with the old grin, was waiting for me. For two days he waited on me with portraits of sons, daughters and brides, and then fitted me out with a nephew for my stay, a good silent nephew who never made a mistake, while I travelled hard.

BOOK III

LIFE AND SPORT

CHAPTER XIV

HOLIDAY AND HEALTH AND HIMALAYA

Who Goes Home?

The secret of health in India lies in two well-defined directions; in ways of living, including dietary, and in sufficient holiday. The climate of India is well enough for those Europeans who make it so, but life in India for the man who himself is in poor health, or who has a delicate wife, is trying enough. The 'grim stepmother' demands good health—too often that she may destroy it. The holidays come under two heads, the short one to the Indian hills, the longer one, usually accumulated, to Great Britain. The Indian officer or official on leave is a well enough known phenomenon in England. During the last thirty years the tendency to rush Home on every opportunity has greatly increased. The hanker for the increased excitement and amusement of Great Britain is not inconsiderable.

Home leave is taken more often than health demands or pockets can stand, and officials are often busy while in India paying back moneys advanced them when they returned. The want of continuity in local administrative personnel due to leave changes, have done much to diminish British influence and even prestige in the last few decades, and the warnings of older hands have been disregarded. However, that is another story.

For many years, when children are at Home, the enhancement of the cost and style of living in the Indian hills makes mothers find it as economical to go Home as to stay in India, while husbands can run Home on very short leave. This again is perhaps one of the reasons that has induced some of the old hill firms to close their businesses.

Up to now, Home leave means by sea, and the wise will ever keep it so. Human frames need rest, and two or three weeks at sea are an excellent restorative and preparation for the period of leave. The fly Home or the racket Home by car through Persia, to which reference has already been made, entrancing adventure though it may be, is not the restorative that the sea voyage certainly is, both to mind and body.

But since this book treats of India it is to Indian holiday resorts that we must take the reader, to the Himalaya and to Kashmir.

The Hill Stations in the Himalaya

It has been said that you cannot rule a house from the kitchen, and for the last eighty years or so the Governments of India, the Punjab, the United Provinces and of Bengal have moved themselves and the bulk of their establishments to hill stations in the Himalaya. These Governmental stations and several others are the summer resorts of the European women and children resident in this side of India, the larking grounds of officers of all services on shorter leave, and of the last few years of many Indians who have now come to appreciate the European views of health and coolth. These hill stations—there are others elsewhere—are situated on the lower slopes of the outer Himalayas, within the line of Siwaliks or foothills. Behind them stands the great massif of the Himalaya proper, the 'Abode of Snow' aforesaid. Besides the summer resorts and those of them which are both resorts and Government stations, are several hill cantonments for British units, for the Gurkha regiments, and for young European soldiers. They vary from 4000 to 7000 feet above the sea, and even in the lowest of them one begins to see vegetation and flora of the West. Gone are the tropical trees and flowers and fruits of the plains, and we are as it were in a European wood and garden, amid the scenery of Switzerland. Let us look at the trees. We shall find the *Cheer* Pine or Terebinth, which is *Pinus longifolia*, and higher up, the Blue Pine or *Pinus excelsa*, the Spruce which is *Picea Morinda*, the Norwegian Fir which is *Abies Webbiana*, and *Cedrus Deodaris*, the Deodar that is first cousin to the Cedar of Lebanon; there are many oaks, *Quercus Indica* and *Quercus sesquicarpifolia*, there are Hazel and Lombardy and White Poplars, there are ferns and dripping wells, and wood strawberries, apples and plums, and many a flower to delight the European eye. British capital and British industry have made them hives of commerce of sorts while the Indian trader has shops galore. In some cases such as Simla, a railway winds up the slopes for sixty miles from the plains, and in these days motors throng the roads which formerly were the territory of galloping chaises, when Kipling wrote his haunting lilt of the 'clanging tonga bar', and the lover's drive.

Now what shall we do with ourselves, if we go to the Himalaya? Well, if you go in winter, go up by car or train to Simla and smell the hills, there will be plenty of room in the hotels, and perhaps heavy snow on the roads, but go see it and such a wall of snow behind it as no Alps can ever show. But we will assume that like Padgett M.P. you have been persuaded to stay through the summer not among the mosquitoes, but among the pines and deodars and the hill captains, the choice young men who spend their leave there for your delectation, if you be of the feminine sex. In that case too, I ought to tell you what to wear, only I dare not, and times change so fast, and what was written when you are down to the ground might be read when you are up to the knees. But for the feminine there is this rule: Wear what you wear in a not too warm summer in Merry England, and have a useful supply of evening dresses, for you will dance or otherwise festivate most nights. Quantity is necessary more than quality, unless you are a top-notcher.

What shall we do? where shall we stay? You may stay in a charming little half-English house on the hillside if you have friends or are enterprising enough to take a house, which will be scantily furnished, for yourself. But in all the hill stations there are hotels, some very good, some atrocious and many betwixt and between. You will find plenty of merry people there, grass widows and families; officials and their wives who shirk a house, and sufficient men to carry on. Simla of course is a bigger matter. There come many folk. You will dance, you will play tennis, you will dine out and give dinners at house or hotel; you will ride and picnic and what not. There will be a man's club where skirts can be eschewed, and remembering that many folk in India are young, and that there are unfortunately no old folk, you will, in a way, find much fun and pleasant intercourse.

In Simla, where there will be two thousand people all on one calling list, there will be plenty to do. There are half a dozen hotels, delightful forest resorts, and places of entertainment in the wooded hinterland; there is a Viceroy to see and be entertained by, and if by chance you will go to a State Ball, you will feel as if you really belonged to some Ruritanian story, what with princes and queens and life-guards and officers in many picturesque uniforms; Rajahs like Carlsbad plums, in kincob and crimson, and in the corner 'ould ladies match-making' and the 'shubadars wid their midals and shtars'. Did you ask about love-making, go to! This is a land of young people, of young women and young wives and cavaliers, and busy clever men and so forth: 'Woman is fire and man is tow, the devil comes and begins to blow'. But not more than elsewhere ye'll ken. Bright pleasant folk there are of both sexes, and a world of action, that is worth your seeing.

Perhaps we had better now leave the hills, but it may be said that young officers, who incidentally, for matrimonial purposes, are usual detrimentals, are hunted from the hill stations by their commanding officers and sent off on shooting quests for wild goat and sheep of immense horns that may adorn mess and club. Nevertheless the said young officers on their way to and from their hunting in the interior, do evade the rules and put in a week or two with the fair on the hill-top.

Autumn in the Himalaya

Before we leave the Himalaya for the South Lands let me show you autumn which is even as autumn in England, red and brown, soughing and wistful, restless and stimulating. The charm of the middle Himalaya to English folk lies in its trees and its flowers that are of Europe; gone are the flora and fauna of the plains and the tropical atmosphere of the Terai and the Doon. The trees stand as old Isaiah put them, the cedar, the pine and the box as aforesaid.

The *Chikor* are calling on the hillside and the pheasants *Kalej* and *Mannal* in the deep glens, the water in the streams below a-gleaming. And because it is all so redolent of Merry England in the fall, one is pleased to be wistful, listening to the wind whispering in the trees and feigning a *heimweh* for which there is no shadow of reason, unless bairns and missis be across the sea.

Down on the cultivated terraces below you, colour is blazing; the orange corncobs on the flat roof-tops, the crops of scarlet crimson amaranth and love-lies-bleeding, illuminate the whole hillside, and the hillmen are bringing up the narcissi to hawk in the roadways. The mule trains are moving to the plains with the potato crop and the hill roads are alive with the jink of the mule bells. Travellers and pleasure seekers who have been far into the mountains are hurrying back, for the snow is coming lower and the great peaks glisten with the fresh falls, and the mantle is already far down on the deodar fringe of the main range. Winter is coming, and those villages in the deep glens that even in summer lose the sun at noon are preparing for their months of gloom with great skins of *ghee* to feed on in their semi-hibernation, amid the gloom and *brouillard* that looks so *triste* to those on the sunny slopes above.

In the hill stations of the Himalaya all is pleasant bustle

for there is no call so joyous as that of the plains to the hills in autumn. To the civil servant of Government there is all the busy touring winter when families have rejoined him, and the interludes when snipe and duck and partridge abound, and the curling smoke of the camp-fires brings back many memories. The Indian traders and all who make their harvest in the summer season are leaving. Simla and Darjeeling may discharge their population by the winding mountain railway, but to other places and even to the masses of Simla it means the roadway, by shrine and rock and long bazaar, with strings of bullock- and pony-carts, of odd and snarling camels, of peasant and coolie families, of pimps and panders, of lepers in the roadway shoving their poor stumps in the faces of the kindly, fearsome lest the police take them to the asylum; such a come and go as must be seen to be believed.

Up in the curling looping railway where the quality journey, there is a new feature. During the last few years the Indian has seen the wisdom of escaping from the stifling plains and he too brings his family to the hills, buying and building many cottages and bungalows. Further it has become the fashion for the timorous purdah lady to come to the hills for her chrysalis act and there emerge from the veil among the other emancipated ones, return to the plains in the autumn as bold as brass, having actually perhaps gone in to dinner on a white man's arm, and found he did not want to stare her out of countenance. And very attractive and charming some of them are, and the daughters of the intelligentsia come with their papas to the Parliament session at Simla. Members of Parliament are rum fish to look at all the world over, but their daughters far otherwise and the Indian lasses follow the rule, and have learnt to dance too, so that in a few years you won't see their heels for the dust.

In the hill cantonments where the British soldier comes o' summer-time for his health and more vigorous climbing and training than he really cares about, and the little Mongol Gurkhas live, the autumn moves are stirring things. There is much gossip; everything is happening, and while further from the frontier the talk is of manœuvres and camps of exercise, and of Christmas shooting camps, in the hills near the frontier it is more exciting. The mountain batteries are on the move from the Gullies.

> A-smokin' my pipe in the mountain,
> A-sniffing the morning cool,
> I climbs in my old brown gaiters
> Along o' my old brown mule.

The Highland regiments are moving too and there is a skirl of pipes as the kilts swing round the Changla road. There is a jam of camels and pack mules, and the dust is rising high while a flight of cars coming down the Kashmir road tries to get through. A battalion is halted by the wayside for a drink o' tea, long known in India as the morning 'coffee-shop'. Half a dozen peripatetic musicians are fiddling hard, fiddling still perhaps what they know as 'Kaki Narth', so popular when the Gordons stormed Dargai, and wounded piper Findlater played 'Cock o' the North' as the kilts rushed by. And from time immemorial the gossip has been the same . . . good stirring exciting gossip and rumour, and the gunners start it no doubt. There is trouble in Kabul . . . no new thing . . . the Afridis are restless, the Mahsuds won't have the motor road through Waziristan, the Commander-in-Chief has been up the Khaiber . . . someone has a pal in Simla who said there would not be much time for polo this year. . . . A Sikh regiment at Ferozepur was restless. . . . The tang in the air, the movement, the sight of snowpeaks which lie far up into Afghanistan, the knowledge that the frontier of the Indus Kohistan is but a dozen miles away, produce a romance and an atmosphere that is most intoxicating; and every autumn it is the same. It is added to as the men from Kashmir pass by hurrying back from their leave, who call for the latest news as they pass, and perhaps show some of their trophies from the mountain-side; and so it has gone on these last hundred years for there is no new thing under the sun. And before the British found the Himalaya and all their charm, the Turks from Central Asia found them too, and the Mogul Emperors traversed the hills with guns and elephants and the daughters of the South in their harems and came down through deodar and juniper and pine for the work of the winter. And what they once said to conquered Hindostan, the British now say in kindlier vein:

> Now my frontiers march on the Himalay snow
> And my landmarks stand on its loftiest crest,
> Where the winds blow soft on the pines below,
> There shall my legions halt and rest.

Kashmir

Did you say Kashmir? Well, you as a visitor shall hear about Kashmir, and some who are not may profit by it. It is a summer proposition and if you have signed that agreement to stay till October, you can do it. At any rate let us run a reel or two through the lantern for you, and then a very special one to follow of an old Mogul garden on the route that the Emperors took when they left Lahore with their wives and whatnots, their guns, their elephants and their court.

Kashmir has been the playground of the rulers of India for many centuries, and it is as all the world should know a valley, an inland upland valley far away in the Himalaya in which the river Jhelum rises and winds its way through an old and fertile lake-bed, set in a ring of snowy and forest-clad hills, with a lake or two still left in its centre. From the valley the Jhelum then cuts its way for a hundred miles or so of gorges until it emerges on the plains as one of the five rivers of the Punjab, on its way to join Mother Indus to which all good northern Indian rivers flow.

The valley of Kashmir is much as parts of Switzerland and its lower hills are like unto the Eigenthal. It has been a seat of Hindu learning and culture from very early times, and the remains of temples dating from the beginning of the Christian era are to be seen, some indeed intact to this day,

By courtesy of Indian Railways Bureau

A high valley in Kashmir

By courtesy of Indian Railways Bureau

How the Kashmir shawl is grown

but most destroyed in the wild hatred of idols that so marked the early Moslem invaders, Turks and Afghans, who overran Northern India in the twelfth century.

As one Moslem dynasty at Delhi fell before another we see Kashmir either subject to local rulers or else fiefs of Delhi and as such chosen by the Moguls, who came from upland Kabul and beyond, as their summer abode. Beautiful were the summer palaces and gardens that they made, modelled, as those in Agra and Delhi and Lahore, on the hanging gardens of Kabul and Ferghana, with rills and fountains and terraces. You will see them all to-day, and if you are clever you will camp in and by them, the 'Garden of Delight'; the 'Garden of Pleasure'; the 'Garden of Sweet Breezes'.

When the Mogul Empire started that crumble that brought the British on to the scene, Kashmir fell to Ahmed Shah Durani who had made an Empire of Kabul as far into India as the Sutlej river, and it remained an Afghan possession till the magpie, acquisitive, hands of the Runjhit Singh aforesaid took it from the Afghans. That was so recently as the Year of Grace 1820, when the Sikh was driving the Afghan back not only across the Indus but actually into the hills.

When that terrible lustrum of disorder and depravity fell on Lahore after the death of Runjhit Singh, which ended in the Sikh Durbar inciting the army that it could not control to expend itself on invading British India, Rajah Gulab Singh of Jammu with his large army on a French model, held aloof. The little Rajput state of Jammu lies the hither side of the Pir Punjal whose snowy peaks divide it and the Punjab from Kashmir. The view of the Pir Punjal from the Punjab, say from Sialkot in winter, is one of the most inspiring things in the world. Gulab Singh of Jammu had long been eating up his lesser Rajput neighbours, and he and his two notorious brothers were the big noise at the Lahore Court. But the wily Rajput was not going to link his fate with the crumbling Sikhs. When Lord Gough had fought his series of fierce battles that ended with the crowning victory which drove the Sikh Army into the Sutlej by the two villages of Sobra, of which the plural is Sobraon, then it was that Gulab Singh appeared as honest broker. Eventually on shouldering the burden of the Sikh war indemnity he was made Maharajah of Jammu and Kashmir. Very soon the British officers who had been on duty in Kashmir brought word of all its beauties and it became and is still the holiday resort of many in Northern India. It is a land of river and house-boat and tent life. Green and attractively treed, covered in spring with apple and plum blossom, wild iris and tulip everywhere, it is a dreamland of holiday for the sun-soaked European from the plains.

How do you get there? There are two good ways with a third from the frontier. The normal visitor will take train to Jammu whence he can drive (or drive from Lahore) straight to Srinagar by the Banihal route which brings him into the upper end of the valley, or he can drive through or from Rawalpindi, through the hill station of Murree, down to the Jhelum valley and then to Baramulla via the Jhelum valley. At Baramulla if he wants the happy leisurely way he will have a boat, either a house-boat or better still the *doonga*, the country boat with its comfortable bed space and its grass mat roof, and then will go leisurely up by lake and river to Srinagar the capital. Because the English are like that, many of them will come all the way from some cantonment in India to stay round Srinagar playing golf and tennis and attending gymkhana races, as if they had never left their happy homes. Others wiser in their generation will be away by boat and tent to the wild valleys that the snow has just left, to camp, to sketch, to read, to enjoy an entirely different life. There are many beautiful valleys to visit, many charming camping-grounds to explore. Later on, after the orgy of the strawberry season and the early fruits, when the valleys get hot—it is only 5000 feet above the sea—then folk take to the upland valleys to camp; many flock to the beautiful hackneyed, half-camp, wholly golfing hill station of Gulmarg and its social delights, which lies 4000 feet more above the valley. But there are less frequented and less hackneyed spots of even greater beauty. Kashmir for its full value, is a land of camp and boat and *alfresco* life. Servants, boatmen, shopkeepers, tent-hirers conspire to make the outdoor life easy. Hotels too there be for the unequipped, in Srinagar and at Gulmarg, and all goes easily and none too expensively, though the old simple life with eggs twopence a dozen and chickens at fourpence and ducks at twopence apiece are gone these fifty years. The days when you brought up half a cask of Army rum, filled it with morello cherries, carried it about with you and drank it at Christmas, those too are gone.

The big-game story of Kashmir I have alluded to elsewhere; the big-game ground is far away into the great hills, but there are poor old black bear to slay, if slay you must, when they be stealing mulberries, and there are the *chikor* to be shot by hard work in the autumn, and *mahseer* in the big river, and trout in the small. And Tommy Moore who had never seen it, wrote *Lalla Rookh*, and yet *you* can see the places from what he wrote; Glory be!

> Who has not heard of the Vale of Cashmere,
>   With its roses the brightest that earth ever gave,
> Its temples, and grottos, and fountains as clear
>   As the love-lighted eyes that hang over their wave?
>
> Oh! to see it at sunset,—when warm o'er the Lake
>   Its splendour at parting a summer eve throws,
> Like a bride, full of blushes, when ling'ring to take
>   A last look of her mirror at night ere she goes!

I cannot perhaps communicate to you the romance of this house or camp life, though I hope it may enter into your bones, but I will try and take you there by the old way. You will perhaps see something of the ruling Prince, great grandson of the Maharajah aforesaid, a player of polo and lover of horses who is somewhat put about politically at the moment. Since the mighty calm that the British brought to India was montagued, political disturbers from outside have been pulling strings of disharmony. Kashmir, a Moslem state, is joined with Jammu, a Hindu one. Too many Hindu servants of state control affairs. Since Hindu and Moslem have been brought to enmity, this gives room for discontent, and if administration is indifferent, the voice of the complainer is loud in the land. Time was when we saw, in a fatherly manner, that Princes governed their states reasonably and disturbers and mischief-makers got short shrift. The trouble however has for the nonce been straightened out. But there is in Lahore a party dreaming a dangerous dream of a Moslem block, and who like to pull strings of mischief.—However, to hell with politics! and come see the beauties of the land!

In an Old Mogul Garden

So much for Kashmir, that is to-day blatant at times with electric light, yet a thing of great beauty. But if you will come with me, you ladies and gentlemen of India, you young officers who want something more interesting than the *piaffe* and as some would rudely say the poodle-fake of a hill station, or you, visitor, who would march and travel, and have signed your contract to stay, I will take you by the old road—the road that is always new.

We will follow the now deserted road of the Mogul Emperors, the great cobbled *pavé* that rose stage by stage, easy Emperor stages, over the Pir Punjal among snow and glacier, down by Shapiyon into old Srinagar, the Holy City of Hindu fame. Think of it! Think of Jehangir and Shah Jehan in all their glory setting forth, wives of Toorkistan and wives of Rajputana, in their hooded conveyance on howdah-ed elephants, the rumble of brass cannon with lion mouths, the soldiery, spears, spiked helm, mail shirts, harquebuses, concubines—and Court feminines, and then the rag-tag that followed the camp, dancing girls, pimps and panders, shoemakers, kincob-sellers—really *kamkwab* or 'rarely seen'—and every sort of food merchant, all kept in reasonable order by the *bakshi* and the bastinado. We will dodge the cavalcade and make by train or car to Gujerat Station, say towards the end of April, and at Bhimber we will take to the road. What do we want for the road? Well if there is a lady, a horse, indeed for both horses or ponies, unless in these hiking days you will march. Good tramping girls can march too, but ponies apiece with their good *saises* are worth having, for sore heels may make them valuable even if you are going to foot it. In days gone by ladies had carrying-chairs. But in any case the smaller the party the better, since supplies of fodder, etc., at the stages are none too plentiful. You will want tents, for the old bungalows and *serais* will be ruined or supremely flea-encumbered. Shelter tents, of the kind that used to be called 'sleeping pāls'—old hands will remember the *Pioneer's* leg being pulled in this connection—are easy loads for coolies. You will want some pack transport, to be hired fairly easily in small quantities, perhaps, as in the good old days, you may hire some Army transport mules. And thus you will start, and all the while the ghosts of the mighty will jostle you by the broadway, even though the dead-and-gone cavalcade cannot gleam like the lightnings.

You will soon march through the foothills and come to Rampur Rajaori with castle atop the hill and below a ruined *serai* of the same old Mogul Emperors, and you will find one at every stage. You've left the plains and there is a sniff of the still distant pines in the air, but if you are of the kind that try to catch fish and you have a rod and a spoon in your outfit maybe you will stay at Rajaori a day or so amid the almond and peach blossom and will spin for *mahseer*.

Marching on we will turn into one of the old *serais*, standing on a low plateau above the road. The old lost gardens of the world are an everlasting pleasure; sometimes in an old priory by an Irish loch, lying to the soft west wind, amid saxifrage and old-world things, some wild and some cultured; sometimes by Hadrian's wall where Iberian Cohorts left their seeds, and sometimes by these Himalayan foothills. Somewhere in Central Asia the garden and fountain cult excelled, using mountain streams and fruit trees with the Persian rose, the narcissus and the *Paighamber gul*, the Prophet's Flower, with its five yellow petals, black where his fingers touched them. Above our road is a low flat hill with a cobbled causeway leading up it, and a partridge running in front of us. Let us follow and we find ourselves in a narrow plateau with a hill behind. There is a walled enclosure, with little bastioned towers and red stone umbrella kiosques on top. A high gateway with plaster peeling admits us, but we will walk round before we go in. Ah, see! a mountain streamlet is taking water to a field below, and should run through that grill into the walled enclosure Let us divert it and see the water push the dead leaves down the channel . . . a hole in the wall will let us through too. Ah! apple and almond trees in blossom and pomegranate overgrown and untrimmed, but rich in colour! A canal runs down the centre and down it now comes our water. See a drop with carved ripple-stones to let the water run over and glisten in the sunlight—and another farther on, across it a marble slab with carved rails, on which a king and his lady might sit and see the trickle catch the light and the goldfish jump over. A few yards on the channel runs under a stone open summer-house—old rings on the wall show where the rich curtains were once festooned. An Emperor's rest-house by the way—and Turkish maidens to sing to him. Hark, even now comes music! Is fancy to play us tricks and show us Shah Jehan and Mumtaz, golden umbrellas and kincob? A zither twangs again and something rustles—and blood runs cold for a moment. It is but some village children, but the girls' loose red trousers flash amid the blossom. A boy is twanging on a *saringhi* and a small bird gilded like a beetle's wing comes out from the undergrowth, looks at the unwonted trickle and flies off, as the surprised children, who have not seen us, hasten to the ripple. The garden is alive again, and the sadness and the beauty are living sensations. As we come down to the gate a very old man comes out and salaams to us. He is the caretaker—no, not the gardener, a gardener would cost ten rupees, he only gets four. What does he take care of? Why, this *Badshahi Bagh* to be sure, this Royal Garden. God be praised that kings have gardens, and that *sahibs* come who gave him *bakhshish*—and then he fell a-mumbling. The children come to see what it is all about, and we make them too happy with coppers, and the boy strikes a plaintive note that is the very essence of the grandeur that is gone.

Now, on with our way! lest we too fall a-dreaming and a-mumbling.

The Glory of the Pir Punjal

Having torn ourselves away from the Lost Garden we must march on to the snows that are still far above, over a lower range and its sweet resinous terebinth, down to Thana Mandi and Baramulla and then up and up through the forest by pine and deodar, by silver birch and juniper, till there is nothing but grass recovering from its fall of snow. The tulip and the violet, the sweet-smelling *banafra* are out by wayside, and at the very top a primula is nearly so. On the north side of the slopes the snow is still deep as you come by Hyderabad and Aliabad Serai, and find one room in a ruined rest-house that will keep you warm if you'll chance the fleas. You decide on a shelter tent, and pile up the fir-cones and dead wood for a good camp-fire. There are glaciers above you, the world is below you and the smell of the bruised wild thyme is in the air—you are really in the Himalaya now, no mistake about it, and the keen mountain air makes you dance for the very joy of it. To-morrow you will breast the pass, 10,000 feet above the sea, and traverse the long wind-swept col before the cobbled way will take you past the old fort and down to Shapiyon on the road to the Happy Valley that once was thronged with pageantry and beauty. There are more forests to traverse as you go down; the deodar and the Norwegian fir growing mightily above you. Look down to the valley that lies far below you with the silver streak of its river winding in deep curves—the curves that some say suggested the 'shawl' pattern, though others attribute it to the date, the fruit of the Tree of Life.

You will enjoy the calm and peace of the valley—with its blossom and its narcissus by the channel and its iris by the tombs—after your hard march over the Pir and your sojourning with the ghosts of other days, for pleasure comes by contrasts. So you will come by this older route to the same Srinagar to which the motor will have brought you, and if so be it has left you in the mood for curious things, to see the mosque and tomb of Jesus, who as some men say survived the Cross—and you may also hear the story of the fake of Nicholas Notovitch,[1] a lieutenant of Cossacks—for in the East eyes and nose and ears will always bring you some interest that is unexpected to the West.

[1] Who astounded the world with a life of Christ found in a lama sarai.

CHAPTER XV

SPORT AND THE SCATTER GUN

Sport in India

The attraction of service with 'the grim stepmother', and undoubtedly what takes many young men of our race to India and attracts them to an Indian career, is the facility for inexpensive sport. The Services, speaking generally, especially the Military Services, but many of the others, come from the cadets of the old county families, and the middle class of the countryside. The heads of families may be able to afford sport in England, the lesser branches cannot, and so the trying climates of India, the swift deaths and the vexatious diseases, appear nought as compared with the opportunities that India offers the leisure moments.

What are the sports of India that a European may enjoy? They come under many heads; but leaving out for the moment games, it is rod, gun and rifle and the chase that are meant here. Speaking generally, I would call rod and gun the lesser sport, and rifle the greater, using these comparisons merely to denote time and effort involved.

The lesser sport of the scatter gun is obtainable in some form round almost every station or within easy hail of it. Hence the old military festival of Thursday, introduced in the seventies of the last century, when the good Lord Napier of Magdala was Commander-in-Chief, and the Sabbath, are days when horse and trap, and now motor car, bear the sportsman to his ground. The motor car brings more distant ground within easy reach. It also crowds grounds that were in days gone by only accessible to the early bird and the more energetic. Happily, to this day the better *jheel* and cover may only be accessible to the horseman.

Duck and snipe and quail in due season, the partridges, the bustards, the sandgrouse and such rarer birds as peafowl, jungle-fowl and guinea-fowl, all game birds in their wild state, and on occasion the pheasant, are within reach of one's twelve-bore, with no cost save cartridges, and the pay of beaters, and a gallon or so of petrol.

Of the greater sport, big game, there is a great variety—some accessible to the empty purse, others only to those who come with their pockets full—tiger and all their cousins of the cat tribe that we know as panther, leopard, cheetah, etc., the bears red and black, deer of many kinds, wild sheep and goats of great horns and mighty climbings, the buffaloes, and even the maneless lion. What a vision for Shikari Smith to dream of! Poor Shikari Smith whose ancestral villa in England will be hard put to it to house ibex heads and Bara Singh horns, the bear-skin and the tiger-skin rug. Nevertheless he will shoot big game and small, and his clubs and his messes will be the richer therefrom.

But when we come to horse and hound there is a lesser story. The foremost, far far the foremost, of all the mounted sports of India, is that of the mighty boar, and hard of seat and head must he be who would see the wild boar die. Great is the charm of the simple jungle camp of the hog hunter—the sport that is ridden in open shirt in the hot season.

Of hounds as we know the word in England there are several packs. The endeavour is to copy this sport of kings as we know it in England, and to have even the scarlet coat of the hunt servant; but save the Peshawur Vale in the misty English winter of the frontier, and the galloping pack on the great down of the Blue Mountains at Ootacamund, there is not so very much in it. Hounds in India are expensive things to import and to look after, but the Indian jackal is first cousin to a fox and gives good sport.

In many of the lesser stations, the small civil stations,

eager young Englishmen, and still more, Irishmen, get great fun from long dogs, who chase hare and the little Indian fox, with what is known as a 'bobbery' pack of all the terriers and oddments that can be assembled. Such indeed beat for a pair of 'long dogs', greyhounds or Rampur hounds, to be loosed from leash when hare or fox is flushed. Nor is the otter quite unknown to more enterprising sportsmen who wander far afield.

Duck and Teal

India is the land of many kinds of duck and teal, as well as the between bird, the pochard of several kinds. They too, like the snipe, come down from the lakes of Central Asia and of Chinese Turkestan when the cold weather begins, and fly through to the south and their feeding-grounds of glorious memory. There are many famous marshes and *jheels* all over the countryside, and great folk have great shoots thereon. At Bhurtpur below the city are marshes of fame where the Maharajah entertains the great, and where large bags are made in the flighting hours. At Hokra in Kashmir is another such, while in Sind, at Gurdaspur in the Punjab are famous places of Christmas pilgrimage.

Duck in India, however, are so numerous that there is hardly a piece of water, great and small, that has not a mallard sitting thereon, or a brace of 'teal duck' to be flushed as you look for snipe and quail. When you and they are not hidden from each other by reeds, devil a shot will you get save at morning or evening flighting, as in all the rest of the world; or if by some low cunning you do get a shot, the birds will then fly close to the sun, and far up in the heavens. Duck shooting at dawn has an element of excitement that is absent from the more deliberate attack on the snipe when the sun is high, and everything connected with it is redolent of some mysterious enterprise. If your camp or traveller's rest-house be near the *jheel*, so much the better. In any case you rise in the night or when the mysterious whispering breezes that herald the false dawn are moving. Even your early tea and your egg has its air of mystery, and the pouring of cartridges into bags and pockets is full of hope; and then you start in pairs for the strategic points, your clump of reeds, your grass shelter or what not. Unless you belong to that let-'em-all-come type who carry 6's, and hope to shoot everything with one size of shot from a jack snipe to a mallard, No. 4 will be your supply, with some 8's in your shikari's hands, lest snipe befall later.

It is rather slow and cold work that waiting in the reeds, especially if you be in water, but there is nothing against a pipe, and so you wait. The sky is brightening. You can see the tops of the distant snow-peaks. Soon one or two will encarnadine as the 'enemy', as we call the old puff-bellied sun in the East, shows first sign of rising from his tomb beneath your world. Phew, a bit parky, eh! and you shove your hands deep in your pockets. Plenty of duck about; you can hear them talking and fluttering their wings. They are waking up and taking their heads from their wing-and-wind snuggle. Do I hear a goose? is that the *raj-hans*, the 'Royal Goose', or further south the *mug*, that is now our English slang for a fool? A gaggle of geese coming down would be more than your battery can tackle, unless close range and a lucky shot break a wing; but their wings are deuced strong. Better a small-bore rifle. The writer has started lying flat in a dugout, on a Kashmir lake, paddling onward with the hand, murder in his heart, for a wounded goose that he thought was dead has shoved up a head and is giving tongue. How hard they are to murder, to strangle with the dugout a-wobbling! But it had to be done or the gaff would be blown. There are not likely to be geese here, but you never know your luck. Much more likely to see them later flying in the arrow-head of the ancient cuneiform, setting out on the day's travel.

Flop! close by the duck are moving and a restless pair have joined the others. Too dark yet to see, but a small white shrine is getting visible on the shore a couple of hundred yards away. No doubt the presentation of Mahadeo stands erect in black basalt within; and women will soon come a-marigolding; the duck will be moving before they come, or before someone drives buffalo to water.

The sky is brightening. Whiz! another one flops in and has come close to your patch of reeds. You had better get ready; you've got your shikari handy with a second gun, the American hammerless—you really prefer the old hammer-gun of your subaltern days that belonged to your best chum long dead of typhoid, and that is in your hand.

Pop! pop! Ah! that d——d fellow Maitland is off. Ah! and a whirr comes your way. Bang! got him! Bang again! Missed! Now they're off. *Dusera bandook jaldi!* ('The second gun sharp!') Five of 'em that time; got 'em both? Believe I did. Blast that fellow; he caught me napping! Bang, bang! Two more—I heard them splash as they fell! *Buldoo!* is that *chowkra* after those birds?

Pop, pop! from Maitland over the way—again and again. Another right and left to you—teal, and you missed them both. Someone is at the far end of the *jheel* too, and getting lots of it seemingly—good biz. He'll send them back to you and Maitland. Ah! that was a heavy old mallard, and now a couple of pin-tail; no, several! tell 'em by the sharp tail against the skyline. Ah! got the last one—ought to have had two.

It's getting lighter and the birds are not yet getting away. They fly round and round, fairly low, and dart in for a secluded spot or what passes as such. Maitland sounds busy, so does the man at the far end. Hulloa! steady, a rush of teal all bunched, must brown 'em—four! no, there's another coming down. Rather cad browning! but then teal are like that. The old Brahminees are waking, and coming up in rows—not worth shooting at that old shoveller coming over with his beak like a Thames barge, peering this way and that. Right and left at mallard, another at a laggard jinking like a snipe—and so forth, till the 'Enemy' is up, and all fighting over.

So while the coolies are wading about among the reeds

and the bag is a-counting you've nothing to do but try the coffee in the thermos flask, and stand by with your eye skinned if you are wise for another stray chance, which will certainly come if you're not looking. Maitland has come round with his bag and you lay them out. Not too bad! Six and a half couple of mallard and their mates—it is curious we have only a name for the male—three and a half couple of pin-tail, one Brahminee (Maitland's), one and a half couple of pochard, of which two are red eye and one crested, and three couple of teal; in all fourteen and a half couple, a pretty fair morning, and we bless the distant gents who kept sending the birds back to us. So, as boots are wet, back to camp for a spell of dry and breakfast, and then to the snipe when the sun is higher, and they've put some food into their suspicious bodies.

The Snipe

Among the most fascinating of the small-game shootings of India is that of the snipe. They are often to be had in far greater numbers than in what once was the United Kingdom. While often in the heat of the late hours they are more sleepy than their wide-awake cousins of the Irish bog, you will as often find to your undoing that they are not. Snipe fly from the breeding-grounds on the lakes and marshes of Central Asia, from the lake of Gakuch beyond Gilgit and elsewhere, to the warm grounds of India over the great mountains in vast numbers—in myriads in fact. They are the Full Snipe, *Gallinago caelestis*, and the Jack; while, lying in the corner of marsh and field, breeding in India, is another bird that sometimes at the end of a day adds numbers to a disappointing bag, the 'Painted Snipe'. 'The Painter'—because of his bright feathers—is really not a snipe at all, but is *Rhynchaea capensis*, and does not even migrate; but he is edible enough and reasonable fun, and, after you have wasted a dozen cartridges in shooting a couple or so of elusive, fun-poking Jack Snipe, comes pleasantly enough as the sun is dropping on the horizon.

Here is a typical lesser bag for a day's work for two guns: twelve and a half couple of Full Snipe, two and a half of Jack, and three Painters. Might be worse, and they hang pleasantly on the game-stick, while, if you've not shirked the borders of your *jheel* and the land between, there may also be a mallard, a couple or so of teal, a hare and a quail or two. Red-letter days may even give you a Florican, which is the small bustard, but as a rule Florican mean a special hunt, with the 'Painted' Partridge perhaps in attendance.

What is snipe-shooting like in India? Well, that is a large order. India is a very big country and snipe fly very far. In spite of the tens of thousands of their coming, you rarely if ever see them come. They fly by night, and they apparently only fly by moonlight, which enables them to come down on the more likely patches of water that they see and get good feeding without a shift; freshly flooded land, glitter it never so alluringly, is no use to them. They fly, generally speaking, from north or north-west to south, and pass on over Northern India to the lush feeding of the rice country. The marshes and wet fields of the North are full of them in November; by Christmas time they are far on their way, and only the Jack and the Painter remain. In March they are coming back to their distant breeding-grounds, fat with the spoil of the South, yet not so much easier to shoot, and seemingly none the fewer for the toll of the busy English guns. I say English guns, for few Indians care for snipe-shooting. Not many, save a few sporting landowners, care for firing several rounds after a mouthful. Most Indians shoot, if they shoot at all, for the pot, and have more the ways of the lesser Frenchman in this connection.

In the wet rice-fields they get up very wild, sometimes clearing out of fields in a whisp, as you enter. In wet grass and rice stubble they lie quieter, especially so as the day gets on. If there is a wind, come down wind. They hate it and are behind cover and don't see you from afar. In Madras they have a fancy for 'making a digestion' in the dry fields, and are to be put up thus in the middle of the day. They do the same sometimes in the Deccan. Perhaps digesting the tough worms of the South is a serious matter to be done in warmth and ease.

The woodcock is so rare a bird in India, that he must crowd in with the snipe. You get him in the forest clearings in the Himalaya at 6000 or 7000 feet. You sometimes get him in Baluchistan and also in the Blue Mountains of the South, and also in the higher parts of the frontier hills. In any case a woodcock day is to be recorded in red letters.

Partridge

Some of the partridges of India are very good fun; and out of the way the best to shoot and the finest birds are the Black Partridge of the grass by the northern river-beds. Their almost virgin soil was the Tigris when the Army first went there, getting up under your feet as your steamer touched the bank. On the Indus, in the Derajat, where the wide beds of grass are interspersed with cultivation you may get them to perfection, save only that the markets of Karachi have set the villagers a-poaching. By poaching one means trapping and killing with the throwing-stick, at which some boys are clever, for there are no shooting rights and no lord of the manor. You may shoot over anyone's land if you shoot as a gentleman should, with consideration for the crops and your owner. Some day the landowner and the tenant may make a fuss, and now and again some non-co-operator will try and spoil sport. The Indian himself is taking to shooting, however, in his own way, and skims off the cream in a none too sportsmanlike manner. The plump Black Partridge naturally is worth his while. Older hands of the landowning type will prefer to hawk, a heartless sport if on foot after little quail; a better sport with partridge, but best with the bustard, and that may take you a-galloping hard.

The other partridge in their commonplace names are the Grey Partridge, good enough shooting in the yellow mustard fields and the neighbouring grass, somewhat doubtful eating if the fields are near to villages, for they are not particular feeders. A 'call bird' in a cage that your shikari may have put out will collect several in its vicinity. In the writer's mind, grey partridge, yellow mustard fields, tall-growing millet and Indian corn, a group of dark mango trees in the distance, a wallow of water buffaloes, stand for the heart and life of ordinary India. Painted Partridge are good shooting in the Deccan and Central India, and elsewhere for ought I know, better in the feather than the homely 'grey', clean feeders, and sharp in flight. Where they gather too will be the Florican, the small bustard, like to the *Khoorhaan*, the 'scolding hen' of the South African veldt. There we call shooting them, the red-wing partridge, and the guinea of the riverside, 'going hunting'. Round this Empire of ours English like Arabic has many meanings, some older and truer than the degenerate use at Home.

In the foot-hills and in Burma is a pleasant little game-bird, the Bamboo Partridge, which is not to be despised, though not easy to flush, and in the same terrain you will get that wonderful jungle cock of brilliant plumage, which is none other than our domestic fowl before man caught and tamed him, and shut his mate in coops, when all the world was young.

Whether it be in the brilliant mustard field, in the grass of the northern river, or whether in the lush of the foot-hills, the clear call of the partridge to his mate is exhilarating, and I like him best when I'm riding, and can neglect the Englishman's duty to shoot something.

Because the 'Black' is the king of them all, we will go Black Partridge shooting on the Indus in the winter, in the country of the 'people who live in tents', the Derajat. If we are to have a good day, we must get far afield, and so we will travel up-stream by the post-boat in the moonlight. We will drive three or four miles from cantonment, with a good bedding roll, a lunch basket and a bearer with kettles and his paraphernalia, for there is no harm in early tea and a breakfast to follow.

The post-boat is a small single-masted vessel, that will

be towed up-stream all night by its crew, while we shooters will be sleeping peacefully in the moonlight, with the ripple and the mutter of the Indus water in our ears. There is no particular virtue in being up with the lark, so we lie snugly in our blankets, and watch the rim of the frontier hills grow lighter, and the rising sun catch on the peak of Shuidar away in Waziristan, and on the lean hills of the Ruttah Koh, where stand the great ruins of the Kafir Kots, the 'castles of the unbelievers'. Coming down-stream under sail are two or three Indus boats, with the crew, hereditary sailors who are so like the boatmen of the Tigris, and who are chanting some shanties in *jatki*, the language of the great river. Massive great boats are they, with a carved stem ten foot in the sheer, and the lady of the boat a-pounding rice on top, and now and again giving shrill tongue.

As they slip past us an island comes abreast, and it is here that we are to land, and beat the high grass alongside the fields of young emerald wheat. A flight of duck swishes past, and up-stream come long streams of the early paddy-birds making for their feeding-ground. The world is awake, and the morning breeze is whispering for the sun to warm it. The good bearers have been busy with the kettle aforesaid, and now comes hot tea and toast, before we need pull on the shooting-boot and wrap the leg puttee. The guns are coming out of the cases, and the cartridge-boxes are being tipped into the bags, while one of the crew has hustled off to his aunt's mud house hard by, to get his nephews and two or three more lads he wots off, to come and beat for coin of the realm.

There are coins of other realms about, and some old man will probably untie a knot in the tail of his shirt and offer you two or three Graeco-Bactrian coins, coins this time of the kingdom on the Indus, when Sacae and Getae and the like had driven the Greek on the Oxus down to India. This may happen anywhere along a thousand miles of border.

By the time we are dressed and guns ready, it is breakfast-time, and getting on for 8 A.M., and the sun well established.

The dawn breeze has dropped, and we stretch and plume ourselves on the mud bank, and then, wonder of wonders, comes Indus fish, fresh fried, the fine *rohu*, with bacon and eggs to follow, which the expert has cooked over an earthen pot of charcoal. By now the coolie lads are perched like a row of crows on the edge of the bank, and all is ready for the start.

The first thing to remember with Black Partridge is that they always take you by surprise, and love to frighten you to death by whirring up under your very nose. When you aim, remember what the old man at the Army and Navy Stores shooting-ground said, 'Blot out your burrd, sir! Blot out your burrd!' Don't fire if you can see him over the barrels!—a sterling rule. Another stirring thing about it is that you don't wait or walk long for the fun; the partridges are in the long grass, before they make for their feeding-ground in the wheat, and, even before the line of beaters is formed, there is an explosion as of a bomb under your feet; you fire wildly and one little speckled feather comes back on the breeze to you in derision, as if to say 'sold again'. However, you've learnt by your lesson, and both hands grab your gun; whirr! there they are on the right, and you shoot back, and get the cock, dead too as a bird should be. You come on a little clearing among the tussocks, and two brace get up. You get a right and a left, a cock and a hen; glorious fun, and a hare starts out hurriedly, to get a shot from you that only knocks up the dust behind her—but you hear the next gun fire twice. She has probably dodged him. And so on. Two more birds rise quietly and make to get off. The cock comes down in a cloud of the speckled feathers aforesaid, no derision this time, and then two more, and a singleton. The bag is mounting up, and the boys are whirling their sticks and making enough noise to put up all the partridges in kingdom-come, but they are lying close and may be walked over.

The shikari comes along and says that there is a break in the grass ahead, and that it will be well if the guns will push on ahead of the beaters, the birds are running, but will get up with a rush to fly over the open to the next cover. You do so. It is exciting hearing the beaters come up; whack, swish and *crash! garrh! smack!* Now the fun begins. Three get up in front of you; half a dozen in front of the other guns; two rocket clear of the grass and break back, you get one, and another right and left in front. Phew! there *are* a lot of birds, more than you can cope with, getting up in bunches before the beaters' din, and both guns are busy. The beaters come through to the open, and another hare jinks across the fallow of last year's stubble. Two from you. Missed her! d——n! but the next gun has her. A lad rushes out in excitement to cut her throat and make her lawful meat, and is cursed back for his pains: a cock partridge pokes his nose out behind a tuft of grass on the edge of the clearing—late for the fair—he does not want to run the gauntlet; a beater pokes him, and up with a flare again. His goose is cooked, for you've seen him on the ground and are waiting. Give him plenty of law, and shoot him cleanly at thirty paces! Nicely, sirr! as your gillie would say, and that glorious dark plumage comes down plump. Dead to make an English holiday! dead at once, happily. But why do we want to kill them? One loves the excitement and sport, and hates oneself at times, but you may reassure yourself with the fact that if you don't shoot them villagers net them and wring their necks. A No. 6 in the heart or brain is a better way than a wrung neck, my glorious cock bird! whose mate will pipe sadly till another takes your place.

That little beat took forty minutes, and there are nine and a half brace—of which more than half are cock birds —and two hares—pretty good. One hare you give to the beaters, who pretend it is not dead so that they may cut its throat and save the Moslem law; nice Moslems won't eat hare for she menstruates like human folk, but all is fish to the net of a hungry village lad. If they beat well, they shall have another.

There will be three or four more such beats before the

hour of twelve, and a spot of lunch, with the village children in the offing, comes along. We won't follow the guns further, but I hope you feel that Black Partridge on the Indus are very good fun—aye, and a wistful thing to look back on as the years roll by, and something reminds you of the dry red grass that was so crisp under your feet.

Chikor and Pheasant in the Himalaya

There are two birds that you shoot with more than usual pride in India because they have got to be worked for, and worked for jolly hard. They are the Chikor, which is one of the partridges, *Caccabis chikor*, and the Himalayan Pheasant, of many kinds, *Manal*, *Kaklas*, *Kalij*, and the like. The pheasant is an Eastern bird, which men say was first brought to England by luxurious Rome. He lives in many Eastern hills, and in India where we pray for the Viceroy, you find him in the great clefts and gullies of the Himalaya, and he wants beating well, for he hates coming out, and you may shoot him clean over a dark deep chine, so that he whirls and falls hundreds of feet below. That however is the beaters' funeral. I know no more glorious sight than the plumage of a cock pheasant as he flies across to the shadow of the depths below from the cover of the deodar whence the beaters have driven him. They lie close, the pheasants, and if you have a tame monkey that likes beating, as a friend of mine once had, and will pull the tail feathers of birds that won't budge, why, all the more fun!

The Chikor is another matter. You find him on the bare slopes in the Himalaya, on the barer hills of the frontier, and at the foot-hills round the lakes in glorious Kashmir. We call him the Chikor because that is the note he makes, and if you are camping near you will hear him very talkative in the early morning. *Chikor! chikor! chikor!* and the sound will get you out of your blankets quickly enough. They are a light brown bird with glorious marking on wing and neck and head. They are fine fighters, and in every hill bazaar a young blood will have his champion in a cage, stuffed on the best grain. Not too glorious a career, my Chikor! but you look well on it!

On the bare frontier it is bitter hard climbing, and your boots will suffer, and in Kashmir the thorn bushes get their own back, but all the better the sport when you get it. *Chikor! chikor! chikor!* hark to the little devils laughing at you on the hillside, and you vow that your legs and your twelve-bore shall be their masters. The young Pathan is a good beater, and you and he will be happy together.

There is another little bird that keeps you busy on the frontier hills, among the Chikor, and that is the *Sisi*, a beggar to run, and to get a shot at him as he flies a gully you must be active too.

While we are on the frontier there is some fun to be had with the Blue Rocks. You must know that water in Baluchistan and other frontier tracts is brought to the surface by an underground channel from adjacent hill springs. The channel is made by sinking a line of wells, and then joining them by a tunnel, a pretty piece of rough yet accurate engineering. Down the wells the Blue Rocks love to hide and drink. Place two or three guns at every other well, and let a beater throw stones. Up will come the birds a-rocketing, and no mean shot either. Also remember that if one pigeon is wounded the others are bound to circle to look at him, in the vain hope perhaps of aiding him. So stand by, as a Pathan sniper waits for the stretcher-bearers; you will get another shot.

CHAPTER XVI

RACING AND GAMES OF INDIA

Polo

Polo is *par excellence* the game of India in that it is from that country that this fascinating and exciting amusement of rich young men came into the world. From the hill principalities of the Northern Himalaya, from Chitral and the statelets that claim Alexandrine descent, was learnt by British officers the fierce fast game of *chaugan-bazi*, played on oblong grounds cut out of the hillside, on mountain ponies that scuttled up and down the *maidan* at top speed amid the shouts and cheers of the spectators.

The keeping of good and fast ponies is a rich man's business, but because, at any rate in the early days in India, ponies, ground, groom and fodder cost far less than in Europe, the athletic young officers of the Army and the Civil Services found the westernized version of *chaugan-bazi* extremely to their liking. Authority saw that it developed and stimulated the qualities desirable in officers, and looked with some approval on it, as a competition to the universal sport of horse-racing with its occasional disastrous effects on purses and characters.

So popular became polo in India, that three times a week in almost every station, from 4 to 6 P.M., it was played, everyone bringing such ponies as he could train and muster. Everyone contributed as now, so many *chukurs*, or quarter-of-an-hour rounds to the game, and the sides were organized by the administration accordingly.

The 'station game' on these lines was and is the rule of life, especially of Army life. But as the years went by and tournaments and first-class players brought the more scientific and higher grade of play into vogue, the class of pony and his cost increased. The game naturally fell into the hands of those who could compete with the growing expense. In the last forty years and more polo has become highly specialized. British cavalry regiments, where officers of means concentrated, usually led the way, followed close by the artillery, and now and again some infantry regiments such as the famous Durham Light Infantry teams of De Lisle's training, making the game almost a life's aim, climbed to the front rank. The intrepid young horsemen of the Indian cavalry trained ponies and paid their expenses by sales to the wealthy. The Princes of India with their unlimited purses took up the game, and the wealthy young men of Europe and America followed suit. Now is polo one of the premier games and glories of the sporting world. The height of the animals used and their speed has increased out of limit, and in horse-flesh it is as developed and as complicated as first-class racing.

It remains the most beautiful and most exciting of the games of the world, and it may be said that the young officers of the Army in India have made it so, from the first excitement of *chaugan-bazi*. The tournaments now stir the whole sporting world, and in India tournaments of all kinds flourish exceedingly. Wherever a horse is loved for itself, there are spectators watching the whirlwind game. The Indian Princes and nobles, and the native officers of Indian cavalry regiments mounted by the regiments, are some of the great players, and here do British and India meet most eagerly in a sport that both understand.

But when all is said and done, perhaps the greatest happiness of the greatest number arrived when almost every pony could be worked into the simpler 'station game', and polo was less the sport of kings.

Cricket

Wherever the British young man of any sort of education and culture has gone in the last century or century and a half, with him has gone cricket. Sometimes on matchless turf, usually on burnt unruly pitches, sometimes on levelled and rolled mud or on coir matting, there in the four quarters of the globe has cricket been played. It is, even in village cricket, a 'gentleman's game'. In the Army it has always been the initiative of the officers which has not only started but kept the cricket ball a-rolling. When in the early nineties of the last century Lord Harris came as Governor to Bombay, cricket in India received a great fillip and its higher side became more seriously studied. Cricket was added to the qualifications which it seemed good to the ambitious young man to acquire, and it was fairly evident to its audience that in the Governor of Bombay's band proficiency on the cricket-pitch and in the Government House team, was more important than that on clarionet and cornet!

But long before Lord Harris had come as great proconsul, cricket had come to stay in the schools and colleges in Bengal and Bombay; curiously enough the entirely unvirile Indian intelligentsia took to the game with zeal, both boys and young men. The old English feeling that all cricketers must have unblemished souls and hearts did not hold good in its entirety, for zeal and considerable proficiency in the game of the Saxons did not produce the results expected. Hardiness and what in India is known as *jawanmardi*, manliness, are not of necessity produced thereby, and timorous natures would stand up to a cricket ball and nothing else, which was and is a paradox. The Parsee community also took to cricket and after many years of endeavour have made a very good fist of it, and hold their own in high-class cricket. Among the lads of the more virile races we have seen some very fine performers indeed, notably the England-famous, nay the world-famous 'Ranji', the Rajput Prince, and his nephew, while even Bengal has produced good cricketers and, what is more mysterious, good Association football players.

At the present moment, therefore, cricket, to which must

now be added tennis, stand out as two Western games in which India is taking a more and more prominent part. Some of the cricket fixtures are now notable, and with the result that of late years the grounds receive far more attention. The Indian of many races seems to have a natural aptitude for ball games, and everyone who has played racquets with the 'marker' will remember what a good game he can put up, and how indefatigable he was and is, as indeed is the lawn-tennis marker.

Tennis

Lawn tennis has long been the game that India favours most by reason of its fine seasons. Hot or cold, tennis can be played, and every club in India, and every station, has at least one, and most several courts and keep them admirably. Grass is often not obtainable and requires much irrigation, but the hard courts of rubble, or what in India is known as '*put*', mud and chopped straw, rewashed with a mud plaster every day, are admirable in their way. Screens and ball boys are always good. Time was when the polo players and riding public sniffed at the 'pat-ballers', but that is a generation and more ago. For forty years tennis has come more and more by its own. Indian tennis tournaments are famous, and the Indian himself is now furnishing players with world-wide reputations. The tennis ground is indeed another field where British and Indian meet very happily and on an equality of performance that adds much to the social amenities and admixture.

In the hill stations there are few other games to play, and tennis is very much the order of the day, while private tennis-courts are much sought after. The courts have usually to be cut out from the hillside and cost a good deal to make. The playing surface is made of what is known in the North as *bădjări*, a very fine sifted shale.

Racquets, alas! for many generations a famous game in India, is dying. Time was when every station in India had its courts, usually covered, and in the days when officers had more leisure they would play racquets for hours together, to the accompaniment, in the old days, of unlimited Bass. The trouble with some of the best-built courts in India was that they were not always of the right size, and of later years they have been costly to keep in repair, while racquets and balls alone are expensive items in these hard times. The coming of the simpler and cheaper squash has done the greater game in, and many courts have been pulled down and squash-courts built in their stead. Old hands will mourn therefor.

India has acquired some skill in the manufacture of tennis gear and racquets, which from mere pat-balling implements have now acquired considerable fame, and are really useful. The Punjab city of Sialkot has especially succeeded in capturing and developing this business, manufacturing indeed all sorts of sports gear.

Badminton in India has always been the lighter form of exercise, popular with women, and now almost a game of high skill and exercise. It is usually played by artificial light in covered courts before dinner, as well as on grass in the open. The game inside can be a severe one.

Golf

When we come to survey the golf of India, we come to a paradox. No game is more desirable or suitable to the conditions of India. It induces the European to do what is so good for him and what he dislikes, viz. walk. It subscribes to the harmless *promenade à deux* which is part of Indian life. It provides an exercise that is not too violent, when the weather is hot, and it has the merit of so few modern games of being inexpensive. You get to the ground without rail or taxi. Your house as often as not abuts the links. But alas, when all is said and done, the whole of Indian climate and terrain are against the game. Rolling field and down on which to plan your links exist not—turf is conspicuous by its absence. Even where, by considerable expenditure of water, money and patience, you can keep a couple of tennis-courts in grass and your cricket-pitch, you have done the most you can do. To keep the golf greens in turf on almost all the links is beyond the powers of man. Therefore are your greens 'browns', plastered each day for you with a fine mud like the Hindu housewife's dining-floor. The accessible ground, for which it is true there is usually nothing to pay, is often flat as a pancake and every feature must be artificial with the flood drainage channels assisting. Yet because we are what we are, and because the game even under such disadvantages is something to do and give exercise, so does every station where Europeans live have its little mud-greened stony links. At places like Peshawur it is true, a water-level close to the surface does give you a little fitful grass on the fairway, but links in the real meaning of the name exist but at a very few places. Nasik on the uplands of the Deccan has a season in the rains when all is green, and golf with a big 'G' has a real vogue, where enthusiasts find it worth while to go. The beautiful upland glens and forest of Gulmarg in Kashmir, 9000 feet above the sea, have a links free from snow for a very short season, where the beauty of the Swiss surroundings and the greenness of the real turf, and the profound hazards of the burns, are a thing of their own. Ootacamund, where they rejoice in three monsoons, 6000 feet up in the Blue Mountains, has a real highland links with Scotch mist complete and there real golf is played under delightful auspices. In the great capitals, where money is available from full membership, watered turf greens and of course a pancake course with made bunkers rather of the Ranelagh type are to be had, or further afield perhaps a real course. The enterprising sports factories of the North try to turn out clubs, but not so successfully as they do tennis-racquets. The Indian who has been in Europe perhaps takes to golf, but, speaking generally, it is not yet his game. He prefers to go, as an Indian gentleman said to me the other day, 'for dog-walk', when tennis is getting past him.

Football and Hockey

Association football is largely played by the Army, British and Indian, and famous tournaments are held, notably the Durand Tournament at Simla. But it is now the game of the Indian schools and universities, who play a very good game indeed. The experimental battalion of Bengalis, largely students, which came to Mesopotamia in the Great War and was perfectly useless as a military unit,[1] for all the stimulant and kindly training it received (a uselessness relieved by an exceptionally fine and unusual Bengali senior Indian officer), was very good at Association and could beat the Scottish regiments in the force. This indeed is another of the Indian anomalies like the student-cricketer, that people who had neither military aptitude, instinct nor hearts, should make so good a shape at so essentially a manly game as Association football. Of Rugby football there is not so much to be said. It has generally been considered the game of men who have learnt to keep their tempers, and it has only recently on occasion become the game of the Army. In Madras and Calcutta, young business men who have played Rugby at college do play with praiseworthy zeal in the great capitals in the rainy season, when alone can a fall without broken bones be possible. It is a game which cannot by the nature of things, therefore, be as much to the fore in the Shiny East as its lovers would wish.

Hockey, the younger sister of football, however, is above all things the cheaper game for the country; soldiers, European and Indian schools and colleges play it with pleasure, profit and success. Hockey tournaments, both civil and military, are legion. The Indian soldier takes eagerly to this inexpensive game, which perhaps gives the maximum of exercise and physical training in the time, and whose time of play can be adapted to the rigours of the hot season.

[1] It was under the writer's command.

Winter Sports

With several thousand miles of snowy mountains and unfailing snowfall on the India borders and in places in which Europeans still winter, it would appear that there might be ample room for winter sports. In the actuality, however, the matter is a disappointment. Nevertheless the instinct is not wanting. In the winter of 1839, at Kabul, when the British Army was in friendly camp and quarters as the restorers of a popular dynasty before all went sour, the winter activities of the British excited much comment. The Afghan is a keen slider on his frozen lakes, but skating was new to him. When the regimental artificers made up skates and the inhabitants of Kabul saw the British officers career off thereon, they said '*Wah! wah!* now we know that you speak truth when you say you are a Northern people and familiar with ice and snow'.

The chief trouble in the matter of ski-ing is that the Indian sun is very powerful even at 15,000 feet if there be no cloud, and the surface is very soft. Further, in so many of the accessible hills, even if there be fog and the surface hard, yet are slopes too abrupt and dangerous. The Gurkha regiments winter on the edge of the snows, and from such places as Dharamsala something is possible on the mountains above. But of late years the enterprising, aided by the motor's coming, have set distance at naught, and made short leave full of possibilities, and ski-ing at Gulmarg in Kashmir, on the slopes around the golf-links, has come into actual being as a sport and custom. Here and there others have been successful also. Gulmarg at 9000 feet and easily accessible is of course a great find, while huts can be opened under ideal Alpine conditions, and toboggan runs are not unknown. In Simla four tennis-courts on the northern side of a steep slope give skating like to an ice-rink in London Town. The courts are reflooded between morning and evening excitements, and skating by electric light on new ice is possible. At Parachenar far up on the Afghan marches, and sometimes at Quetta skating too is possible. The motor and the desire to go further afield will no doubt open up a little more, but on a large scale the disabilities I have mentioned will prevent anything extended. Besides, the Army at any rate, is pretty busy in these winter months and a week at Christmas is about all there is to it. But Christmas, unless you 'give us back our eleven days', is early for accessible snowfall in most years.

Boating and Sailing

India is a country of sea-coast and harbours, and, as might be expected, there are many places where sailing is in vogue. Bombay with its yacht club is the home of fine sailing both in the spacious harbour and out into the ocean and down the coast, and those who live in Bombay who wish to sail will find themselves among a particularly charming community, and can sail anything from tom-tits upwards. Karachi does some sailing too, and various other places, where the community is sufficiently numerous to be able to support it. Unfortunately many of the lagoons and other possible sailing waters of the South have too sparse a European population. To Indians sailing as an amusement is almost unknown, as in fact as yet are many other things that pass the time harmlessly. But many thousands sail the sea.

Away up in the Himalaya is a hill station, Naini Tal, with a famous landslide-formed lake, and there boating and sailing is fast and furious, in its small inland way, and very good fun it is with a yacht club complete. It is one of those places where you are safest sailing in your bathing-dress. The Woolar Lake in Kashmir should be a place for keen sailors, and now and again the enthusiast gets down to it there. It is larger than most Indian lakes and not too gusty. Close to Poona there is a lake, Karakwasla, where sailing has long taken place, but it is a highland loch, and those who won't remember the fact and the dire consequences of not keeping your eye skinned and your centre-board down have suffered sad fatalities.

Boating in India has always been a difficulty. The big rivers are too fiercely raging when snow is melting and rains falling, or in winter the long stretches of sand, always new each year, make boats and boathouses a difficulty. They boat a little on the Adiyar in Madras, they row on Naini Tal, but Poona is probably the only place that has a suitable sort of water. There there are four miles of really good and beautiful rowing river, the result of a dam. The Indrayani not far off, since it has been dammed, might produce the same, but there are no sailors near its banks. This Poona river, the Mulla-mutha, Poona Boat Club, and the Rosherville Gardens where once the dead and gone Crawford held revel and dispensed a generous hospitality, make a rowing life there a real one. Here and there a few of the Princes have lakes and boats thereon, but a motor boat is more the Princes' idea of how a river or lake should be travelled on. In Kashmir, while there is little boating on the river, there is a very full ornate and charming houseboat life, and plenty of boats are to be hired for the summer. Sign that contract, O visitor, to stay till November, only sniff the hot weather, and defeat the mosquito by summering in Kashmir, and roam the happy valley a while in a small houseboat. The big ones are hard to move, though perhaps outboard engines make such doings easier.

Horse-Racing

Horse-racing, it has been said, is neither a sport nor a game, but an industry. From time immemorial the Englishman introduced this national sport into India, which there also has become an industry, and there is no innovation from the West that has been more eagerly adopted by the East. Rich merchants and princes own first-class horses, and follow their bent to England, where the Agha Khan is a household word. Tens of thousands flock to the racecourses. Betting in all its forms is hugely popular, whether by bookmaker or totalizator, by street or by course betting. Many Indians have made useful jockeys, and even as trainers some measure of reliance and success has been obtained.

The courses at Bombay, Madras and Calcutta are as well equipped and as well cared for as any in the Empire. At Poona, at Lahore and at Lucknow and a few other of the up-country centres the courses are famous, while almost every station has a course of sorts and many of the ruling chiefs also.

Before the advent of polo, almost every officer and civil servant knew something of racing and what was far more important, how to get a horse fit. 'Sky races', so arranged that the winner should not incur penalties by his victory, were very frequent occurrences. The number of officers who owned and trained the lesser racehorses and who rode their own horses between the flags and sported their own colours was considerable. But just as tournaments and professionalism have spoiled some of the amenities of games even if gaining advantages that more than compensate, so have wealth and competition almost driven the gentleman owner and gentleman jockey from the course. Better far is the horse-racing in speed and performance, but the owners are now largely the wealthy Indian owners and the jockeys are professionals. Gone are those universal 'sky races', gymkhana races are almost entirely given up to fancy competitions, and the lesser horse-racing has gone down before the greater, and also, as has been said, perhaps polo has equally contributed to the death of regimental racing. There will be many an old hand who will regret the cheery lotteries at the clubs before the local races and all the other concomitants of non-professional and inter-regimental racing.

But apart from that, the modern racing is very good, very well worth seeing and a very great feature, and for all colours, creeds and purses. On many of the first-class courses now no bookmakers are allowed and the totalizators are organized with an efficiency and a promptness that cannot be beaten in Europe. The horses racing are now largely Australian and English, though there is still happily a special class of events and even special meetings for Arab racing, even though the Arab for other purposes has largely disappeared from the land. There are some few classes for country-breds, but the country-bred as a racehorse has yet to come. It was only in the earlier days of universal racing on a humble scale that he was a common object of the course, and despite the good Arab and English blood now in the indigenous horse, it is only as an Army remount that he has a great place in the land.

Motoring and Aviation

Motoring and aviation are such special matters with such a literature of their own, that I hardly need allude to them here. But aviation, it should be said, is peculiarly suited for the climate in India. The mountain flying is another and a special story and those who do it are worthy of our very great admiration. Motoring as a real amusement and sport is hampered by the roads. To make good roads is to waste the Indian taxpayer's money. He does not want good roads, and except a very few main routes they should not be made. It is great fun to drive from Bombay to Peshawur by the old marching road, but there is no reason for it to be made luxurious, to bridge the rivers for you, or even to spend money on better ferries. But to travel from Bombay up-country by road has a charm and an interest that is all its own, especially if you are aware of and care for the history of the English and if wayside battle cemeteries and the like intrigue you. The ways to the summer hill stations were always good driving roads, and these now carry many cars and are kept up accordingly.

The Indian Government has been as short-sighted as the Home Government, if not so radically criminal, in the matter of road and rail competition in Britain. Here by allowing the uncontrolled competition of motor with rail not only has the capital of all who made railways possible for the State been largely destroyed, but the vast source of revenue that its dividends afford has been lost. On the Simla road the capital involved on the costly sixty miles has been depreciated by allowing an unrestricted and cheaper car industry to compete. In fact we have now the spectacle of the capitalists and even the small-holders eating each other up! The Indian makes a good chauffeur within certain limits, and the Indian intelligentsia seem like to make good in the air. There is of course no car manufactory in the East, nor indeed outside the Army shops, anything to write Home about in the repair industry. In fact it is in much the same state as that of the gentleman who repairs your watch, save that there are no jewels in car bearings to rob. The tin-lizzie buses that take folk packed like sardines from rail to village on the fair weather mud road get no repairs and little oil. When done with they merely lie down like the camel by the wayside to die.

CHAPTER XVII

HOG-HUNTING AND BIG GAME

Hog-hunting

Hog-hunting, more colloquially pig-sticking, is easily the premier sport of India, being something fresher, newer, more daring and more exciting than anything else, save perhaps 'walking up' a wounded tiger on foot. In the early days of the Company the officers of regiments on the march are constantly depicted as chasing the wild boar. There are many charming old coloured prints, the legend in both French and English depicting the sport, and always a marching scarlet-clad column in the distance.

Hog-hunting, the chasing and killing of the wild boar, is perhaps the greatest test of courage of horse and rider, of skill and activity. Among its many merits it takes the officer away from dusty polo and hockey ground and puts him out in the countryside among the people. His knowledge of the real folk of India who matter, of ground generally, and of the rougher camp life are all improved thereby.

The best time for pig-sticking is in the early hot weather when all who camp have come to rough it in some sense. India is covered with wild tracts of shrub and jungle, and the wide beds of river covered with high grass, interspersed with open spaces are the best of riding-grounds. The wild pig is the peasants' great enemy. He is an astounding destructive agent among root crops, his long tushes being given him for digging rather than for battle. Shooting wild pig is the protective action of the farmer, and the sport of the baron and rajah, who love to have them beaten across shooting glades and valleys, but to shoot a pig in a rideable country is as big a crime as shooting a fox in England.

The wild boar, for his mate is immune to the hog-hunter, is the most sporting of animals, fast, clever and immensely game. So long as he can get away, get away he will, but once pricked with a spear, and cornered, it is no slaughter of the fleeing beast. He then turns at bay with his fierce tusks set, and dares you to kill him, ready to charge fiercely at horse and rider on every opportunity. His glorious fighting courage is the admiration of his pursuers, and the sport, cruel as blood sports must be, is sung with far deeper admiration than anyone can have for even the staunchest dog fox. 'The boar, the boar, the mighty boar', is roared round many a camp-fire, to the auld Scots air of 'My love is like the red, red rose', and a very stirring stimulative thing it is, which can bring many a man's memory to a gulp in the throat.

The horse, the good pig-sticker, must be fast, extremely handy and staunch to the core. There is many a useful horse that will not face the boar when he stops at bay for his death stand, defiantly glaring and waiting for whoever will ride in at him. There he stands! to charge in his turn, ripping tendons and bellies of horses, goring at times the rider he has brought down.

Hog-hunting has the merit that it is the sport of the simplest pair of energetic subalterns who can boast a rag of courage, to that of a numerous well-organized tent club. There was a time when, except in the most famous places, the sport was dying. Cultivation was encroaching on their habitats, the farmers were shooting freely, it required more energy to get pig and farther to go, and polo, with its demand for better and high-priced horses, was calling another way. Then the tide turned; wherever there was a mounted unit, the fashion came back. Cavalry and artillery vied with each other to revive the tent club. District officers and village headmen were approached and enlisted, and since the young Indian civilian is almost always a sportsman, and the Indian country gentleman too, hog-hunting has come by its own once more. The Royal Artillery, often the only mounted unit, have taken a leading part, and if there is a pig to be found in a rideable country it is the subaltern of artillery who will discover it. The Meerut Tent Club is the most famous in the land from time immemorial. There the *kadirs*, viz. the river-beds, are adjacent, and there the sport has never flagged. The 'Kadir Cup', run in the end of March, is one of the world's famous sporting events, and attracts sportsmen from far and wide. It takes place some miles away from the well-known cantonment, where the presence of cavalry and artillery units ensures a large local support as well as that of competitors from the rest of India. Here the riding is for the famous cup, and the winner is he who wins the greatest number of heats. The riding is as in all other pig-sticking, and is run by heats. Pig are usually 'ridden' by pairs, the long line of riders and beaters advancing through the jungle till a boar breaks. There is no mistaking a boar. The rider who first wounds, and in the case of a competition does so to the umpire's satisfaction, has 'the spear', viz. wins the heat, but then the boar must be killed . . . the fierce dogged despairing creature, who as explained, if sharply speared, will turn at once on his pursuer.

The riding is rough, the horse alone can save you. Rocks, pebbles, buffalo wallows are all waiting and all the while the boar is galloping all he knows . . . those short powerful legs having an astonishing turn of speed. If you know your business, you ride a bit wide on his flank, lest he jink across your horse's path and bring him down, and you will have your spear low and ready for him to jink on to, rather than be brought to the ground by his sudden turn.

At the end of the day when the boar are laid out and measured, before your beaters feast on them, you will realize how hard you and your friends have ridden to take that gallant life. You may console yourself, if you think of such matters, that you have but destroyed the peasant's enemy and that if you don't do it the latter will, even as the farmer must shoot foxes. The great fierce head of the boar is the trophy; a more handy token is these curly tushes which await you when you face him.

To the Moslem, the slaying of boars is a peculiar satisfaction, '*Hamara dushman hai!*' ('He is my enemy!'), but only the low-caste Hindu will feast on him. A clean feeder is the wild boar and his mate, but the flesh is too coarse for European taste.

The pig-sticking camp is a cheery place, whether of the small local tent club, or such famous places as Meerut and Muttra, and the great grouped camps of the Kadir, born of summer clothing and simple ways. The start at the Kadir will give you lines of elephants carrying spectators and waiting competitors; the small meets, just a camp under a mango grove, and a few villagers as beaters with an old know-all shikari in charge. The latter meet has quite a different charm from the excitement and splendour of the long lines of elephants and competitors seen through the jungle of the Kadir country.

The row of spears racked upright in the corner of a hog-hunter's bungalow, or better still hanging with a weight on them, interspersed with trophies and spur rack, are stirring mementoes of the field and its occasions. The Bombay and Bengal hog-hunters used to pride themselves on different kinds of weapons. The latter used a long spear but slightly weighted, grasping their weapons for an underhand stroke as a man rides at a tent-peg, as often as not letting the weight of the boar do the work. The Bombay hunter prided himself on a short spear balanced by a heavy round counter-weight, and held near the weight, the weapon as often as not used for an overhand jabbing blow. In fact this spear is often known as the 'jabbing spear'. Controversy as to the merits of respective weapons would often run acute.

The Big Game of India

To write graphically of big-game shooting in India one must have taken part in it more than a little, and my own humble experiences do not entitle me to claim that. But among my friends have been many that were great shikaris, and my own experiences do allow me to interpret theirs with sufficient colour for that cinema of Indian life which this book aims to produce.

Great game of India stands to my mind in two great divisions, the Mountain Game and the Jungle Game, the denizens of the swamps and forests and those of the Himalayas, for it is with small exceptions in the Himalayas that the mountain game dwell. I would put among the second tiger and leopard, bison and buffalo, the great *sambhur*, the *cheeta* and the black bear, and so far as they exist the lion and the rhino. Among the denizens of the mountains come the sheep and goats, the *markhor* and the ibex, the *Ovis ammon*, *Hodgsonii*, and the *Ovis poli*, and to them may be added the jolly old red bear and the snow-leopard, while the *barasingh*, a twelve-pointer of the higher Kashmir forest, is one of the biggest heads in the world.

Practically all big mountain game must be shot by licence, a measure introduced for preservation, and in most parts of the tiger country the area is divided into blocks, and a block must be obtained from the forest officer of the district, who hands out licences to shoot in any unallotted block at his disposal. I do not propose to enter into detail as to the shooting *bandobust*, as the visitor who is intent on sport will have studied the books on the subject; at any rate, have consulted 'the man from Cook's'. But while we are about it I think I might introduce the English reader to the all-important and useful word '*bandobust*', much in use with regard to shikar as well as to many other matters. It is Persian, *band o bast*, 'the closing and the binding', and means the complete 'arrangement' of any undertaking. If you tell your servant to make the *bandobust*, it means that he is to have everything ready for some occasion in question. . . . There are half a dozen Indian words which the world would be the better for and *bandobust* is one of them. It is almost worthy a study as to what words in the English language are derived from India. Those in the sear and yellow will remember the school phrase, for aught I know not in use now, 'quite the cheese' [1] or 'thing', and then 'the hot rum shrub' [2] of the public-house o' winter-time.

Tiger and Panther

First among the big game of the jungle must come the tiger and panther, for all they mean in difficulty and also in danger. The lion, it is true, exists in Kathiawar and has lately increased, but he is outside the normal range. In this enormous India while the march of civilization has steadily cleared away jungle and extended cultivation, nevertheless there are still vast tracts of forest and jungle, both in Central India, the Central Provinces and at the foot of the Himalayas, where there are plenty of tiger. There are more now in many parts of India than there were twenty years ago, and they breed freely. The Kumaon jungles on the edge of Nepal are kept in tiger from the Nepalese jungles, where the tiger knows not the frontier line, and the fastnesses of some of the Rajputana states are the breeding-grounds whence many of the Central Indian tigers emerge. In Northern India the *sal* forests, though full of tiger, are not easy to beat, since nowadays elephants for the purpose are hard to come by. There are many ways of shooting the King of the Jungles, from the lordly method when you are invited to shoot with a chief or some high official, when it is elephants all the way, downwards. Then the line of elephants, the beaters, and the thick forest and grass, give all the romance of the India of our dreams. Tiger-shooting from elephants is not devoid of danger, for more than occasionally do tigers, especially wounded tigers, charge and spring on the great beasts, to be shot perhaps at the very mouth of the rifle. Tigers are anathema to elephants, who fear them greatly and loathe their feral odour, and will bolt if frightened. A bolting elephant in a forest may be disastrous to all who are seated thereon. Tigers are as a rule only to be had in the

[1] *Chiz* = thing. [2] *Sharāb* = wine.

hot season before the rains. The reason thereof is that they roam so much when water is plentiful that yesterday's *khabar* ('news') may be of no use to-day. When a tiger has killed some beast and has not finished it, he or she will return to eat it after retiring to cover to sleep off his meal by day. That is why a sportsman sits up in trees hard by a half-devoured 'kill', on a rough platform made by day for him to sit on. Thereon, through the night, the expectant shikari will sit waiting for a sound. Then again sometimes, especially in a hill country, tigers are driven, and guns are posted at places where they are likely to pass as the beaters move them on. The writer has a very lively remembrance of sitting on a rock overlooking a valley, in a beat in which four other guns were posted. The tiger had killed the day before, and was now, according to the native shikari, down in the gorge. The writer took post on a huge rock overhanging a road, and sat with rifle on lap, as an hour passed and then a second. It began to rain and he got off, uncocking his rifle, sat down on the road under the rock and dozed, his uncocked rifle by his side, feeling that there were no tigers in India at all. He looked up, and there sitting on *his* rock looking down on *him* was the tiger, who had been *outside* instead of *inside* the beat. The tiger leapt lightly on to the road, with a deep *wunff*, and stood a moment looking at the writer six feet away, who raised his rifle, happily still uncocked, and pulled a futile and fortunate trigger. With another *wunff* the beast leapt lightly to the bushes below. As I could not have shot him dead, he would have probably got me had I fired, and I must have had a mighty let-off. He was shot a few minutes later by the next gun. That is one form of tiger-shooting or tiger-missing.

There are two rules in tiger-shooting: the first that a beginner go out with an old hand; it is too dangerous a game to play alone and unskilled. The other applies to old and young: 'Never follow up a wounded beast on foot, unless you have dogs and another gun with you'. A wounded tiger is the fiercest, bravest beast alive, save perhaps a wild boar, and he charges from the lair in which he is licking his wounds. The only occasion when a man may follow a wounded tiger, without such concomitants, is to save the beaters among whom a wounded beast may have gone. Then *noblesse oblige!* Also be it remembered that a tiger's claw is, bacteriologically speaking, terribly foul. The least scratch from it is very likely to mean blood-poisoning, and the strongest antiseptics should be at hand.

This great cat, graceful and attractive as we see him in captivity, is ten times the more so when we see him from our elephant. It is to be remembered that except in very rare cases it is the old tiger, toothless and stiff, that preys on dull and tasteless man. The tiger in his prime wants venison and veal, and the best of everything is just good enough for him. But venison takes some getting, while any mug can catch a man.

The other felines are the panther or leopard and the cheetah, the hunting leopard. The famous tiger-shikari Faunthorpe thought that the leopard, whom he considered a nasty sneaking brute, often took to man-eating, and that the tiger got the blame. It is found in almost any jungle and while feeding on game will often hang round villages and live on their goats and cattle and their dogs. A goat or two tied up near any hill station will usually attract a panther. Man-killing panthers will terrify a whole district, and the panther has not the instinctive dread of man that characterizes the tiger. He will boldly enter farm or house to carry off his victim. There is a book published a year or so ago by Colonel Stewart which is full of tiger lore and excitements and well worth the reading of all who would know more of 'Spots' or 'Stripes'.

The Bison and Deer

Whereas the tiger must generally be looked for in the hot season when want of water curtails his wanderings, the other great game of the plains must be sought in the rainy and none too healthy season. Anything living in forest—and forest does not necessarily mean wood as we so often forget, the 'flowers of the forest' are more the moorland than the wood product—that needs stalking, cannot be approached when every dry twig snaps like a rifle-shot. The sportsman must wait till he and his shikari, be they ever so snakelike, can move without making noise, hence it is that we must in most places wait for the rainy season. Happily some of the game lies in those parts of India where the first burst of the rain is followed by fine weather under a cloudy sky and the further bursts may be fitful.

First among the great game of the jungle is of course the elephant, but they exist in places where they are beyond the reach of the ordinary visitor or sportsman in Government service. There are, however, plenty of this wild leviathan in India; on the other hand, the rhino is almost extinct, there being a few in the Assam but a good many outside India in Nepal where they are strictly preserved. The buffaloes of the Central Provinces are almost extinct, partly as Faunthorpe says from reckless shooting and partly from rinderpest. The bison, however, have recovered and are still to be found in Canara and in the Central Provinces. It is perhaps in Canara in the Southern jungles near the western coast that the bison in the rainy season can be best shot. Here again it is the wounded beast who is dangerous, and several sportsmen have lost their lives from such. The officer commanding a battery to which the writer succeeded was gored and died in Raipur. The massive heads of bison and buffalo adorn many a mess and club.

The *sambhar*, the great deer of the Indian jungles, is a magnificent beast and his head a glorious trophy only equalled by that of the *barasingh* of the Kashmir forests. He will be found perhaps at his best in the jungles of the United Provinces. There is next the swamp deer of the same areas; besides these there are many handsome deer and antelope of various sizes all over India. The greatest of all, that one will find numerous enough in Hindu areas is the blue bull, or *nilgai*, who is really an antelope. His horns are trivial, but a great blue bull has a magnificent pelt. Because in the vernacular he is erroneously called a 'blue bull', Hindus will not kill him. The Moslem has no such scruple. The black buck, which is practically the spring-buck or bok of South Africa, abounds in many places, and is about the most accessible of the four-legged game. But his horns vary greatly in size according to the district, and what may be a record in one district is nothing at all elsewhere.

The charm of this type of shooting, for those who can feel it, apart from the excitement of the sport, is the jungle life and the jungle people, the aboriginal and outcaste tribes to whom some of the beasts are almost relatives, who study their ways to an extent that is a great joy and mine of information to the naturalist. The marches to one's ground, the elephant lent by a *thakur*—'Thank you very much for asking the elephant', as a chief once wrote to an officer who had asked him to join him with his elephant—the bullock-cart in which one must sleep and jolt, the old bungalow, the grave perhaps in the yard, the deserted old-world shrine in the woods, the smell of the wood fire, the chanting of the beaters, the long dogs of the *Bheels*, they are the things that live for Shikari Smith when all the world is brown. I never smell a bit of burning grass, but I am carried back so vividly to a shoot in Burma, nor do I tread on a piece of wild thyme without feeling the Kashmir hills underfoot.

The Game of the Mountainside

The Himalayas and the Mountains of Solomon, that lesser brother which fringes the Indus from the Pamirs and tumbled Kohistan, on its long road to the sea, are the home of wild sheep and goats. Even the domestic variety grows great horns, and the beast that has been wild since time was, grows magnificent trophies. Further, he lives in places inaccessible, so that to slay him and bring home his head stirs that strange spirit of the chase which the British people seem to possess so keenly.

The Kashmir hills before all others, take pride of place

as the best of shooting-grounds, though to get to them means a journey far beyond the slothful delights of the Valley of Kashmir itself. The game of Kashmir and the Suleiman Mountains is largely the sheep and goats aforesaid and the great forest stag. The goats are the ibex (*Capra ibex*) and the *markhor* (*Capra falconera*). The former is almost confined to Kashmir, but the latter is to be found all along the Suleiman Mountains. For some unknown reason, or some strange freak, he is known as the 'Eater of Snakes', since *mar* is Persian for a snake and *khordan* means to eat. I have never yet heard of a *markhor* who did eat snakes, but then times are not what they were. The biggest *markhor* head is found in Kashmir and curls to a height of close on sixty inches straight up from the skull in beautiful great spirals, but the farther down the Indus, curiously enough, the straighter and the less free the curl. The ibex on the contrary has great horns of the shape we perhaps associate with pictures of the chamois, viz. curled directly back in one graceful curve. Along such ranges of the Himalayas to the east and south of Kashmir as are accessible, only the small sheep and goats such as *bharal* and *tarh* are found and anything of the Kashmir variety must be far behind in inaccessible Tibet. They are the fair sport of those who dwell adjacent, but the sportsman who wants the big heads and the great mountains will make for Kashmir and the high hills that 'hop' so gloriously. The Valley of Kashmir runs roughly from south to north, and between it and the plain runs the great snowy range of the Pir Punjal, far higher than most of the Alps. In the early days of the British in the Punjab, the Pir Punjal was full of big heads, but the comparative accessibility of the Pir resulted in their being shot out fifty years ago and more. For forty years, shooting in Kashmir under judicious game laws has been controlled by licence, and while the game farther afield has been prevented from extermination, that in the Pir Punjal has to some extent regrown.

If you drive in by the road from Murree, as you get near the Valley you will see on your right an immense mass of mountains, the Kajnag, where game has always been and still is. In the higher forests of Kashmir where Norwegian pine mingles with the deodar that gives place to the silver birch, feeds the great stag known as the *barasingh*, the twelve pointer, *bara* meaning twelve. To shoot *barasingh* in the autumn 7000 to 10,000 feet above the sea, is a joy and a feat, especially to those who prefer glorious forest glens to the bare open hill-tops and valleys, where live the sheep and goat.

Sheep, the *Ovis ammon*, and others are harder to come by than the goats, while the great sheep of the Pamirs with the triple curled horn is almost inaccessible for political as well as geographical reasons. The Pamirs is where three Empires meet, and since Russia and China are out of business, they are not always healthy.

Among the bare hills above the juniper, you also get, if you are enterprising enough, the great red bear, which is a very different matter from the poor old black bear whom you shoot a-mulberry-stealing, and if you are lucky a snow-leopard.

The great hills and valleys above the forest are two or three weeks' march from Srinagar, the Kashmir capital, where you meet your shikari and make your *bandobust*.

The stages will mean steady hard foot-slogging over great passes, fifteen miles a day, your kit on mule or coolies, the less the better, and by the time you have got to your *nullah*, the valley assigned you by your licence, you should have sweated off the fat of ordinary life, and be already twice the man or woman you were. I say woman, for now and again adventurous women will come too. There was a story once of the Deosai Plains . . . no, that story is better untold . . . but any way, hardy women do march and shoot *markhor* and ibex, for 'thy *nullah* shall be my *nullah* and thy *kiltas* [1] my *kiltas*', all the world over.

Unless you know really great mountains, mountains beyond the pine and the deodar, beyond even the silver birch,

[1] The leather-covered baskets of Kashmir.

where the juniper creeps to the snow, you cannot realize the desolation of the hillside, when the snow is just off it, before the grass grows or the primula shows, or the wild thyme makes a move. It is desolation personified, but at the mouth of your *nullah*, where the stream is bridged by snow, there will be some stony patch where the grass is just showing, where you pitch your base camp, and your 'sleeping pāl' of the *Pioneer* leg-pull. If you love the keen wind down the pass, and the high mountain air, and if your heart-muscles have risen to the occasion, you will be all agog with excitement, telescope in hand, planning with your cunning old Kashmiri shikari, while he plaits your grass shoes, how you will seek your *markhor* or your ibex—you won't get both in the same country.

With your grass shoes on, you will be 'seized' of the Himalaya, and let us hope that when you have climbed up and down several thousand feet you will hit the great head that fortune has put in your way. Some can't. Also until you are a very old hand listen to your shikari. And there we will leave you. Perhaps you are out on the new and bloodless sport—telephotography. *Bon!* as Marshal Foch would have said. Also, be it remarked, those three weeks' march to your *nullah* have still to be marched, a pony perhaps assisting; no tin-lizzie can help the modern on his arduous way. *Verbum sap.*, stay away if you can't hike!

And that ends a scamper through the subject of Sport in India. There are numerous books that dwell on the subject at length, both of birds and beasts.

BOOK IV

THE SEEING OF INDIA

CHAPTER XVIII

THE GREAT GAZETTE

The Reel of 'The Way'

I use perhaps this term 'The Way' too lightly seeing that it is the name of the holy rule of Life that Prince Gautama the Buddha taught, but it does express what the true sight-seer, the *tamasha bin* in the pleasant-sounding Persian, should feel. The earlier chapters of this book aim at showing the living India, in its facts of history and daily life, its colourful yet simple details, its vast peasantry waiting on the sun and the rain and the Will of God, and the life of our British people who have restored the edifice. If they have been at all helpful to those who would understand the great problem to which fate has married Britain, perhaps it may now be useful to suggest how to get there, and to present what may be worth seeing to those who come.

To see India as a visitor is of course a contradiction in terms. Who can see 1,800,000 square miles and 353,000 peoples or 500,000 villages? Even those who spend their lives there do not do that. Those who live for ever in the land see little more than their own corner, at best their own province. Perhaps the question of 'seeing' India resolves itself into 'What can I see in the time', and too often 'with the money at my disposal?' To this must be added another quite different question, perhaps a self-searching one, 'What do I want to see?' Do I want to go where the English go?

Do I want to see cantonments and capitals, soldiers at work or play, councils and governors at work, semi-bogus parliaments discussing details even more feebly than at Westminster? Very interesting things to see, and if you can see it with the eye of one Abereigh MacKay, long since dead, but whose humour lives, and with him can laugh as we sometimes still do, to our shame, at the Cee-Aye-Ees (Companions of the most eminent order of the Indian Empire), and see good polo and bad cricket, well and good. Do you want to see some of the history of India, the great Buddhist remains, and see where Gautama Siddartha taught 'The Way', and seek, as the pilgrims sought, the 'deer park' and the Boddhi tree? Do you want to see the great carved rock temples of Hindu reformation and recreation as Buddhism faded from the land, the temples carved with great curved dairymaids, and dancing girls who dance with breasts like towers, for the glory of Krishna and other incarnations of the great God of All? Do you want to see the stately remains of Islam, or the great mosques that remain to this day? Do we want to see the Seven Cities of Delhi and the Great Eighth? Do we want to see the 'gloomy portals' of the Khaiber, the mighty Indus, and the rugged outline of the Mountains of Solomon, or the ruins of the great city where Alexander tarried a while, and the remains of the Greek Kingdoms with their two hundred mints?

Or would you like to see the peoples in their villages, the great canals that British engineers have made from the waters of the five rivers, the great canal colonies with their sturdy soldier sons, and see millions and millions of acres of ripening wheat, and thousands of miles of canals with shady avenues alongside, for the sight of the living is better than a sight of tabernacles of the dead? Or the Deccan villages in the land that depends on rain, with the ruined bastions that once kept Mahratta and Pindari spearmen from carrying off their girls? The villages where the most beautiful of all the *prakrits* is talked, the *prakrits* that once were Sanskrit, the dialect that tells the story of the people, as distinct from the written word of the dead hand.

I would differentiate those who go to see, from those who go on a mission or a professional visit, who go from one learned body to exchange bouquets and presidential addresses with other learned bodies, universities and the like, for that is another story. Nor do I talk to those who go for special science such as to see Dr. Mattley a-digging out dinosaurs in Central India, or such like, for that too is another story. To all such India is but just another field for the exercise of profession, hobby or complex; not for them, save in their lighter and more natural curiosity, is this section written.

To the general visitor for visiting's sake, to the tourist, who neither wilful nor bl——dy, but inquiring, with an earnest desire to see, to know, to understand and to sympathize, the Gazette of 'The Way' will endeavour to appeal.

The Ways to India

The ways to India are many. The modern spirit to marry time and space, may take you by air, but that is not the restful way of the *tamasha bin*. It will take you through Bagdad, it is true, and touch you at other places of romance where your sensations can be sated. But most of the while you must snooze, with nothing to look at save below you a map, a very dull map at that. Nor is the way of the motor car satisfying in itself unless your insatiable instincts want dust and travel.

To and from India by car is not the method of the traveller for pleasure, but rather of the experienced traveller who wants a new way. You go, via Europe, to Italy or Egypt or perhaps by 'Constant' and bring your car by sea. Then you travel by such of the Syrian routes as you may choose, taking Jerusalem by the way if you are so greedy of sensation, and by Nazareth and Galilee over the 'Bridge of the Daughters of Jacob' to Damascus and across the desert by the famous Nairn route—'Nairn' since that enterprising modernist set the desert at nought with the road car—to the

City of the Caliphs; incidentally, be it remarked, the real City of the Caliphs is long dead at Seljuk hands, and it was at the opposite side of the Tigris. Thence, not for you the swift flight to Karachi down the Persian Gulf, but a climb by the Persian uplands by the long long road of Hamadan, Teheran, Meshed, Duzdap and Quetta to the horrible dusts of Sind. No, the motor road is better as a way home for the old hand.

There is nothing wrong with the ancient ways of our fathers who ruled the waves. So let us take ship, at London and Liverpool, or at Marseilles if we would cut out the Atlantic rollers. But if we go the full way, why, we see the Rock of Gibraltar, and all that therein is, and get the first lesson, if we are stay-at-home folk, in Briton's heritage and the story of those who go down to the sea in ships. The sea voyage is health-giving and restful, not tiring and dustful, and you will see strange lawless and criminal Marseilles, a princess of watering-places, and also a lure of all the evil that came out of ancient Phoenicia. You will make by Malta or Stromboli for the most romantic sight of old—the lowland of ancient Egypt, rising, literally rising, from the waves in, if you are lucky, the soft creamy light of an Eastern dawn. The romance of the Canal and the desert of Sinai is supreme. The glorious winter air of Suez and the hazard of Red Sea weather will intrigue you, and the harbour of Aden will give you another lesson on Admiralty, and what the Flag of Britain really means on the high seas.

How shall you take ship? That depends on your purse. There is the luxury and over-burdened tables of the greater liners and the merry company. But there is just as good company on the liners who provide the one-class steamers of to-day and make it very agreeable. The chastened P. & O. and other liners have made this way of travel extremely good value for money, and a return ticket at £50 will land you in Bombay, and if you are of the beach-pyjama age, you certainly won't be bored. In one of these, from the cheery three-berth cabin and scramble for your clothes to the dignity of a first-class single berth, the sea and all that therein is yours; till in the pearly light of early dawn you enter Bombay Harbour and fairyland.

The Gateway of India

In making our entry to India, we shall start according to rule at the Gateway of the East, the great archway and portal on the Apollo Bundar where Viceroys arrive with their hearts a-tingle and go as in that delightful story called *India in 1983* written in 1883 amid enthusiastic shouts of '*Are Badmash*' and '*Jao Soor*'. As I shan't interpret those for you, you must ask your courier or your neighbour at dinner if so be he comes from the East. It was through this gateway that Lord Willingdon stepped on his great mission of restoration 'once again the "Captain of Pop" in his grey frock-coat, walked up the red-carpeted steps of the Apollo Bundar and by his side the Great Proconsul' (evening paper), and all India shouted 'Welcome'.

As a matter of fact you, as an ordinary visitor, having sailed into this magnificent land-locked harbour, and seen the towers and spires of Bombay arriving through the haze at dawn—and the glamour of the East will really and truly, if you are lucky, cast its spell upon you—will land at the quay. The express for Calcutta and the North will be alongside, but only Americans will scamper, and you should, before you land, look at the old Portuguese castle on your right and the old battlements with guns that still frown therefrom. The business part of the modern defences you will have passed on the islands in the harbour, but these old stone walls tell you of a tiny country, hardly the size of Wales, that dreamed and indeed strove mightily to be a world-compeller and Empire-builder. Wherever you go round the world, even to far Cathay, you will see the derelict stone castles of the Portuguese. These old battlements in Bombay Harbour should remind you of the great king who tried to rebuild a broken kingdom and train a cursedly pragmatic people. When Charles II. married his bride Catherine of Braganza it was this island of Bombay—for Bombay is not only an island but has another island between it and the mainland—which came in her dowry. You will see the great arms of Portugal carved over the gateway, and they are worth seeing, though at present, for military reasons, the castle has not yet been given up to be a public site and garden as it should be some day. Landing in Bombay is the most tiring affair, and if you are wise you will at once give your keys and your customs papers to your agent, bother no more about your boxes, and drive off at once to your hotel, and thus avoid the splitting headache which the noise and the heat and glare of the quayside so readily engender.

If you are not in a hurry, stay, I pray you, a day. A taxi drive round the Back Bay and Malabar Hill will interest and will thrill you for its new sights, and you should ask your agent to give you someone to show you the real bazaars. Also if you want pith hats, veils and any kind of travelling gear there are plenty of shops in Bombay where you can get them reasonably enough, but those are not the bazaars. A guide will take you to the real native city and you will see crowds and crowds of peoples of many races, bewilderingly new. You will see the women of Bombay with baskets on their heads and breasts like the lotus, who teach you how to walk, and you will see Afghans and frontiersmen chaffering and peddling, and come a-labouring, and policemen keeping their eyes on such swaggering troublesome gentlemen. There will be Arab horse-dealers and grooms about, who bring horses down the Tigris from Mosul far away, recognizable by the handkerchief (the *kafiyeh*) on their head with a rope round it (*aghal*). There will be merchants with little basket caps and a handkerchief round who belong to that heretical and rather mystical Islamic sect the Ismailis, of which the Agha Khan is head and whose pence provide his ample revenues. There will be Parsees about with curious high japanned hats or funny round felt ones with a bunt round the forehead. If you are in the wealthier portions of the city you will see the beautiful fair Parsee ladies in coloured silks a-riding in costly motors, charming to look on, the women-folk of the great Parsee merchants of Bombay. Did you ask who are the Parsees? They are the remnant of the old Fire-worshippers of Persia driven out by Islam without their real women, several centuries ago, who have already been described.

In the bazaars again you may see some Muhammadan woman tight-veiled in a white *burqa* down to her toes, with only little smocked eyelet-holes for the eyes and breath. Very convenient for intrigue, very convenient because you need not bother what you wear under it, damnably hot, and yet without it no old-fashioned and orthodox Moslem woman dare venture abroad. She has this advantage over the Hindu purdah woman, who can never move abroad at all. If you have ever felt a hesitating pat on your arm from a woman in a *burqa* and wondered quite what it means and what you should do about it, you may know too how convenient the said hood is.

The Road to the North

If you look at the map of India you will see that Queen Catherine's Island of Bombay lies about in the middle of the West Coast. North-east runs the rail to Agra, if we go by the G.I.P. (the Great Indian Peninsula Railway), to Delhi, or north for a while if we go by the B.B.C.I. (the Bombay Baroda and Central India line). As in England so in India we know the railways by their initials. In fact there is the nice story of an officer who met somewhere in Oudh a former soldier of his regiment now in the employ of the railways.

Said he, 'Hullo, Brown, I thought you were employed nearer Calcutta?'

'Sir, I used to be in the Hee-Hi-Har (East India Railway) but now I am in the Ho-Har-Har (Oudh and Rohilkand Railway).'

East runs the G.I.P. till it meets the E.I.R. on the way to Calcutta, or southwards via Poona and the more southernly part of the Deccan plateau to Madras and the Southern Railway.

Indian trains are very comfortable, and the only trouble is the dust, and in summer the heat. The real time for travel is in the rainy season, when all the world is green, cattle fat again and the dust is laid, from July to September. But if you are the ordinary T.G., *i.e.* travelling-gent, which is less offensive than G.T., or globe-trotter, you will be coming to India between November and February and therefore dust will be your portion, and if, oh lady fair! your hair be long and therefore unwashable in the bright plated basin in the bathroom, I pray you wrap it in a green travelling veil. If your hair be bobbed or cropped or what not, it is another matter—you can shove it under the shower-bath that all good railways now provide and watch the mud roll off. Except for that, the accommodation is good: four to six may lie comfortably at night, with their bedding spread thereon—and you can sit comfortably by day. There may be one or two armchairs, and plenty of room under the seats for the lesser boxes. The bathrooms are well equipped to hold your dressing gear. There are electric fans if it be hot, and on one or two of the special mail trains there may even be bedding of sorts obtainable. Otherwise all travellers need a valise and bedding, and in most private houses visitors bring their own sheets, blankets and pillows. Even the spacious days that are gone, did not provide bedding, and in many hotels your own is necessary, but not in the largest hotels of to-day.

The more modern bogies also have coupés as well as the large carriage, but these are hotter. In days gone by the larger number of Europeans travelled first class, but harder times have brought the second into vogue. For a family a reserved second is as comfortable a form of travel as could be wished for.

The mail trains now usually have a dining-car on the main routes, where the meals are good. On the lesser routes the older system of halting at certain stations where there are refreshment rooms obtains, and on certain routes, such as the new line from Madras to Delhi, certain stations put baskets with a hot meal on board if ordered through the guard. All sorts of arrangements will be noticed for the Indian humbler traveller, and great selling of all sorts of confections and curries at the train windows. Fruit-sellers are always on the platform, where oranges and bananas at least will be available, and in the North, grapes and the Kashmiri apples. The mango will be very much to the fore in May and June, green and yellow to look upon, yet often horribly turpentiny to the European taste, unless near Bombay. The station fruit-stall is often a picturesque sight. In the hot weather melons are in great demand, the huge green water melons with the pink insides being more than picturesque. To cut out a block, scrape out the seeds, and fill with ice and a glass of liqueur is the old hand's way of using them. They can be so big that on a very hot day half the rind can be used as a hat and half the rind sat on. At many of the larger stations Indian toys and curios have been hawked from time immemorial, from a long horn back-scratcher with a hand at the end to a marble model of the Taj at Agra—the former of more use to you. But all and sundry go to make up the charm and interest of an Indian railway journey even to an old hand. Here I will give my own simple tip for Eastern railway travel amid heat, dust and flies, for peace in camp or anywhere. Hot air can be very hot, and punkahs give no relief, therefore I always carry one or two pieces of fine muslin, some three foot square; one of these dipped in water, wrung out and shaken, becomes icy cold when put over the face in a hot breeze or under punkah-driven hot air. You are asleep before it is dry, and flies cannot use your face as a fly-walk. Sitting reading or writing in camp, or in the countryside in an English summer, the same tucked back over each ear like an ancient Egyptian head-dress, keeps off the flies from head and neck equally comfortably. Travelling on the steamer in the height of summer on the Tigris, I have even sat wrapped in wet muslin, a bucket by my side to wet it again and again as it dried, and in an Indian train when hot it is especially comforting. On the other hand the T.G. rarely stays till such comforts are necessary.

The road to the North be it hot or cold, by the G.I.P., will carry you first up through the Ghats over the arms of the sea that make the twin islands of Bombay, or Mumbhai to give it its true name, and Salsette. If you keep a sharp look-out you will see two grey stone Portuguese castlets that guarded the old-time mainland ferry, and then you run up the Ghats, overriding the pink ice-cream that vendors at Kalian may offer you, made of doubtful milk, and you will note the queer deep golden-brown colour of the long grass by the rail-side and up in the whirls and corners of the mountain railway cutting. The first really exciting place is Fortress Gwalior, which stands out of the plain carved and embattled, a fortress of very great antiquity, home of old gnarled trees and rocks and ancient carved temples, with ancient cameos on its wall, the Maharajah's guards at its gate. Many a siege has it seen and thrice have the British stormed it, last time in 1858, when the mutineers of the Gwalior contingent held it. If you have plenty of time in India, it is worth while stopping a day or two, but if not let it go—there are heaps of others like it—and make for Agra. There is more there that is worth your tarrying awhile, besides the Taj, the tomb of the 'Crown of the Palace', whose description all the world knows; you have first the great palace fortress of the Moguls, with the pearl mosque, the halls of public and private audience, the great red sandstone wall and bastions. You may reflect how it was the centre of Count De Boigne's military system, which he built for Sindiah Maharajah of Gwalior, and how Lord Lake took it in 1803, how Scotch Sangster there cast cannon for Sindiah, and how French officers and many English and Eurasian cadets then entered this remarkable service.

You may also care to remember that in 1857 it was the seat of Government of what was then called the 'North-West

Provinces', and that there, protected by the 3rd Battalion of Bengal Europeans, ladies, children, refugee officers, civil and military, and numerous unofficial civilians white and half-breed, sought refuge for many dreary months, till the victorious troops from Delhi marched down to their release.

But another marvel awaits you besides Agra and its Taj, its fortress, its palace and its city, for a few miles off lies the deserted city of Fatehpur Sikri, the new capital for himself built by the Emperor Akbar, with the usual halls and mosques, deserted for reasons that are not quite clear, not long after its completion. The palace walls of red sandstone, the mosques of marble are something like those of Agra, but save for a few peasants' hovels of those who till the interior, all is silent as the grave.

Among the sights is the tomb of the Moslem saint Salim Chisti, and on the walls of the entrance porch, carved in the flowing Arabic script known as the *Khata Kufi*, is written this astounding and unexpected sentence—astounding for its beauty and its 'likeliness', unexpected for its place: *And Jesus said, 'The world is a bridge, you must not build on it'*.

But as you have moved north you will perhaps have noticed the changing people; they are perhaps taller, and rather different of feature. The women with protruding teeth will have changed to those of a better-looking people. About Agra, the Moslem, and the Turkish *tarbush* will be more in evidence, and the northern soldier will be on the platforms. You are passing from semi-Dravidian land to Aryana. The trees of the villages are larger, monkeys and perhaps peacocks are by the wayside and carved temples at times are visible with the villagers' mud huts clustered round. Both nearer the coast and inland the handsome deep green foliage of the mango groves is at all times to be admired. From Agra runs the line to Delhi by both banks of the Jumna, and on and by the way are many points of great interest which few trouble to see. At Aligarh for instance, there is the really famous Moslem University. It is also famous in British annals for the storming by Lord Lake, his

76th Foot as always leading, in the war with the Mahrattas of 1803–4, when it had become the question whether Britain or Mahratta was to predominate in India. The story thereof is one worthy of perusal. In fact all the way to Delhi from Agra on both sides of the river history, especially Anglo-Indian history, is to be met with on all sides.

Perhaps here one may turn aside to say that in this connection by 'Mahratta' we talk not so much of the people, as of certain Mahratta chiefs, who from being soldiers of fortune had carved their principalities out of Hindustan, Central India or Guzerat. They, together with the Peishwa, the hereditary Prime Minister of what was once Sivaji's kingdom, who alone ruled in true Mahratta land, were ruling with some few true Mahratta followers large foreign tracts, and were using the poor figure-head of the once great Turkish Empire as their puppet and sign-manual. The puppet, blinded by a previous minister, was in sorry durance in their hands, from which Lord Lake rescued him and restored him to his personal conveniences, of which some outline is given in Chapter XX. It but remains to say that this country between Agra and Delhi is full of the scenes by which the Mahratta spear was driven by the British from the countryside and the King's peace put over all, where save for the Sepoy madness of '57 it endureth to this day.

When you come to Delhi it is a long and a big story, which guide-books more than cover, save that in the telling of the drama of '57, the colour should be so vivid that I try to give it in more wealth.

CHAPTER XIX

THE CINEMA OF THE KHAIBER

The Way to the Indus

If you are to travel north of the capital of the Punjab, you will find yourself passing slowly from the land of the warlike Sikhs to that of the Muhammadans of the Punjab, men who still call themselves Rajput, glorying in the fact that, belonging to the old Hindu Rajput clans of India, they have kept the descent honoured and revered, but rejoice to be within the cleaner fold of Islam. Fine faces they are, those clean-cut profiles, sturdy chins and grizzled beards, of small landowners and yeoman peasants. Men with whom a blow soon follows a word; and the women among them are sturdy and sonsy, and comely withal, fit mothers of men, and very different from the puny chatterers of the South with an infant astraddle their half-formed hips. For in the North we don't let our boys and girls go a-chambering too early.

You will be going north into the cold, and on your right will be the great snowy ranges of the Pir Punjal that run perhaps as high as Mont Blanc, and will almost hit you in the eye, so sharp and white and near do they seem as you gaze out of your carriage in the morning. You will roll over the mighty Chenab running shallow in its bed, since its waters are spread on the land, till the snows melt or the mountain rains come, when it must be let free in its bed once more lest worse befall. It was here that John Nicholson in his young days found the ford that took Lord Gough's army over the Chenab or Chinab, veritable 'waters of China' where it rises. It was to that bitter battle-field of Chillianwallah that he was marching, that veritable soldiers' battle where

British pluck pulled their chief out of a bad mess, and Bengal Sepoys were very wobbly. He was fighting the flower of the Sikh Army, an army in both British and French uniforms, with horse artillery in British braided jackets, and drilling to the French word of command, the command of the pre-revolutionary Royal Army of France, the troopers with cuirasses that were hammered at Lille. Then a few miles on you will see, nay you will run through, the actual battle-field of Goojerat, which the wags called in the diction of old Cromwell 'the Crowning Mercy'. There Lord Gough really did beat the Sikh Army once and for all, driving it before him, to surrender a little later for its pains, every man to receive a kindly rupee and blanket in return for his arms, so that he might get to his home. Then did the British and Indian cavalry chase the jackal Afghan Horse that had come down the Khaiber to see what they could get, over the Indus at Attock, which you will presently see, and through the portals of the Khaiber where you could not see their heels for the dust.

There you go every yard over a battle-field—'tread soft o'er the dead in the valley'; you are now passing in your great steel double-bogie saloon where marched the phalanx of Alexander of the Two Crowns. In 1849 the British Army knew it when fighting rebel Sher Singh, where Western Alexander fought Eastern Porus, and this is what Lord Gough's soldiers roared round the camp-fires:

> Oh! sabres drawn and bayonets fixed,
> Fight where fought Alexander.
> Oh, Paddy Gough's a cross betwixt
> Bulldog and Salamander.

And they fought so that India might once more be a land of peace and plenty, and return to the Mogul fold whence it broke away, only the New Mogul was to be better than the old, and bring peace and law and prosperity behind the thousand bayonets marching as one.

But you have not done with history yet; as your train runs you on, there is the mighty Jhelum, the Hydaspes to cross over, on one of the great steel girder bridges which alone are worth coming north to see, and you then pass through the cantonment of Jhelum, the scene of a little fight with Mutineers in '57, and on to the great Aldershot of the North, the cantonment of Rawalpindi. But before you get there you will have climbed a bit through the raw red jagged spurs and scarred ravines of the famous Salt Range, which lies chiefly farther to your left, with its fortresses, its temples of a dead Hindu Raj and its marvellous red rock salt mines, which some folk care to go and see. On the great plain of Rawalpindi the Sikh Army as aforesaid laid down its arms to the British Army drawn up in a scarlet line, and passed by the pile of arms and the rupee table of cunning, kindly John Bull.

Rawalpindi is not a bad place to stop at in some hotel for a few days, merely to see this great army at its everyday life. There will be something more of romance to its trimming than at the Aldershot of the West, with its buglers a-sounding and sheepskins a-beating, its réveillés, its retreat, its tattoos and its last posts. Perhaps then you can realize the saying that the British 'retreat' or 'tattoo' follows the sundown to its sinking the whole world around. If you are a good Briton and not bitten of the Little-Britain-kiss-mammy-complex you will thank God therefor, especially if you see the lame and the halt and the blind flocking to a hospital in Rawalpindi city.

But to see a cantonment in its inner life, you must have an introduction, or in Pindi if you stay in one of the hotels, you are sure to meet some officers and their wives who will do the needful for you, unless you suffer from the said complex, when you may 'warm your own piece of board', for you are not worth the powder and shot of *camaraderie*.

The Dress of the North

To those who demand a guide that shall help them tell one race or one religion from another as they pass them on the street or platform, let it be said that such is a complication. Dress is usually racial, but also is prescribed for religion.

Since the endeavour to revive the Moslem cult, when Abdul Hamid engaged to appear as the Caliph of *Al Islam*, and to some extent a Moslem revival in India took place, the red *tarbush* suddenly appeared as the fashion for Musalmans. That in Turkey and Turkish countries, other than Egypt, this was many years ago relegated as the wear of the Nazara, *i.e.* Nazarene (Christian), and the Jew did not matter. Many Indian Moslems, especially those of inferior status, wear the *tarbush*, and still think it the glory and badge of Islam. When attempts were made to raise regiments from among the fanatical but un-martial Moplahs, the *tarbush* was selected as their military head-dress. 'Our Coons', as the Army on the Frontier called them, looked quaint enough in what is really a very effective military head-dress, in which, however, protection for the eyes and neck was omitted.

To distinguish a Sikh or Dogra head-dress, always a puggaree, from that of a Musalman of the Punjab or Pathan, is easy enough to the accustomed eye, but not to the newcomer. Perhaps it may be said that the up-country Moslem usually ties his round a *kulla* or small pointed skull-cap, that a down-country Moslem of the trading and clerkly class often wears a *tarbush*, and that Moslems usually wear some form of trousering, and Hindus some form of loin-cloth. A cloth round the loin caught up between the legs and the ends tucked into the waist is the convenient garment that most Hindu men, and many outdoor women, affect.

The caste-mark on the forehead, put on fresh each day after prayers by the religious, appertains to the Hindu, and by it he denotes the particular form or aspect of the deity that he specially worships.

When Western or semi-Western forms of dress are worn, it is still harder to distinguish. Until comparatively recent years many Moslems wore a trimmed beard; now many shave all but the moustache, and many Hindus, especially the higher castes of the South, shave altogether. In fact as in the West the changing customs and fashions of the day are taking the place of the ways of the 'old time afore'. A Sikh grows his beard, and for the last sixty or seventy years twists it up neatly on a thread and ties it behind his ear, as do many Rajputs from whom the Sikhs took the custom. The Govindi Sikh's hair and beard is uncut, because it is one of the strict rules of his faith. Most Sikhs met with are Govindis, the followers of the Tenth Guru, Govind.

The Frontier

By common inaccurate parlance the term 'Frontier' is used for a thousand miles of the North-West Frontier of India; yet there are three thousand miles of North-Eastern Frontier that has plenty of watch and ward, and many wars of the past on its record. If you go up the Brahmaputra and into Assam, you will see plenty of Military Police who watch a turbulent set of border tribes and raiders, with a military force for their support. That however is another story, and now we are making for the Khaiber, which we used to write Khyber.

Having a few notes about peoples, you will not perhaps write as one of our most distinguished globe-trotting writers has done—I would not give his name lest he have the law on me—of red-bearded Sikhs at Amritsar, but will mark and learn who be Pathan, and who be Sikh or Dogra, or Indian Moslem. Thus equipped, avoiding fear on one side and rashness on the other, you may safely start from Rawalpindi for the great fortified Indus bridge at Attock, through the Pass of Margalla, where stands the high monument to Nicholson, over the pleasant flats by Hasan Abdal—but stay! you should have seen the city of Taxila, a short drive from Rawalpindi, before you passed by in the train. It is the city of that good King Taxiles who joined himself with Sekunder Badshah, Alexander of Macedon in all his glory, and with him marched against Porus aforesaid to the Jhelum river—Taxila that became the city of a million folk—Taxila the centre of Graeco-Buddhist learning and culture. If you have been there, you will see the most charming museum in India, with all the jewelry and culture and carved shrines and beautiful Buddhas that have lain beneath the soil for two thousand years. How destroyed? Ah! India's invaders have so often wrought destruction on hands that could not keep their head, as Sultan Mahmud Ghaznavi destroyed Holy Somnath and sacred Bindraban. But Taxila must have fallen to Tartars—more properly Tătārs, and pronounced like a postman's knock—to Toramun and his Tătārs, to Mihrahulla and the White Huns! Can you see and feel the tramp and the yell of the murderous thousands, spears and mail and leathern helm, void of any ruth whatever—tramp and slash and gallop, and the scream of the girls and the children—so different from the orderly march of the Alexandrine Western phalanx. You are passing by car, where all the world's drama has been played, and all the world's tears wept.

When you come to the mighty Indus, that has just emerged from the snows, by the old Attock fortress, Afghan and Mogul built, that guards the passage, you may picture much. You may picture two Victorian scenes, one in 1842, the British avenging army returning from Jalalabad and Kabul, in high shakos and scarlet coatees, sepoy and Atkins alike, stepping high with the sense of much endured and victory won, the rescued ladies in their midst, the armies of Victoria *Vindex*, to quote from the exergue of the old medal. Or perhaps more dramatic, the escape of the Afghan Horse from Sir John Gilbert in 1849, the dreaded Afghan Horse that had so long overrun the Punjab, who had for the moment struck up an incestuous friendship with the Sikhs, and were now being chased back through the Khaiber 'like dogs'. But the race is not always to the swift. Sir John Gilbert, the 14th Light Dragoons, two troops of Bengal Horse Artillery, and some Irregular Indian Cavalry, stand on the heights above the bridge of boats; the Afghans have cut it away and set fire to the boats, and are brandishing their spears on the far side. Sold again! The guns fire a few rounds in vain chagrin, but the sappers are at work below—

By courtesy of Indian Railways Bureau

The grim portals of the Khaiber

retrieving the bumping boats, poling, lashing, sweating—and by nightfall the pursuers are over. Then the discomfited Afghans are riding hard again for the safety of the great black gorge of the Khaiber, that tunnel below the snows of the mountain ring, but they scuttle through by the skin of their teeth, with a handful of spattering shrapnel to give them god-speed. And in March 1932 died Troop-Sergt.-Major Stratford of the 14th Light Dragoons, at the age of 104, who had seen it with the young eyes of a trooper. But you, gentle reader, will go there in the comfort of your first-class saloon, wrapped in your warm rugs, sniffing the glorious winter air of a frontier morning, unless so be, which it is to be hoped will not be the case, that you be going in the inferno of midsummer.

Looking out from your carriage window as the train clangs over the great iron bridge, you will notice its fortified entrances, and the armed guards at the gate, and you will look up the Indus, the mighty Indus, to the frontier snows, and the Rock of Aornos that Alexander stormed. On your right, too, half a mile away will be the said old fortress of Attock that watched the Afghan marches, since you are now in Afghanistan, though the Afghans lost the Peshawur valley a century ago to the Sikhs. So, marvelling at the long-haired, hook-nosed gentry at the station, in their sheepskin coats, and the loose Pathan trouserings, we rumble on to Peshawur—the Peshawur that the Sikh Governor, who was an Italian, General Avitabile, kept in order by four be-tasselled gibbets at the four corners of his garden.

Now the mouth of the Khaiber lies some ten miles on, beyond the old Sikh fortress of Jamrud, and we can stay in Peshawur with friends or at a hotel, and drive up the Khaiber by car. Or we can go through by the new broad-gauge train to Landi Kotal, on the far side of the Pass, where a British brigade makes sure that we shall not again be Amanullah-ed as in 1919 to make an Afghan holiday. The great trains on the graded way winding above the gorges are a magnificent way of going, but you will see the human side rather more by road. You will meet the long strings of Bactrian camels, the fierce Ghilzai tribesmen and their women, and the levies who by way of blackmail keep order on the trade route. You will see too how gloriously dirty a tribesman likes to be, such things as baths, that 'hopen the pores', being anathema from boyhood to eld.

After twenty miles or so, past old Ali Musjid and other defensive posts perched high on the hill-top, you climb to the plateau where dwells the British advanced brigade. There bugles ring, and pipes skirl, and mountain guns on their pack mules will jink past you. Atkins as smart as paint and as hard as nails, and little squat Mongoloid Gurkhas emulating him; tall Punjabi soldiers of all kinds, and a rattle of armoured cars and lorries. It is a modern force, two miles away from an Afghan brigade, which less than twelve years ago led an Afghan invasion, an event indeed which had not taken place since the British first closed the Khaiber in 1849. And lest cars and tin-lizzies on their way to Kabul obsess you with their incongruity, you may if you drive on a mile or so, look down into Afghanistan and see high above you the long stone wall of a *kafir kot*, an '*unbeliever's castle*', which may have been old when Alexander's young men came a-venturing to India.

If you are bright and comely to look upon, you may even engineer a very pleasant lunch with officers of the garrison, to whom a skirt *in situ* is taboo.

A Bit of Afridi Land

When you come back to the main cantonment of Peshawur, and see the wire defences within which it lives, you may like to think of that day when stout British hearts, old Sidney Cotton and Herbert Edwardes, blew red-coated Sepoy mutineers from the guns on a public parade, and all the wild rebel young men from the hills flocked down to be led to Delhi by the white men who could show so daring a face to their troubles. You have now glimpsed the Frontier, but to finish your *coup d'œil*, without troubling to go far afield—the Frontier stretches for a thousand miles—you might very comfortably drive through the Kohat Pass in a hired motor and skim Afridi land. You will meet the armed tribesman, a well-kept stolen rifle on his shoulder, you will see the loopholed farm-house towers, and you will get the real tang of the Frontier even more than in the Khaiber, and you will see a small Frontier cantonment. If you would like to read something of the Frontier hazard, 'ye gentlemen and ladies of England, who sit at Home at ease', why, turn into the beautiful, peaceful little Kohat church, read the tablets and how the subjects thereof came by their end. The writer once went round with a new chaplain straight from peaceful Madras, whose nerve was not braced thereby. You can return by train from Kohat to Lahore.

There is one fact in Peshawur that is worth your remembering. The Valley, as we call the country round, was once Buddhist, and a Graeco-Bactrian Kingdom, as was the adjacent Frontier valley of Swat across the Malakand, as you look north from Peshawur. The Peshawur valley and Swat have many Greek-like carvings on shrines and temples; in fact an Irish doctor once remarked to the author, 'You could tell they were Graeco-Bactrian by the Roman tōgas (with the long Irish 'o', please) depicted'! Quaint old cultivators will untie the tail of their shirts, and offer you Graeco-Bactrian coins, and there were 212 kings who minted them. Now, alas, some smart Alec in Peshawur city counterfeits them in good silver. But the crown of it all is this. No one knew where the ashes of the Buddha were deposited. The extant itineraries of the Chinese pilgrims, however, of the fifth and sixth centuries A.D. described how they came to see a certain shrine. Dr. Spooner of the Indian Archaeological Department, by much search and thought and some trial-and-error, thought a certain mud mound, like the usual city brick-kilns, must be the place. There he dug, there he found the shrine, alabaster casket and gold reliquary just as the pilgrims described it . . . and now the monks of Ceylon hold the precious relic. Since Tutankhamen's slung pent-roof ark is older than the Ark of the Covenant, and like thereunto, that Ark may still be, as the *Negus negasta* [1] says, somewhere in Abyssinia—that strange 'secret' which is somewhere there. With the Buddha's ashes revealed, the tomb of Alexander's ashes is still perhaps to be found. If you are fond of controversy you might like to discuss the matter of Greek influence on Indian art.

But now unless you really wish to steep yourself in Frontier lore and Frontier ways and to say 'Don't be tired' and 'Don't be cast down' and the like in the Pushto metaphor, to attractive if verminous passers-by, or know what to say to sonsy Ghilzai girls in the lacquered *khajawahs*,[2] it is time you set your face for Hindustan once more.

[1] The Abyssinian 'Book of Kings'.

[2] Camel panniers.

CHAPTER XX

IMPERIAL INDIA AND DELHI

Imperial India

There have only been two Empires in India during the Christian era, for even mighty Harsha in the seventh century could not pretend to more than Northern India. Those two Indias are conspicuously foreign; the first, the great Turkish Empire of the Moguls, was doubly so, for as well as being foreign, it was Turkish, that is to say, it was entirely foreign in its psychological make-up, to either Aryan or non-Aryan India. Not that Turkish psychology or Turkish rule was anything new, for India, quarrelling feckless India, which Brahmins could bully but never bind, had been in Turkish hands in a yearly increasing degree. Increasing since Mahmud of Ghuzni, that *Sultan Mahmud Ghaznavi* as the epic runs, brought his fierce Moslems and pagans out of the tumbled Mountains of Solomon from the uplands of Ghuzni over the mighty Indus into the plains of the Punjab and the Ganges, as already outlined in Chapter I. Mahmud of Ghuzni was the son of a Turkish slave, Sabaktagin, son of Alptagin, and *tagin* is the 'Slave' appellation, and is much as that of 'Mameluke'. More and more did the Turks spread their rule, and all the way from the time of Mahmud of Ghuzni till the other great Empire arose, the rulers of the major portion of India were Turks or Tartars, people of the mysterious 'Mongol fold', and of that strange, savage, ruthless psychology we see so strongly marked in our time in that of the 'Grey Wolf'. This last Turkish Empire ceased to be great when Aurungzebe Alamgir died in the reign of Anne and the British Empire arose, by that strange series of chances which set her a-picking up and piecing together the countless fragments into which this Turkish dominion crashed, though it lasted in name and in puppetry till 1857. For those who care for such things it might be of interest here to note how four great Turkish Empires dominated Asia from the Pacific to the Bosphorus, all of which except the Mogul lasted till after the World War, and the latter nominally till, as aforesaid, 1857. They were the Manchus at Pekin who alone escaped Islam, the Moguls at Delhi, the Khajjars at Teheran and the Ottomans at Stamboul.

Recent as their dominion has been, there are now none so poor to do them reverence.

If we accept that most of the stories of Genesis, even when not quite intelligible to us, do record some historic germ, then it is also of interest to think that there is quite a possibility that the story of Cain tells the commencement of the almond-eyed race who are as much taboo as Cain himself and his descendants after the Seventh Chapter, and for whom the brand of warning may have been that twitch of the eyelid born perhaps of a boil, which men call the Mongol fold.

It might also be suggested to our Aryan friends to-day, that to be led by another Aryan race who puts their advantage in the forefront of their programme and offers them a condominium, is a very different matter to being ruled for so many hundreds of ruthless years by Turkish and Afghan invaders from the north, who cared not two hoots for them, save to convert them at the point of the sword and exploit them as the fount of revenue and treasure and women.

The Seven Cities of Delhi

The whole of the stories of ancient Delhi, the stories, the dramas and the tragedies of the Seven Cities, are told at great length, or at as much length as sightseers require, in the many books published to that end. It is not therefore necessary to try and do so again here, but as we are speaking of Imperial Delhi, the Eighth City that has its seven forbears in direct succession, some mention of the seven, that number of mystic meaning, can hardly be omitted. The city that you will probably stay at is the Seventh or last, of which the story of its latest drama is told in this chapter. Its real name is Shahjehanabad, because that builder, to entomb whose heart's desire the Taj at Agra was built, was its founder. It should be realized that the founding of new cities is one of the vanities of Eastern monarchs, who must often build afresh and move their capital that their pride may be duly fed.

The Seven Cities, however, minister to Moslem pride only, for the first of this series is by general convention 'Old Delhi', built by the 'Slave' dynasty. There was an older Hindu city still, perhaps several, that fell before the Moslem invaders. We don't count that, though when in 1857, the 54th Bengal Native Infantry let the mutineers from Meerut murder their officers close by the Kashmir Gate, as is shortly to be described, and the 38th left the new magazine, it was to the shout of '*Rajah Pritwi ki Jai!*' (Victory to Rajah Pritwi!'), the Rajput king before Islam smote the land, that they marched off.

Of the seven Moslem Delhis some are but enlargements or bulgings of older ones, but seven is the accepted number.

The *First*, this old Delhi of the Slaves, was built towards the end of the twelfth century, and below it lies the captured Hindu capital. 'Old Delhi' is chiefly represented to-day by Qutab Minar and its surroundings built by the slave Qutb-ud-din Aibuk, or the 'moon-faced', a Turk, like most of the rulers of Delhi.

The *Second* is Siri, built by Ala-ud-Din of the Khilji Dynasty, and is some three miles to the north-east of 'Old Delhi'. There is not too much to it save walls that were built to keep out the Mongols, as Calcutta built the Mahratta Ditch.

The *Third* lies some miles east of the Qutb, and is known as Tuglaqabad, built by the first emperor of this Turkish line in 1321. This is a town of dour workmanlike bastions and mosques of a stern and simple style.

Tuglaqabad did not last long, for the next emperor built the *Fourth* Delhi known as Jahan-pannah, the 'World's Shelter', to include in its enceinte the remains of both the *First* and *Second* Delhis.

The *Fifth*, Firozabad, is just outside the present Delhi, its fortress palace remaining and known as Feroz-Shah Ki Kotila. It is probably contemporary with the mosque known as the Kalan Masjid which is within the boundary of Shahjehanabad, the present Delhi.

The *Sixth* City, of which again only the fortress palace remains, viz. its citadel, is the magnificent Indrapat usually known as the Purana Qilla, or 'Old Fort' on which, as a vista of great beauty, the Eighth City's lay-out is oriented. It stands straight ahead of the great King's way and the plinth on which stands the Viceroy's palace and the Government of India's offices, which is known to the native mind as the 'New Fort'. It resembles to some extent the citadel and kernel of all earlier Delhis. Indrapat was built by the Emperor Humayun, the son of Baber, who could not keep the throne that his father won. Perhaps his share lay in the laugh and kiss that bore him Akbar:

> You played and lost the game? Perhaps your share
> Lay in the hour you laughed and kissed,
> Your son shall bear the honours
> That his father missed.

And it was so.

The Afghan usurping dynasty of Sher Shah, if usurping is a fair word for a newcomer at Delhi, occupied the Purana Qilla till Humayun's son came by his own, and became the greatest of all India's rulers save Asoka and George Windsor of England, who built the Eighth Delhi.

The *Seventh* City, the Shahjehanabad aforesaid, was built between 1638 and 1658, and its glories are its citadel, the Red Palace and marble buildings therein, and the great mosque or Jama Musjid. Its walls and bastions were repaired and improved by British military engineers after the siege by Holkar, and defence by the British in 1804.

The number of Delhis is not necessarily the measure of the many Turkish and Afghan Dynasties that sat on the throne, and any exploration of these may be left to the guide-books. The visitor, after glancing at the story of Lord Lake's victory at Patparganj across the Jumna from Humayun's tomb, will find the real drama and the stirring of his blood at the Delhi of 1857. Lest some squeamish over-kindly mind may think that he is making bad blood with India by glorying in the deeds and sorrowing in the tragedy of his countrymen, let him realize that the Mutiny of the Bengal Army was put down by Indian soldiers with Indian help, as will be explained. They did so lest the best rulers India had seen, despite their mistakes, should be 'outed' from the land they had saved.

Delhi of the British and the Rescue of the Mogul, 1803

How the British came to Delhi is too long a story, except to tell in very brief guise. The Mogul Empire was dead, the Emperor had sometimes been a fugitive with the British, sometimes with the Mahratta, sometimes in the hands of the Rohillas or Afghan colonist barons in Rohilkund hard by. The Mahratta freebooting confederacy, which had arisen from the state which Sivaji created, had two objects; to expel or cripple the British and to dominate the Mogul Empire, if not actually proclaim a Mahratta chief as Emperor. So recently as 1761 their endeavour to do so had resulted in the Afghan Emperor, Ahmed Shah, and the Rohillas destroying the Mahratta host at the 'Battle of the Black Mango Tree', the last of the many battles of Panipat fought fifty miles north of Delhi. A whole generation had passed before they had again raised their heads, and by the beginning of the nineteenth century they had got into their hands practically as prisoner the Emperor who had been blinded by a Rohilla eunuch baron. Having seized the power at Delhi, Scindiah, to use the old spelling, the chief of Gwalior, who had a powerful army trained and largely officered by Europeans and Eurasians, had with the other Mahratta chiefs planned the outing of the British. British India was then governed by the remarkable Lord Mornington, afterwards Marquis Wellesley, whose first work of self-preservation was the destruction of Tippu, the Afghan usurper in the South, who had refused every chance to live at peace with the English. Wellesley saw that until the Mahratta chiefs had been taught a lesson and made to keep within their own territories as ruling but not paramount chiefs, there could be no peace in India, and in fact that the only way of prosperity was a federated India of the broken Mogul lands, bound in some bonds of goodwill under the British aegis.

Among the great combination of British Indian troops and British allies, Sir Gerald Lake, then Commander-in-Chief in Bengal, led the 'Grand Army' north from Agra to meet Scindiah and rescue the miserable Emperor who had once been the ally of the British. Another army, under Sir Arthur Wellesley, came up from the south of India through the Deccan.

Lake met the French-trained Mahratta Army outside Delhi at Patparganj, some three miles on the opposite bank facing Humayun's tomb, defeated them heavily, drove them through Delhi, rescued the old Emperor, restored him to comfort and dignity and all his old titles, and left him to rule, within his palace, with sufficient means. The old blinded man was pathetically happy, conferred all the great titles of the dead Empire on General Lake, and passed his few remaining years in honour and comfort, his son and grandson remaining, as we shall see, in the same position. All the derelict territories round Delhi that the Mahrattas were persecuting, were annexed to the Company's dominions, and the British frontier now touched the Sikh chiefs of the Southern Punjab whom they were later to protect from the conquering clutch of Runjhit Singh of Lahore.

The next year the Mahratta chieftain, Holkar, who had refrained from joining Scindiah and the Rajah of Nagpur against the British, suddenly declared war, inflicted a crushing defeat in Central India on Monson's force, incidentally the first to our fortunate arms, and actually besieged the British in Delhi.

After this period the cantonment behind the Ridge at Delhi was constructed, while forty miles away in support was inaugurated the great station of Meerut with its British garrison of all arms as well as Indian corps.

The Delhi of the Mutiny

There will be few among the visitors to India, and especially to Delhi, who will not know something of the story of the great Mutiny of the Bengal Army in 1857, and the drama that was enacted there.

The story of the Indian Mutiny, as just remarked, need not be locked up among the skeletons in the cupboard. That mutiny was not a real attempt to throw off the British dominion and leading by India. It was the mutiny of a pampered army mishandled by theorists who had forgotten how men are managed. The great armies of the Madras and Bombay Presidencies stood staunch, the fighting folk of the Punjab hurried to join in its suppression and gave their lives freely to that end. The peoples of India hurried also with all their resources to help suppress it as soon as they saw that we would not thus be turned against. Even in the districts where the mutineers were in possession the mass of the people stood quiet. True, every bad-hat and rowdy made the most of the occasion and most of those who had a grievance joined the soldiery. But the Princes held aloof, and only the same sour leaven which has kept alive for thousands of years and now pulls the Congress strings, joined in and fanned, or perhaps started, the flame.

The most kindly Liberal hearts need not fear when seeing or studying the tragedy and drama which their countrymen shared in that time of stress, that they are stirring up the flames of strife. The statue of Nicholson and Alex. Taylor before the gates of Delhi remind the traders and shopkeepers of that city of those who saved them from the unbearable dominion of swashbuckling mutineers and the riff-raff of the bazaars. So, free of compunction, let us study this so recent past and sorrow therewith as well as glory therein.

Visitors will certainly want to see the sites and hear the story, but they will probably concentrate their attention to such episodes as the camp behind the Ridge, the siege, the storming of the Kashmir Gate and the like. If they do they will miss the real drama, and it is essential to realize that this has two entirely different scenes and occasions, separated by several weeks. *First*, the agony and tragedy of the entirely unexpected outbreak at the very commencement of the trouble in India with the pitiful massacres that resulted. *Second*, the glory of the return of the masters, the setting-up of the flag on the Ridge, and three months later, the death-grip on the throat of the guilty city which ended in the final strangling, when the Kashmir Gate was stormed and the heroic Nicholson gave his life.

It is of course to be remembered that the people of Delhi were much as now, traders, merchants and the like, but that there was a rabble of decadent Mogul pensioners, a few hundred Afghans and the usual horde of bazaar ruffians who, just as to-day they will slice off women's breasts with the butcher's fleshing knife, were ready for any riot and bloodshed that did not involve their own skins. It was they as a rule and seldom the mutinous soldiery who were so active in those cruel massacres of Christian women and children that so stained the annals of the Bengal Army and of modern India.

So let us try to follow in our mind's eye the story of this tragedy which came to quite unsuspecting English and all Christian folk that 11th May 1857, not eighty years ago.

To get the atmosphere let us get out of our car near the Kashmir Gate and clamber up, if in energetic mood, to the bastion and look down into the ditch. There let us reconstruct. The troops and their officers and families, three regular battalions of Bengal infantry, and a native horsed field battery, were cantoned up on the far side of the Ridge, over two miles from the gate. If you drive along the road parallel to the Ridge and quarter of a mile beyond it, you will come on the bells of arms of the regiments, ten to each, where the arms of each ten companies were lodged, standing to this day. They with the little magazine and quarter guard, were the only masonry buildings, the lines were behind them.

On the Ridge is the Flagstaff Tower, but it is not visible from the Kashmir Gate. In those days there was at the Kashmir Gate that rare thing an 'officer's guard'. A company from one of the regiments with a British officer was always at the gate. There were little barrack-rooms for the men within the gate and the officer's quarter on top. Looking to the shops from the gate, there was then nothing till you came to the church, old James Sekunder's (Skinner's) presentation. Between the Kashmir Gate and the church, terminating as it were the military precincts, were white timber posts and rails with a gate. Having the gate and the church in your mind, now drive on towards the fort, and you will pass the buildings with high pillars and green jill-mills of the old Delhi College, and the Press, and between it and the city wall, a wall which at that time was often washed by the river, were and still are a dozen or so bungalows in which the officials of the arsenal, and other Government servants, with a business man or two lived. Then you will come to the gates of the big Delhi arsenal. Only the two little castellated gateways thereof remain as a glorious memorial. The most important arsenal in northern India lay between these gates and the city wall, left without any British guard, inside a city known to harbour many bad-hats and not half a mile from the great Palace fortress where the puppet relic of the Empire was allowed to hold his bogus court!

Inside the arsenal were large stocks of cannon and other equipment. There had been also a large magazine, but when Sir Charles Napier was Commander-in-Chief, he had protested against the whole illogical proceeding of this unprotected arsenal. He was not listened to, but at least he was allowed to move the magazine to an isolated point on the river some three miles higher up. Just inside the white gates where the big post office and the telegraph office now stand, and where some of the old arsenal buildings with their vaulted roofs may be noticed, stood the small expense magazine where fifty barrels of powder were kept for making up practice ammunition. Just outside it, in a quiet corner before going under the railway bridge, stands to this day the original old British burial-ground. There is another up in the cantonment where most of the deceased of the avenging forces were buried, and there is a modern cemetery near the Kashmir Gate inaugurated with the burial of John Nicholson and those who fell at the assault. Driving under the railway bridge you come to the *champ de Mars*, the name given to the fort glacis by the French officers with the Mahrattas, which still remains, and to the left goes off the road to Meerut through the now non-existent Calcutta Gate. You then come to the rose-red palace built by the Mogul Emperor, Shah Jehan, and you drive in by the Lahore Gate. Here, in the latticed windows above, were in 1857 the quarters of Captain Douglas, a political officer on special duty with the King of Delhi, as the descendant of the Moguls was then called. Captain Douglas commanded also the King's own guard, 400 strong, dressed in scarlet like the British Sepoys, but with pugarees and not shakos, and a small detachment of saluting artillerymen. Spending the week-end of 9th–11th May up in these cool quarters with Douglas was the Chaplain of Delhi, his daughter and a girl friend. You can go and see in the quarters the bullet-holes in the bathroom door where the rabble and the King's Sepoys fired into the girls' bathroom.

Inside the fort you pass through the great bazaar, in those days crowded with the crafts that hedge a court, and beyond where the barracks now are, was an immense crowded city of houses, lanes and courts, where lived all the retainers of the dying court and the relatives and barons and their following to the *n*th degree. As has been just said, the King ruled within the precincts, having even power of life and death.

When he died they were all to go, and the heir was to drop the title of King, go live at the Qutb, and be known as 'The *Shazadah*', the 'Prince of Blood', but to receive as usual his pensions.

The great gardens and *diwans*, etc., were as now; the present entry is at the Naubut Khana, the 'drum house'.

The Palace fort was atop a high open plinth on the riverside, which when at high water washed the walls thereof. From the plinth a stair and wicker gate led out to the *beyla* below where Royalty might take to boats, and overhanging the river, as now, was the beautiful *Mussammum Burj*, a towerlet, with its marble grills.

Outside the Palace was, and is still, a suburb known as Darya Ganj, with also as now several bungalows, some owned by Rajahs, some occupied by European and Eurasian subordinates.

Now let us turn to the drama. On Monday morning, the 11th May, everyone in Delhi went about their ordinary business. It happened to be a cooler summer than usual, and the ladies had to some extent put off the usual tiring exodus to the hills . . . that exodus that was made by carriage and chair through several days of heat and dust, so different from the modern ways of rail and motor car. There were thus ladies and children in most of the houses in cantonments and civil lines this Monday, while there were always the women and children of the humble white and the half-blood folk who would in any case seldom be able to get out of the summer inferno. The women this summer morning were about their household business, some actually shopping in the bazaars, the scholars were at school, the officers of the arsenal had gone to their work, the magistrates were just starting their courts. Up on the Ridge the whole garrison, of three Indian battalions and a battery, had paraded early to hear read out the sentence for murder and mutiny on certain men of the garrison of Barrackpur, and the officers after the dismiss had gone to their messes for breakfast and something cold to drink. Fairly early, somewhere between 7 and 8 A.M., half a dozen cavalry troopers from the great cantonment of Meerut forty miles away had galloped up the river-bed below the Imperial gardens where the private apartments overhung the river, and were calling on the King to come and lead them.

What had happened? Nobody knew! The excited troopers said the Indian regiments had killed all the European troops in Meerut, something over two thousand. The aged Mogul King, grandson of the last nominal Great Mogul, a slippered pantaloon if ever there was one, was sore afraid, and he summoned to his presence the British political officer in attendance on him, who was also, as explained, captain of the royal red-coat regiment and the saluting artillerymen attached thereto. Captain Douglas hurried to the King, who went with him to the marble *Mussammum Burj* that overhangs the *beyla*—you may see it any day—and there the Captain asked the troopers what they wanted, and said that if they had a petition to the King they knew how to make it, rather than kicking up a dust below the Queen's quarter . . . it was really *zer jaroka* 'below the private windows', the traditional place of suppliants. The troopers answered impertinently and one unslung his carbine and fired at the Captain, justifying the King's action who a minute before had prevented Douglas going down to them by the wicket. The men galloped off to the small Rajghat Gate outside the Palace that led to the *champ de Mars* without.

At that moment came a summons to Douglas to join the Commissioner of Delhi who was outside the Palace at the Calcutta Gate of the city, which has now gone, but which was below the Palace walls on the way to the railway bridge. The Commissioner of Delhi was also Resident at the dummy Imperial court and he too had heard that mutineers from Meerut were coming into the city. He went down with two or three Europeans to order the closing of the Calcutta Gate from Meerut-wards. There was some story that he had news of the trouble in Meerut, where there had been terrible scenes late the night before, and had not acted, but that he had sent

The grim architecture of Turkish Delhi
The Begumpur Mosque

By courtesy of Indian Railways Bureau

The Delhi Gate of Delhi Fort

In the quarters under the chatris on the left were murdered Captain Douglas, the Chaplain of Delhi, two English girls and others, May 11, 1857

word very early to the Brigadier in the cantonment. Death closed soon enough all possibility of verification. He ordered the British Sepoy guard to close the gate. They refused; some troopers of a native Prince's retinue rode at him. He snatched a rifle from a Sepoy and shot a trooper. Douglas had joined him just then, and fired at by the guard, jumped into the fort ditch with Mr. Hutchinson, the assistant magistrate, spraining his ankle. The Commissioner, Simon Fraser, jumped into his dog-cart and galloped off to the Lahore Gate, went up to Douglas' quarters, to which their owner was carried a little later by his servants, and summoned the Royal litters to take the ladies to safety in the Palace harem.

Then come oblivion and hearsay. The Palace infantry opened the gates to the mutineer cavalry, the men in the french-grey light dragoon uniforms, and a wild armed crowd surged up to those quarters over the gateway—you can still see the bullet-marks in the door—and massacred the commissioner and his assistant, the injured captain, the chaplain and the two young English girls. The Royal litters arrived for the girls. They had come too late. That was at the gate of the Palace, where you may see the gateway and the bullet-marks upstairs aforesaid, and on in the Royal gardens you can picture the excited mutinous troopers, the frightened old King and the puzzled British officer standing by the *Mussammum Burj*. A telegraph line to Meerut existed, the 'Electric' telegraph.[1] But the wire was often down and no one attached anything to that.

Now we will go back to the Kashmir Gate and the site of the Arsenal, premising, however, that the Brigadier had heard of a disturbance, had sent the 54th Bengal Native Infantry with two guns, who had all marched off happily citywards with the usual cry of '*Companee Bahadur ki Jai*' ('Victory to the gallant Company').

From the cantonments to the Palace fort was the best part of three miles, but as the 54th marched through the

[1] To distinguish it from the old 'Semaphore' telegraph installed all over England, worked by the Navy, and over part of India.

Kashmir Gate, and exchanged compliments with the guard of the 38th, all was quiet enough.

The 54th marched on, and so simple had been the first news that the colonel had not thought it necessary to load his muzzle-loading muskets, the good percussion Brown Bess. The officers were mostly riding at the head of the regiment, when, some little way beyond the Kashmir Gate they met a crowd of armed ruffians with a party of the now augmented mutineer cavalry at their head. Immediately the colonel of the regiment was cut down, three or four officers were pistolled, and the astonished, possibly disloyal, unloaded regiment melted away. The 38th Guard at the Gate would not even fire. The surviving officers escaped to the main guard; the dead bodies were collected into a bullock-cart, covered with some ladies' dresses from a bungalow hard by, and sent to the cantonment. The cart-driver when he had got close to the Flagstaff Tower, where the rest of the troops were now parading, and ladies and children assembling, drove the cart into the scrub, took out his bullocks and fled. A month later the avenging force found them there and they lie buried in a small enclosure which you may see close to the Tower on the Ridge.

Now the trouble was beginning everywhere; frightened ladies and children helped by their servants were escaping from the old bungalows that still stand not far from the gate; the butchers, the Afghans in the city, the criminal population were pouring out from the bazaar. Any ladies who were in vehicles drove on up to the Tower, and also any unarmed civilians on horseback or in buggy. Those who had no conveyance remained in the main guard, an anxious questioning crowd. No one knew what was wrong. Presently a wing of a staunch regiment, the 74th, came down from the Ridge with two more guns, only to be recalled by the Brigadier, who was flummoxed at the story of the behaviour of the 54th and the vague rumours from Meerut.

All round him gathered refugees, ladies, ayahs, servants,

petulant and tearful children, the little baking interior of the lower part of the Tower their only shelter.

The thermometers mounted, the day wore on. The conspirators in the Palace and the mutineers now sent and demanded the surrender of the arsenal, while the few intrepid young artillery officers and half a dozen staunch warrant and non-commissioned officers prepared for defence, laid a train to the small expense magazine, loaded their guns with grape and stood by defiantly. The rebels had brought ladders and tried to scale the walls. The defenders turning out their Sepoy guard, defended themselves fiercely, and at four in the afternoon, when all was lost save honour, blew up the magazine, causing much damage to the attacking crowd. The survivors blackened with smoke arrived by a wicket at the main guard.

All communication with the Ridge was closed and no orders came. As it grew to dusk the guard, a company of the 38th N.I., fired on the officers and ladies taking shelter. There was something of a *sauve qui peut.* The ladies and men not too badly wounded were helped over the ramparts into the ditch and on again to get into the jungle, whence they got to Meerut after terrible cross-country wanderings for which they were quite unequipped.

That is the story of the Palace and the Kashmir Gate which the visitor should try and understand and envisage. On the other side of the Palace, a different tragedy was in progress. There the Eurasians and the humble Europeans were entirely cut off from even the precarious rendezvous of the Kashmir Gate, and were out in the bazaars a-marketing or at work. Many were ruthlessly cut down without regard to age or sex, others had collected in one or two of the bungalows, all eventually to be gathered as prisoners within the Palace save the lucky ones who were dead. One bungalow's crew held out for several days, and in any case few but women and children were taken to the Palace. There a few days later, after being confined in an underground department near the Naubat Khana, which you will see for yourselves, they were taken out to an open space near by, surrounded by a rope and hacked to pieces in cold blood to the number of nine-and-forty,[1] of whom perhaps half a dozen were men, some of the old King's sons being present with his seal as their authority. Who did it does not matter, it was done *coram publico* with the most cold-blooded cruelty and want of ruth, as evil in its way as the better-known massacre of Cawnpore. Nor was it done in hot blood, for it was four or five days since the last sign of British authority had disappeared from Delhi and the countryside. It is an eternal example of that same Eastern want of ruth that thrusts unwilling widows on the funeral pyre, that injures child brides, and cuts its neighbour's children to pieces in times of communal strife, or even to cure a sore throat!

With the dirge of this misery in our hearts we may pass by the Bank House, which is still a bank, at the Palace end of the Chandni Chowk, and through the now silent Kashmir Gate to the Ridge. There stood the Brigadier—with his 54th melted away, the few companies left of the 38th which that week had all the guards and detachments elsewhere, but which was obviously sulky, and with his loyal 74th recalled from the gate—by the Flagstaff Tower, there were crowds of refugees around him and his remaining troops, so many as had not slunk away. When the sullen roar and the clouds of dust showed that the artillerymen in the arsenal had blown up their little magazine, he sent off to try the same on the great magazine at the edge of the Ridge, near the Jumna, now or till recently the kennels of the Delhi hunt. A guard of the 38th chased and shot the would-be exploding party away from the gate. It was not blown up and the ammunitions therein fell to mutineer hands.

The Delhi of the Ridge

Then the Brigadier, urged by the native officers that the men still quiescent could not hold together long, ordered all and sundry to save themselves. Some made off

[1] Or some count two-and-fifty.

in conveyance or horseback to Umballa and others to Meerut. Their adventures are another story. It is said that the Brigadier, his brigade-major and his bugler went to the brigade parade-ground in the gloaming and sounded the Assembly—and that one loyal soldier fell in! Then he rode away very sorrowful, for he had served over forty years with his Indian soldiers. When he went, no Englishman was left alive in Delhi, save perhaps a few with the miserables in the Palace yet destined to make a Mogul holiday. The Raj had disappeared! That is the drama and tragedy of the 11th May 1857.

But something had gone wrong with the plan. The British were not dead nor likely to be. All round, it is true, for many miles the regiments were mutinying and marching on Delhi, but four weeks later the Europeans from Meerut—whose inaction on the night of the 10th is also another story—with the troops from Umballa and the Simla hills were marching, marching through the summer's heat, to Delhi, the Commander-in-Chief at their head, till he died of cholera. Four weeks after the drama just described, the Sepoys now swollen to many thousands, were fiercely defeated at Aliabad-serai, and the avengers swung on to the old Ridge parade-ground and rehoisted the British Jack. The British who hope had said were all massacred were back again, but it was three months before they could storm the place when every British and available Punjabi soldier had been sent them, and there were forty thousand mutineers in the city. Heat, disease and the scarcity of numbers as well as lack of siege guns were responsible for the delay. At last Nemesis came on 13th September, when three columns stormed the Kashmir Gate and its vicinity, over the breaches to be seen to this day. At their head was the famous John Nicholson, who fell in the hour of his triumph. It is this story of the long fighting on the Ridge and the storming that fills men's minds and attracts visitors, but the drama of that day of May in the Palace at the Kashmir Gate and up by the Tower on the Ridge is emphatically the greater. If you doubt anything here said of the said day, go to the south door of the old Skinner's Church within the gate and see the memorial to one family alone unto the third and the fourth generation, old folk and children, all ages and sexes, who fell in that holocaust in the Darya Ganj and by the Naubat Khana.

The Great Eighth

To add to these seven ancient cities of Delhi, the British have now built the Eighth. The really important point is that prophecy and tradition are agreed that to build a new capital is to end the Raj—which is as may be. For many years the problem of a suitable capital for all India had been exciting men's minds. Delhi had faded with the last of the real Moguls Alamgir, whose name was Aurungzebe. Calcutta had grown to be the British capital, and after 1860 Simla had become the summer capital, but the biennial exodus so far away was becoming a great strain.

Delhi, which is more accurately Dehli, is among the worst of the Indian climates, but its place on the map was decided for it by nature. Just as London grew at the first ford on the Thames estuary, so Delhi was the first place where watered caravan routes from the Punjab could strike the river Jumna. So there dynasty after dynasty had its capital; first the ancient Rajput rulers, and then the Turkish, Afghan and Mogul conquerors and dynasties.

The guide-book will detail them all with accuracy and gusto from the ancient Pithori and Jahan Punna to the dour Tuglaqabad, and the Shahjehanabad which is the Delhi we know to-day. When in 1912, during the King's visit to India, Government announced their intention of making Delhi the capital of India, His Majesty laid the foundation-stone of the new Parliament House on the spot where he held the Great Durbar, and it was intended to make the new Delhi more or less adjacent to the sacred Ridge. Alas! they had not thought of the Jumna floods, and the spot selected was said to be within the flood area. The town planners and experts sought diligently among the masses of tombs

Reception of the Viceroy and Lady Irwin at the unveiling of the Dominion Columns at New Delhi, February 10, 1931

and graves that surround Delhi, and selected the piece of countryside some five miles out of Shahjehanabad that has now at immense expense and immense labour become the official Eighth Delhi.

Like all deserts in India, water will make it into a garden, and the new Delhi, with its marvellous Government Offices, its Viceroy's Palace, its Parliament House and its miles of residences, is a wonderful thing. Thousands of labourers and many million users of water have made it all a green garden and possible to reside in for six months in the year. The critics will tell you that the designer has put an 'o' too many on to all measurcments and distances—which is only their way of saying that the lay-out is vast, generous and no doubt unavoidably costly. The lay-out of the main roads, alleys and vistas have been designed with great skill to give an aspect of ancient gateways or the giant domes of tombs—and has much that is beautiful about it, while electric light and motors minimize the difficulties of distance. The great public audience-hall attached to the Viceroy's Palace is probably one of the most beautiful buildings in the world, and the Palace itself is a marvel. A thousand years hence it will perhaps compare in interest with some of the works that are now antiquities.

If you want to see the Great Eighth, you will, if you are wise, stay at a hotel in the vicinity of the older Delhi, and to see modern British India disport itself, and vie in 'All India' cricket and polo matches, cold weather sessions of Parliament and the like, you should be there in January and February. You may easily see too some state function and the organization of the West mingle with the splendour of the East. But the Taj by moonlight, the villager in his village, the human jumble at Lahore station, or elephants and Princes in Rajputana will probably please you more.

Rajputana or Rajasthan

Some outline has been given of the events which led the Rajput clans of Hindustan to 'up-sticks' and run before the

Moslem storm to the arid deserts and stony mountains of that part of Central India known as Rajasthan.

As has been explained, some of the Princes of India are but moss-trooping upstarts born of the crash of the Mogul throne, others derelict Mogul officials, and such state as they keep is but the memory of the Imperial customs. In Rajasthan we have the old clans, chiefs and clansmen living in many ways as India lived when Macedon knew it. Therefore it is that many a visitor packs himself into the little metre-gauge train and makes for one of the well-known centres, Ujein, Oodepore and the like. Some of the Princes have thrown themselves into the hurly-burly of Western invention, electric lights blaze in their capitals, 'cars', as the Prophet Nahum has it, 'run like the lightnings', and 'justle one another in the broad ways', but off the main street is the feudal life of centuries ago. The Royal gatherings and ceremonies and feudal customs are those of extreme antiquity. Behind the scenes of modernity, the ages beckon, and real India of the past is awaiting your pleasure: great hill castles, lakes, deserted fortresses, palaces—dead when Europe was young—clansmen, dunniwassals, foster-mothers, priests, temples; all are there in a profusion that is missing from much of British India.

For Romance with a big 'R' you will go to Rajasthan, even if romance comes with the night mail, the car and the aeroplane. Unless you are taken by someone who knows, it is best to go by the beaten path of the continental itinerary, for novices otherwise may get queerly lost. If someone will tell you, ask of 'Saccas' of Chitoor, of *Johur*, the great burning of wives, to save them from the Moslem, and the like, and then wonder—wonder at all there has been and all that shall be, and perhaps realize that India is something more than even you dreamed of.

CHAPTER XXI

SOME SIGHTS BY THE WAY

Pilgrims

Peace on the uttermost borders,
Strength on a road untold.

Let us turn to a different vision. The scene of a march of Pilgrims into the Himalaya.

'*Challo Bhayan! challo!*' ('Hurry, brothers! hurry!') and the eager jostling crowd cast their eyes to the snows above and jingled and tramped along the mountain paths. The peasants and even the traders had left their shacks and their booths and had come tramping up from the plains of India, through the passes and over the snows of the outer Himalaya. Old and young, men and matrons, lads and maidens, cowherds and farmers, fishers and spearmen, ascetic and *faqir*, parents and children, '*Un qui marche, un qui tette, un qui vient*, they streamed out of the Holy City. From Baramullah they crowded, over the Pir through Shapiyon, down the valley from Verinag, eager to ease the heartache by the cool tarn and the sacred shrine amid the glaciers on Holy Haramuk. And as they pressed, these tens of thousands of Hindus, the world of Islam in the villages watched and wondered, cursing in their hearts the misbegotten idolaters. Far away into the plains of the Happy Valley tailed the crowds that surged from Punjab and from Hindustan, past the ruined Pandav temples, past the almond orchards, past the mosques of Allah, who shared worshippers with no partner gods, out on to the *karewa* plateau by the dog-rose, the wild thyme, and the iris blooming in the graveyards.

Come, brothers, come! for the snows are far,
Come, brothers, come! to the healing shrine,
Come, brothers, come! for the peace that endures.

. . . .

The great pilgrimage, the yearly pilgrimage to Haramukh in Kashmir, was in full force, and all the yearning for release and peace on a road untold, that lies at the bottom of the heart of man and woman, but most especially man, seemed released in that hurrying crowd, that had been marching for days, or driving by the cart road in bullock-wagon and pony-cart.

Many there were who dropped by the roadway, and here and there a family stepped aside that the mother might give birth behind the blanket screen to the '*un qui vient*' . . . a few hours and she, with her shouldered babe, would be tramping on again. Past pine and fir spruce, past cedar *deodaris*, and out of the forest to the scattered silver birch, the juniper scrub and the bilberry, past the wayside cairn that some pious Moslem may have built, on to the tarn and the deep black pool and the bubbling well and the grey stone shrine. There would be the promised peace, and the balm.

And down on the road where the press lay heaviest an aged Jesuit priest, in white soutane and black skull-cap, moved and worked. Here a word and there a hand, and in his hand the keys of all the creeds, while far above a poised eagle scanned the depth.

Indian Dancing Girls

Pilgrims and shrines are all very well. Let us now see something of the pleasure of the East. It may well be that you wish to see one of those Indian nautches, those performances by professional dancers and Indian beauties, of which you have heard. Perhaps that may be arranged, but the normal nautch as easily hired and presented may be singularly dull to Western eyes. Not for them does the substratum of posture and suggestion carry its purport. Nevertheless nautches there are and nautch girls of extreme grace and beauty. But whether you see the inferior dancer or whether you see the stars you will have been struck by the beauty, the curious haunting beauty and grace, of at any rate the principals if not of their seconds.

Dancing girls have been the bane of princes since princes and girls existed, long ere Salome danced before Herod. Who and what are these women who flash across the pages of history and serve so prominent a part in the underworld of India? The story is as strange and inhuman as any in the history of the world. Whence do they come, in their silk attire and their jewels, for all who choose to hire and possess. And the answer is the foam and the froth of the sea and no more.

> Headpiece and ear-rings and anklets of gold,
> Heartless one, why do you glitter?

It is all part of the curious racial development of the Aryan and of the position of the honourable women. Whereas in Europe dancing is a profession which any woman may adopt, in the East it lies so low that none may do them reverence. The dancer and the courtesan come of the outcaste races, the conquered and ejected inhabitants of India whom thousands of years ago the Aryans drove from their heritage and have kept in social servitude ever since. Women are born and brought up to these trades or sometimes sold into them by parents with surplus daughters.

For many reasons, principally good, women are born and brought up to the honourable condition of marriage, and there are no unmarried women. There are no reputable women who dance and act, and there are no women in any profession. The dancer and the courtesan come from the outcaste tribes. These walks of life usually proceed in matriarchal descent devoted to the trade from infancy. A dancer brought up to dance and to charm from childhood and descended from a line of ancestresses of the same cult may possess very remarkable skill and lissomness, and will often have the predatory instinct very highly developed.

In an Eastern city, if some with inner knowledge can take

you, perhaps in disguise, down below the latticed verandahs that overhang the streets, and into the arched courts, you may find a famous dancer holding her salon. The men of the East see no women in social intercourse save their own. The chat on affairs with a well-informed woman, or the lighter persiflage of the Western tea-table are almost unknown. So men will frequent the dancers' salon for talk and jest and *espièglerie.* Reclined on cushions on the floor, half a dozen visitors may be smoking their *huqqas* prepared for them by the dancer's girls, while the lady of the salon may remain on her divan telling the latest gossip from the markets. One of the girls may be singing a Persian song to a zither's notes, or in the courtyard pipe and tambour may be playing some evil-haunting, amorous air.

If you are privileged to see a star troop dance, you may see some very graceful and beautiful performances, but you are not likely to have enough inner knowledge to follow half that is done, fortunately for you perhaps. In an open arched court the *première danseuse* will stand with her girls, two tom-tom players and a couple of pipers squat in the corner and start their evil-haunting, seductive music. First the leaders and then the others will slowly join in the dance, their bangles and anklets jinking. The dance may illustrate some Eastern story,—a soldier in some frontier castle longing for the charms of the city. Fiercely in love with some woman, some dancer of the town perhaps, his feelings and desires are explained and developed in song and rhythm. Perhaps the charmer has no place in her heart for the absent and has a new lover, perhaps the first one returns to attempt her recovery. Or again he may console himself afresh. It is all done for you by pipe and tambour, and the clever rhythmic dancing and the maddening jink of the anklets.

Lucknow

Lucknow, the capital of the United Provinces, is one of the sights of India for several reasons. Until 1856 it was the capital of the state of Oudh. This old Hindu kingdom had long been a province of the Delhi Empire, and when that Empire collapsed the Mogul Governor, who was also the Nawab Vizier, that is to say, hereditary Vizier of the Empire, set up as an independent ruler, more or less with the assistance of the British, who wanted stability, and in the early days a counter-balance to the Nawab of Bengal, another broken-away Mogul Governor.

Later, with British approval, the Nawab Vizier took the style of 'King of Oudh', and was supported by a 'subsidiary' British force at his capital, as were all the greater Princes under the Marquis Wellesley's wise and constructive policy. Lucknow thus became a city of great palaces and mosques in the Muhammadan style—often a modern florid and over-decorated style—but still a city of picturesque palaces deep-set in groves of trees. Islam with all its beauty and tradition was magnificent in and round the city, and since the Nawab Vizier and King was of Persian descent, one of the Lords of Iran, as distinct from the Turkish Lord of Turan, the Shiah form of Islam was predominant, and to Lucknow came many of that schism.

But evil on evil were the ways and policy of this long-decadent family of Oudh and devoid for many years of justice and right. For many years also the British Resident had made protest and rendered advice! At last in 1856 the Company, *i.e.* the British Government, reluctantly decided to remove the King and annex and recondition the vast province.

The visitor therefore will see all the relics and all the palaces of the old Moslem capital, and the beauty of its setting, but above all will he want to see and to understand the story of the Residency, which has been a household word since his childhood. He will see a battered ruin hung with bougainvillaea and Japanese honeysuckle, and a flag-pole on top with the Union Jack, a flag that is flown day and night and never taken down save for renewal. It is the memory of that drama and that heroism which so thrilled the British Empire.

Lucknow in 1857

The situation in 1857 at Lucknow was a new and interesting one. In 1856 the Kingdom of Oudh had been annexed for many reasons, justified a thousand times, aforesaid. The group of buildings of which the Residency was the centre was the house in which the Resident at the court of Oudh with his staff had long resided. By now it had become the seat of Government. The Resident had become the Chief Commissioner, and his high officials occupied the European houses in the vicinity, which from the Residency group has been referred to as 'The Residency' for the purpose of memory and of history. To India it was known and *is still known to those who remember, as 'The Baillie Guard'*, when a guard of British Sepoys was instituted to guard and escort the Resident. 'The Baillie Guard' was the quarters of the Resident's escort, and if you care for the drama and romance of the old story, you should assimilate this point.

Before the annexation there was stationed at Mariaon, two or three miles from Lucknow, a force of British Sepoys known as the subsidiary force. After the annexation, a British battalion, the 32nd Queen's, was transferred from the adjacent principal cantonment at Cawnpore to Lucknow, and it was quartered half in Mariaon and half near the Residency. Oudh itself was garrisoned by a new and popular *force d'élite*, known as the Oudh Irregular Force, modelled on the Punjab Irregular Force, and officered by some picked officers from that force. It lasted one year and then disappeared in the Mutiny.

The arrangements for the administration of the newly annexed Oudh were not very happy. General Sir James Outram had been appointed Chief Commissioner, but had left in ill-health; there had been a futile interregnum, and then the famous political officer, Colonel Sir Henry Lawrence, an ex-Bengal artilleryman, was sent. A man of intense sympathy with Indians, of great friendship for all Indian nobility and gentry, no better man could have been found, and the whole of the great province, seething with upset of the annexation, answered to his hand on the helm. But it was too late; disgruntled Oudh, whose landowners were perplexed, even if its peasantry were content, was to be whirled into the conflagration of the Bengal Army.

The beloved Sir Henry made preparations to victual and defend the Residency group of buildings and adjacent bungalows, and also took many forcible measures to restore confidence. The local units of Oudh Irregulars mutinied. He dispersed them and held his own. The regular garrison mutinied. He drove the mutineers off, and close on a thousand of them remained staunch to the end. All through May and well into June he kept the place going without concentrating in his siege position. At Cawnpore, forty miles away, where Sir Hugh Wheeler commanded, were four Indian regiments. Wheeler kept them staunch some time and Lawrence sent him some Europeans. Then some reinforcements from below began to arrive. The loyal Wheeler sent back half the Europeans and some of the new arrivals. Then his troops mutinied and marched to Delhi, but returned in two days to attack his little refugee entrenchment. Lucknow still kept itself going until Sir Henry made his great mistake. Several mutineer corps had advanced on the city, and on the 29th of June Sir Henry, who had asked the Viceroy to make him a brigadier-general and put him in military command over the local brigadier, took out part of the 32nd and some details to fight them some ten miles out. Every military and administrative error was made. His exhausted Europeans were defeated, and in the retreat lost their best officers and men and some of their guns.

The Residency position was then hurriedly occupied, although it was not yet complete, and the next day, 1st July, the siege began. There, some 800 British soldiers and officers, 712 loyal Indian soldiers, 200 armed civilian Europeans and Eurasians, began this famous defence. The miserable yet super-gallant Cawnpore episode was over. Wheeler and all his garrison, and the hundreds of women and children he endeavoured to protect, were all dead. But the Residency held out. Two days after its investment, a rebel shell killed poor Sir Henry. Brigadier Inglis of the 32nd took command.

On 16th July General Havelock had reached Cawnpore, but after several attempts it was not till 25th September that he was able to force his way through.

By this time Lucknow, where the rebels had declared a scion of the old family as King, had become the centre to which many of the mutinous troops had marched from many miles round. A vast force of trained soldiery, reinforced by a host of irregulars from the force of the big landowners, held the city and invested the Residency, on to which a considerable artillery fired day and night. The Sepoys had loopholed countless walls and kept up an incessant musketry, while the Afghans in the city and other Eastern rabble led several hand-to-hand attacks.

When Havelock entered after severe fighting, he was too weak to remove the garrison and the many hundreds of noncombatants. He took up a wider *enceinte*, and continued the defence.

General Sir Colin Campbell had now arrived from Home, to succeed the dead Commander-in-Chief, and with him came all the veterans of the Crimea. By the 12th of November he started for Lucknow and by the 17th entered the Residency after severe fighting. He forthwith carried off the whole force, sent the refugees to Calcutta, and had a big fight at Cawnpore with the Gwalior rebels. It was not till March 1858 that he returned to reconquer Lucknow and the Kingdom of Oudh and to reinstate British authority.

That, shorn of detail, is the story of Lucknow and the city where the flag flies day and night. The gallantry of the defence, the miseries and endurance of the women and children, cannot be dwelt on here, but no flight of imagination can soar too high concerning it. Two historical facts are worth remembering.

The first fact, the tactical disaster of Chinhut, where Sir

Henry Lawrence, practically a civilian, not in touch with the handling of troops, led out his small force in person to disaster, when soldier brigadiers could have done it ten times better, and have fed their men. Without this disaster the siege of the Residency might never have occurred.

The second is the strategical folly of the Government of India in not securing the vast fortress of Allahabad. The stream of reinforcements to Cawnpore and Lucknow had now begun to arrive at both places; the machinery of hot weather movements had been established, when the one Indian regiment allowed to remain unwatched at Allahabad mutinied, and the whole forward movement snapped for four weeks. Had Allahabad been strengthened 'Cawnpore' and 'Lucknow' would not have occurred.

These are the points which should be remembered for instruction as well as the others for glory. The story of the faithful and devoted Indian Sepoys, without whom *the Residency could not have been held*, is as worthy of remembrance as anything else in the episode.

Cawnpore

The Cawnpore story is largely the story of Lucknow. From the beginning of the nineteenth century, it has been the great military cantonment watching the troublesome unhappy Kingdom of Oudh. It was famous in India for its military life and its social amenities. It and Meerut were then the Aldershots of upper India, and at this time Sir Hugh Wheeler commanded the military district which included Lucknow. It was also a growing manufacturing city, and in the summer season was reached by steamer. In 1857 it was full of engineers at work on the new railway, which now ran up from Calcutta for 120 miles as far as Raniganj.

It is not worth going to see from sentimental or historical reasons unless you can go in a hot June in heavy pea-soup haze of heat and dust, when some of the local horror and drama may be presented to you. This is the story in outline. Sir Hugh Wheeler, over seventy years of age, was most experienced in Indian Army matters, and was famous among the Sepoys. He kept his troops steady for several weeks after the trouble began, but on the 4th of June, as related, they mutinied and marched to Delhi. Then later they returned to attack him and his odd military details.

Sir Hugh was hampered with the families of engineers and the European and Eurasian communities. He selected as a place of refuge and concentration for them two big hospital barracks near his own house, because hospitals have many outhouses suited for such a purpose. He wanted to be near the road from Calcutta and the steamer ghats which would be available as soon as the rainy season commenced. His own judgment and the advice of his friend the Nana (with whom Lady Wheeler, a high-caste Indian lady, was perhaps connected) told him that the troops would march off for Delhi (which they did).

He considered that an entrenchment round the hospital barracks would give him a suitable rallying-point against rabble forces, till he was reinforced and his non-combatants removed. But alas, the rebel troops and the Nana returned. His plans for blowing up his arsenal miscarried; the gun and the ammunition fell into the rebel hands, and Sir Hugh, now fairly broken down with age, heat and anxiety, found himself heavily bombarded and beleaguered in his crazy entrenchment. For twenty days his 210 British soldiers, his 40 volunteers and Eurasian drummers, with his huge burden of non-combatants, held out with supreme gallantry and consummate patience and endurance.

At last the Nana offered terms. Sir Hugh reluctantly, on the advice of his younger and more daring officers, who knew that they could do no more, accepted.

Boats for their withdrawal were arranged, and were inspected and taken over by a committee of officers. On the early morning of the 28th June the miserable, worn, dejected cavalcade left the entrenchments, helped by conveyances provided by the Nana, and by the Sepoys who could not withhold their admiration of the defenders.

Just as the packing into the big covered boats on the Ganges was finished, firing broke out, which ended in a complete massacre, save that one or two boats got away for a while and some 200-odd women and children were saved. There is some probability that this massacre was not intended: that someone fired by accident, that the highly strung British replied, and that at once the crowd of watching Sepoys were involved. There would be some slight whitewashing of an indelible stain on the Indian character were this so.

What can never be wiped out is that those 200-odd[1] women and children were massacred by ruffians with the Nana's connivance the night before Havelock's avengers marched in.

If you go to Cawnpore you may see the marble memorial and the angel forgiving over the well into which their bodies, living and dead, were pitched by the sweepers who cleared up the place of butchery. The site of the entrenchment is marked by a privet hedge and the beautiful memorial church stands close by.

Curiously enough, in 1930, the inhabitants of Cawnpore butchered themselves to the number of many hundreds in a fit of communal hysteria, rending each other's children as they had rended the pitiful ones in '57.

Mother Ganges

Down from the Himalaya, all through the *Old Ajudhiya*, that Oudh which is now part of the great district known as the United Provinces, and through Bengal to the sea, runs the Holy Mother, the Ganges, the sacred river of the Hindus. Into Mother Ganges must a high-caste Hindu's ashes be thrown, even if it is years before they can be taken there by the son. Only the son or adopted son can perform this rite. To bathe in Mother *Gunga* is to have all your sins washed white. It is a marvellous great river, many hundred miles in length, and in the rainy season, and when the snows

[1] Exact number never known, but 375 went into the entrenchment.

are melting, rolls down in immense force. From time immemorial boatmen have sailed its courses, and because it is such a highway for commerce all the famous cities of this part of India lie on its bank, or that of its great tributary the Jumna; Delhi, Agra, Cawnpore, Allahabad, Chunar, Patna, Benares and many more. For the same reason the great English cantonments in Bengal were established on its banks, and for many years a steamer flotilla was a forerunner of a railway system, and indeed to this day it is still a steamer highway for many places that are not on the railway line.

The Ganges sent her steamers to conquer the Tigris, with the Irrawaddi, the Nile, the Indus and the Thames. Besides the entirely holy, priest-ridden and temple-laden city of Benares, many a holy place and shrine are on its shores. Allahabad that was the Hindu Prag, where Ganges and Jumna mingle, is especially revered, and holds high revel with pilgrimage and fair. So much is this so that within the British and erstwhile Moslem fortress of Allahabad, where there is a Hindu temple, a special subway, open though guarded, admits the pilgrim under the very fortress walls to the shrine within.

Travellers' tales have often told of the half-burned corpses floating on its waters. Firewood is dear, Hindus are poor even when high-caste, and a half-scorched body on the holy river is as well on its way to heaven as a wholly burnt one elsewhere.

For a century, troops, especially European troops, were moved on its waters, in a form of vast houseboat, and those who have ever read *Little Henry and his Bearer*, written perhaps a hundred years ago, will remember the description of a Queen's regiment sailing up the stream. It is an extremely life-like and accurate record of the Ganges of that period, and how folk moved thereon.

The Ganges boatman, like the Arab-descended mariners of the Indus, is a hardy and venturous man of his craft.

Calcutta in all its Glory

Not far from the course of the Ganges and to the west of it runs the river Hooghly, which enters the sea by one of the mouths of the Ganges. The Hooghly, navigable to ocean shipping, is the river on which stands Calcutta, the greatest city of British India, and until a few years ago its capital.

It is the capital of Bengal in any case, still perhaps one of the wealthiest cities of the world, lying for the moment like all great cities in the trough of the world's depression, and allowed by some strange inconsistency to be in the hands of a rebel municipality. As a whole, there is little of the rebel about it, but where no public opinion is plucky enough to stand out, a few of the rebel set are able to establish themselves. There are the leading scholars, the scientists, and the professors of Bengal, the gallant Vice-Chancellor of the University who stood between the Governor and an assassin, and the Indian High Court judges. There are the great Indian *shroffs* [1] and traders, the still big English firms, the stockbrokers, the company directors and their offices like to other great capital and business centres; there are tens of thousands of impudent Bengal students who, secure in the British law-giving, are a nuisance to their betters, an irritation and a joke.

The merchants' palaces line the river-bank. Easterns in all their glory drive in great cars and still in carriages; ships' captains and pilots are seen in the clubs, the Hooghly is full of shipping, but more in the great modern docks than in the fairway of sailing times. Calcutta lies great as ever, waiting for the revival of trade, and the chiefs of police who hunt the murderers sleep in different rooms o' nights, and all the while the European Associations vary between the hope of saving business and the danger of losing India, as do stronger men than they.

If you really want to dream of underground Calcutta, why, read Mr. Kipling's *City of Dreadful Nights*, the name

[1] Banker and bill-broker.

which the wags also gave it after the King's visit and his accolades. If you drive over the Iron Bridge from Howrah station in the fog of a December morning, why, there is a smell of sea and river mud and also even of sewage that might be London Bridge in the older days, and does for the moment bring the heart of an exile from up-country into his mouth, till he runs into an Aryan brother of Bengal with the tails of his dress shirt a-hanging out.

Such is Calcutta, the city of merchant princes and of seditionists, of great ships and warehouses, and the monuments to the Black Hole, of Warren Hastings and Lord Cornwallis. Aye, and of Job Charnock who founded it from a small Indian village 236 years ago (1698). You will remember the story of Job Charnock, the good John Bull of days gone by, who rescued a terrified Hindu widow from a funeral pyre and married her good and proper, and lived happily ever afterwards, which is not the least of the many stories of the East. And if you would linger for a moment on the old times of John Company and his Writers, why, read from the same Mr. Kipling's pen *The Dream of Duncan Parrenness*, and perhaps if you have time look into one of the old burial-grounds. In these old burial-grounds the length and breadth of India lie the story and the drama and the glory of the British re-mending of India, and Calcutta is their monument despite a Bengal revolutionary mayor and other warts on the wheel of time.

And when your Bengali lesser lights worry you, if perchance they do, why, stroll across the Maidan and see Fort William and listen to the drums and fifes of a British battalion and see the Union Jack a-flying as it has flown this century and a half and more. Fort William is an interesting example of the reformed Vauban system of fortification as complete and scientific in its time as any in the world, and now very suitable to its position as a citadel.

But when you have done with Calcutta you will feel that India is a busy, prosperous, well-governed country, and also that a craven or foolish hand on the rudder or on the wheel might easily upset it. Indeed, as your train will have borne you Calcutta-wards the same thought will have been in your mind as you survey the sugar-cane, and the green fertile rice-fields and the peaceful industrious peasantry, that there is little wrong, and that knife-and-pistol lodges must be but a nightmare that a Seidlitz should cure. For some time have the doctors urged the Seidlitz while the housekeepers have insisted on dietary which but made matters worse.

When you have seen the glories and the queernesses and the old-world sights of Calcutta, and perhaps listened to Warren Hastings' carriage drive in o' nights to Hastings House, and thought of Madame Grand at Chandernagore up the river, why, you have come to the end of all the reels that can be shown you in the time. If you are in a very thoughtful mood, you will try and wonder where the trouble is, and what the end is to be, and I wish I could tell you. *Le Bon Dieu sait*, and at present He won't tell.

CHAPTER XXII

TO THE SOUTH LANDS OF SIVA AND VISHNU

To the South Lands

But it may be that you will turn to the South Lands from Bombay first, which you may properly do, and eventually find your way to the ancient English bride city of Madras, whence you will find a through carriage will carry you north of the East Coast route and then by a recently constructed line across the heart of India to Delhi. And as you go up the East Coast it is no bad thing to remember the constant come-and-go of British and French fleets on this coast from Pondicherry to Fort St. David or Masulipatam in the days when the two struggled for Eastern supremacy. However, before we can dwell on the deeds of Admiral Suffren, or think of the final French struggles, and of the final downing of fierce bitter Tippu, we have a long way to go. This time there is only one main route, the G.I.P., which runs on the same track as the route to Delhi and Calcutta as far as Kalyan junction on the mainland. From thence the Southern branch climbs resolutely up the rocky wall of the Ghats, past the great rock of the Duke's Nose, the separate hill on the right of Materan, to the hill station of Khandala 2000 feet above the sea. The great gorges up which the broad Indian gauge 5′ 6″, as compared with the 4′ 8½″ of the world's universal gauge, by gallery and tunnel are more than splendid, as canyons they are at times sublime. It is worth leaving Bombay by an early afternoon train, rather than a tea-time one that climbs in the dark.

Khandala used to be a reversing station, where having run into a dead end with two or three engines pushing you, the train would slowly run down the opposite way by easy grades to the plateau of the Deccan. Electrification and better lay-out now permit of continuous running.

Before you gain the top you should see on your left, perched high on the hill-tops, the outer walls and inner citadel of the great hill fortress of Raj Machee. Between Khandala and Poona two more great black stone fortresses of Lohoghar and Visapur, and they and Raj Machee will help you to realize that for generations the staple industry of India has been war, and the support of war. War against the conquered, war against the invader, war against your neighbour and war against the King. You are also amongst the country of religion, solid religion, whose builders carved for the future to the glory of gods and the content of men. Close to Khandala is Lonauli, and at both places are simple forms of hotel and rest-houses, and if you would like to see one phase of ancient India, tarry here a day or two—view the magnificent ancient Hindu caves of Karli, the fort of Raj Machee, and of Lohoghar, and see even the Buddhist caves of Baja and Bhensi under the precipitous sides of Visaghur and how men carved and built in patience for all time.

You will see stupa and cells, you will see statues of the Hindu gods and saints, and rows of dancing girls with the big bosoms that the East loves, dancing all in a row. It is as the old religious nursery rhyme of Queen Mary's day:

> Mary, Mary, quite contrary—
> With her pretty maids [nuns] all in a row.

So with the *devi-dasis* of Elephanta and Karli. From these fortresses, you will see how pirate barons as well as legitimate governors controlled the countryside and saw that traders, and gor-bellied knaves with full purses, paid fair, and more often unfair, cess.

If you pass by the foot of Lohoghar, on your right-hand side, whether you have tarried a while for sight-seeing, best done by car and pony—or by car and shank's mare, with a coolie carrying on his head a basket of wet grass and mineral waters behind you—you will see a long spur of black rock, with bastions on top, and at the end a gun-tower. It is a very narrow spur jutting out from the flat terreplein interior of the fort, for many yards. At the end of it there is a hole in the rock through which you see sky, and it has the sinister name of *Bichu ka Kanta*—'The Scorpion's Sting'. The hole in the rock gives you exactly the feeling of the tight tucked-in sting of a black scorpion. From its top prisoners were hurled several hundred feet on to the prickly cactus below.

If you climb up the graded ascent to the fortress entrance you will find yourself climbing through five successive bastioned loopholed gateways, each with decaying teak, iron-bound gates with triple row of elephant spikes. Eastern gates not thus defended would be forced by elephants placing their heads against them and heaving. Rows of spikes forbade this simple method.

You may notice, if you care for such things, that you make your ascent with the right hand to the cliff-side; that means the builder knew his job, for it meant that the assailant could not cover himself with his shield from boiling oil and cross-bow bolts, stones and what not, as well as if he could advance shield-arm to the wall, and well crouched beneath its cover.

Upon the top is a Hindu shrine with rows of the little stone horses of the hunting gods alongside, a half-dry tank, a Moslem tomb, the ruins of the governor's house or office, and cannon lying dismounted half over the battlements where in 1819 one Brigadier Pritzler, who took the place, had thrown them to lie, with lizards agog in their old iron muzzles, to this day. Curiously enough, you may see that an old bronze cannon lies higher up on the sward carrying the Rose and Portcullis and the old monogram of fame, E.R. But what does a cannon of Good Queen Bess do lying in a dismantled Mahratta hill-fort? Nobody has any idea, but maybe 'tis a portent. Possibly some merchant-factor made present of it—even may the original pirates have taken it from some captured caravel. But there it lies and no man knows its story.

The author once tried to carry it off to adorn the Artillery mess at Kirkee near Poona, but was fain to be content with two lesser ones. And as you peer and roam and pile romance on tragedy, a hare will start from between your feet, and a quail startle your nerves. If you take a terrier dog, beware lest a panther steal it.

Having seen one fort, you may yearn for Raj Machee or you may think enough makes a feast and drive off to Karli, interesting but more hackneyed than the desolate Scorpion's Sting.

The Heart of Mahratta Land

Down the railway five-and-twenty miles you come through fertile rice-fields, terraced in mountain wall to Poona, the summer capital of the Government of Bombay, and erstwhile capital of the Peishwa, whose ten thousand horse may still be heard o' nights on the Deccan Plain.

It is a picturesque city of winding river, wooded streets and gardens, ancient temples. It is also a big military centre for all arms, and it rings of British Indian history and of far older dramas of Eastern quarrels and tragedy. It also speaks of Arthur Wellesley, who marched there from the south to support the Peishwa, our ally who was not forsworn. Wellesley was doing in the west what Lord Lake was doing in the north-east, fighting part of the Mahratta federation, Scindiah and the Rajah of Nagpur, 'The Bhonsla', being his opponent. He gained further north the great victories of Assaye and Argaum in 1803, stormed Ghawilghar and trained himself thereby to win his Waterloo—then but a 'Sepoy' general. But the drama of Poona came not then, when a subsidiary British force to protect the Peishwas was established, but when in 1817 that erratic Prince changed his mind. The last great combine, this time of Mahrattas with the robber Pindari bands, to once more break the British, was in hand. The Peishwa, forgetting his friends who had saved him, allowed his forces to collect, and suddenly turned on the British. The small Subsidiary Force moved by the old grey Holkar's bridge from Poona to Kirkee, the

Resident Mr. Elphinstone escaped and the Residency of the Sangam was burned and there the Mahrattas endeavoured to envelope the British force. It later left its baggage at Kirkee, and advanced across what is now the railway line to where the long line of Mahratta cannon was deployed by the camel's hump that is known as Ganesh-kind. It was that day of immemorial trouble, the 5th of November, to be also the day of Inkerman, that the battle was fought that decided the fate of western India. The Peishwa had watched his troops in the prayer of safety at the Golden Temple on Parbatti Hill that you may see beyond Poona city, and when they fled he fled. The end was annexation; and Baji Rao II. ended his days in wealth and peace as the Baron of Bithoor near Cawnpore, whence by some topsyturvydom of fate his adopted son the Nana became by the chance of the Bengal Sepoy the leader in the Cawnpore tragedy.

Poona is a great centre of modern learning and education. There you will see the choice young men and goodly, the students of the universities and colleges on bicycles by the thousand busy in all the ways of youth, but for the moment in politics. Remember you are making your way now to the South Land from the country of the white people to that of the black, that is from Aryan majority to Dravidian majority and Aryan minority. The Mahratta is a half-breed whose Aryan origin is at any rate suspect, but the true Mahratta is a landowner great or small. Among them, overlaid in the work of education and intelligence for centuries, has been the Brahmin settler in the land, a white overlayer, suspect of the people, yet more than usually full of the brains and subtlety of that gifted white layer. It is the Brahmin and the old white trading class who throng the colleges, have given admirable Government service under British leading, after doing the educated work for earlier Indian Governments, giving the sacred Peishwa, originally Sivaji's Prime Minister and leader of the free-booting Mahratta Confederacy. The Brahmins and high-caste traders brim over with brains. I had the privilege, early in '33, of hearing

Mr. Jayakar, a lawyer and member of His Majesty's trusty Round Table Conference, address two thousand students on bicycles. He told them that while he regretted the reserved powers it was proposed to give the Viceroy, they did not matter, as His Excellency would have no machinery to use them! . . . and all the young men were mightily pleased. But the tragedy as one looked and knew, was not the froth of the Deccani Brahmin and how he could down his enemies, but how all these eager young students could keep themselves and their child wives in a country in which the basis of production is so inevitably low as that of sun-dried India. But if you are an educationist you will enjoy meeting these students and their college dons, and wish them well. You may also enjoy Colonel Seton Graham Hutchinson's story of how a committee of them invited him to be first headmaster of a semi-public school on Kingston or West Point Military Academy lines, for Brahmin and Mahratta youths. The Indian intelligentsia hopes that its known reputation for lack of all military courage and qualities may be schooled away. Perhaps they are right, and no doubt Hutchinson was a good pioneer. His lads were devoted to him, and the story of refusal of his committee to supply any of the necessities to make their experiment a workable one is all told in his *olla podrida* of memories.

The good Mahratta countryside, that supplies the eager bayonets that have so often carried the Union Jack to victory, has very distinct ideas as to where it places the Brahmin intelligentsia, who are often fiercely disliked—which is a pity.

But Mahratta Land, and the sweet countryside, and the real, not the town people, and the charm of its melodious and superhuman *prakrit* tongue, is a matter that the passer-by can but little know, even if he can imagine. It must be sojourned among to love it, so we will leave Poona, and the Bhore Ghat and the fortress of Sri-Sivaji on the hill-tops round, and pass on to the South Lands. But I should like to think that a visitor in the cooler if dried-up winter should stop to see the land one vast green carpet in July, when the European for days may wear his trilby hat, and still keep his head cool.

I have spoken of Poona as the heart of Mahratta Land, but perhaps not quite truly, for the little mountain rats of Sivaji and the British Army come more from the seaside of the Ghats, hardy athletic villagers and stout lasses, or down the Southern Mahratta hills. But you are in the land of the Kelkars and Endulkars, of the *ikeri-ye* and *tickeri-za*, or *kai sangitla*, which is a very different tongue from that of Hindustan.

A Glimpse of the Mogulai

So because we mustn't stay messing about the Deccan or find it too attractive, or enjoy the good social life and the Poona river and the English boats, and the parakeets at even, we will climb once more into our G.I.P. and the Madras Mail and swing out into the great upland plain. We shall run down the edge of what folk still called the Mogulai, the country of the Moguls, otherwise the great dominions of the Turk-descended Nizam of Hyderabad. There the descendant of the Great Azaf Jah, the Warwick of Mogul history, whose name was Chin Chillik Khan, still reigns, in Moslem state in a Moslem capital over what is largely a Hindu people. Because we sight-seers should be our own master, we might well after running for twenty-four hours over a somewhat arid and poorly cultivated part of the Deccan, turn aside at Wadi, which is the junction for Hyderabad, the Nizam's capital. The crowd on the platform are worthy of study. Because it has been the only Moslem state left in India of great size and importance, it has special features of its own, and if you like noticing races you will see many Islamic types. There will be some Afghans who penetrate everywhere, some Arabs perhaps in *kafiyeh* and *aghal*, the head-kerchief and the head-rope, and also a keen eye will see an Indian-born Arab, in Indian guise, but of typical Arab features or more often the half-Arab, half-negro slave face; in any case there will be an air about somewhat redolent of older Turkey or Egypt. Hyderabad is a mighty city, with a good few things of interest, notably the great fort of Golconda set high on a hill, and is an example of the Marquis Wellesley's policy of subsidiary forces, in the large cantonment of Secunderabad close to the capital, which it at one time protected from the hatred of Mahratta neighbours. Its cantonment is now the Aldershot of Southern India, contains many British and Indian soldiers, artillery, cavalry, etc., and splendid training-grounds in a moderate climate. Hard by, round the city, are the Nizam's own troops, which still have the old tradition of employing some Europeans among its officers, a relic of the days when the Indian Princes found that Western military training and equipments were a surer anchor than their own older *gol* and *rissalah*. The powerful artillery which the Western gun-founders of Turkey and Portugal taught them to make, was their ancient stand-by.

At His Highness's court dwells the British Resident, who deals with the civil affairs of the cantonment, and is the medium of communication between the Nizam's and the Imperial Government. There are plenty of lesser sights in Hyderabad city, and a few miles out is the mighty ancient fortress of Golconda aforesaid, whose lofty towers afford a magnificent panorama of the countryside. The history of Golconda alone would fill *Arabian Nights'* tales for many weeks, and there is a diamond which bears the name which has no mean history behind it. But to those who know history, it is the spectacle of the original Turkish Raj still in being that is so intriguing, and to those who think of tinder-boxes loose in a magazine, and the forces that we are loosing from the trammels in which they have run so long, the future of a Moslem crown on a Hindu people bears some pondering over. The signs are already accumulating in the Last Land of the Mogulai.

Dravidian India

Having sped away from the Mogulai and its strange and in many ways exotic conditions, we will get back once more to the way of the South and Dravidian India. Here let it be remarked that the Madras Presidency, which it pleased my English lords of the North to call the 'Benighted' Presidency, has for at least a century been far ahead of the rest of India in civilization, advancement, and amenities, Western and Eastern. The educated Brahmin and high-caste people, numbering many scientists and scholars and men of all learning in their ranks, are in many ways the most advanced and broad-minded in India. Madras alone in the opinion of many is nearly fitted for an autonomous provincial government. Partly is this so because years of the *Pax Britannica* have cleared out and subdued the lawless elements. The Afghan and Turk settler of Haider and Tippu have been man-handled long ago into reasonableness, and the climate has taken the Northern fire from their veins.

But just as progress and modern-mindedness has permeated among some of the educated and higher folk, so still do the old ways lie deep among the simple, homely and by no means unprosperous peasantry. Indeed as you travel down in Madras proper, south let us say of the Mysore plateau, you will be surprised at the look of the countryside: the well-cared-for forests, the red-tiled villages and the general air of the best being made of climate, soil and tillage.

Here you will notice even more than elsewhere how *les enfants poussent toujours* and how a fat baby is astride the thigh of every comely matron, and matronhood here begins very early.

The city of Madras, the old presidential capital, has its great Vauban-like fortress as has Calcutta, the Fort of St. George—from which the Province is still known as the Presidency of Fort St. George—and its great merchant houses, its churches and its temples. Here Christianity in varying forms, some of great antiquity, holds considerable sway. Here the British tradition holds great grip—from the days when Britain and France fought hard for dominion, the length and breadth of the coast.

If you want to see vast ecstatic crowds, and the gigantic idols in their cars drawn out by the priests among the engrossed million, it is in the South—the South Lands where Vishnu and Siva are worshipped in savage lusciousness and intense fervour—that you may see them. There are many such places of pilgrimage and festival, and perhaps the age-old temples of Kambakonam city are among the most famous. There are many priest-engendered miracles to give occasion for such festival. Every twelve years or so, for instance, the waters of nine sacred rivers unite in the Maha-makam tank in Kambakonam. In this tank are nine wells each fed by one of the sacred rivers of Hindustan. Kambakonam is on the river Kaveri, but no matter. To the sacred wells in Maha-makam comes to her as well as Mother Ganges herself, the lost Saraswati from the Punjab basin, the mighty Nerbudda, all the way from Central India. To see the flow millions will come, and the railway companies will run long sardine-trains packed with human Skippers. It is a Vishnuvite ceremony and thanksgiving, and some of the most learned modern and western Brahmin gentlemen of your acquaintance will like to wear but a *cachette*, with the white mark of Vishnu fresh on their foreheads, and will be leading the procession that is moving literally in millions to ecstasy.

There may be doubts in visitors' minds as to the mystery—there will be none in those of the pilgrims. The writer once in Jerusalem, after a good dinner and good wine had loosened the ecclesiastical tongue, heard the Latin bishop asked, 'What about the miracle of the sacred fire at Easter-tide, the fire from which ten thousand light their lamps of faith to carry back round the world?' 'Well,' said he, 'what about it? Would you destroy with your Western science this beautiful faith and tradition that bring joy and peace to so many hearts?'

And if you see the ecstasy and joy in the pilgrims' faces at any of the great festivals and in the Gopi-rams you too would say with *Monseigneur*, 'Would you?'

You may dream of Clive at Arcot; of French Rocks and Tanjore; of the battles which finally destroyed the French influence, and if you like you can find many French traces.

You may think of Admiral Suffren, the great French sailor, who would have saved France's Indian Empire, helpless in face of Louis XV.'s Government, and the British frigates that dogged his heels, and helped the *débâcle* that the French Government had begun. It is all living under your eyes if you can see it.

Here Brahminism has taken all the old Dravidian faiths into its bosom and devised cults and castes galore, of which many millions are depressed, and others half-way up and down, wrapped in a strange medley of Hinduism and savage earlier cults. But Siva, the other great *persona* of the Hindu *Trimurti*, is not to be unrepresented at this miracle of the nine rivers, and his priests and devotees will now bring the procession, the great *idolons*, and the stone carriage of Siva. With Siva will come the blood sacrifice that is anathema to the gentle Vishnu. The people of the Siva persuasion will have brought kids to the sacrifice and a great black savage of negro extraction will rend their living throats for you, while you wait as the blood spurts from the bleating victim. A thousand kids a day will those great white teeth tear, till you, a Saxon, almost long to see some tiger rend his in turn, for the blood lust is infectious.

Of the temple dancing-girl, and worse than dancing-girl, and the practical way of exorcising desire before devotion, we will not discourse here, but suffice it to say that you may see in living existence all that you have read of Phoenicia and Sodom three thousand years ago.

The temples of the great Gopi-rams are marvellously ornate, great tributes to what the pious will spend in the earthly glory of the deity, many to Western ideas symbolic of the grossest following of all that pertains to the spark of life.

It is Lyall who sings of the

> Organs of birth and the circlet of bones
> And the light loves carved on the temple stones—

of the temples of the North—but it is Laurence Hope, who

ended her own life on the tomb of the distinguished general who was her husband, here in this very Mysore of the South, who wrote:

> An elephant hunt, a magicians' feast
> And curious mating of man and beast.

But look now at the people, and see the tense crowds, thousands of men exactly alike, bare-headed, with hair combed back, gleaming white caste-marks of Vishnu and Siva and all so different from the North, where fervour takes hold otherwise. And all the while the women, the good round-about women, the best ornaments in nose and hair *champak* flowers behind the ears, amused, white teeth showing, infants on hip, are wondering really why the men are so tense about it.

The good Christian ſaith, even though it teach an out-caste soul that it counts with God, cannot give shows like that! Ah! look at the big idol, how it sways and does not care—superb! *Jai! Jai! Kali Ma!* and so it goes on. All over the Madras Presidency—vast Gopi-rams, clever priests, simple enthusiastic people! You may see it all, gentle reader, if gentle still you be! and perhaps you may thank your stars that Tower Hill and Tyburn Corner and even Guy Fawkes Day are different; or perhaps you won't, for here is life, colour and death and birth, *tout mêlé* as it were.

But you have seen the teeming millions of the South and can imagine missionaries at a catch-penny meeting at Home letting themselves go, as well they might. The negro tearing kids' throats, alone should draw money, and the harvest of souls in the South is growing.

Before we go, let us run up to the Mysore plateau and see Mysore, the state conquered by Hyder Ali, and Tippu Sultan, conquered from a decadent Hindu dynasty which their servant the said Hyder had deposed. But Hyder Ali and Tippu could not let well alone. Five Mysore wars! At last the twittering Government in Fort St. George were made to do the job thoroughly, and in 1792 Lord Cornwallis led a properly organized British army upon the magnificent uplands of

Mysore, captured Bangalore fortified city and Srinagapatam. Tippu, the circumciser of Hindus, the torturer of prisoners, the bitter enemy of the English, Citizen Tippu, as Napoleon wrote him, was humbled in his own capital, Srinagapatam. Terms were dictated, his sons taken as hostages, and Lord Cornwallis marched away. But not for long could Tippu, mad fanatic Tippu, keep faith. Perhaps fate would not let him. By 1793 he was at it again once and for ever. The great Lord Mornington was Governor-General, and he saw that Tippu must go—Tippu, who was calling to the Durani Emperor at Kabul to roll the drum ecclesiastic and come to save him. Lord Harris now marched up the ghats once again with his Grand Army—a real army—organized in eight divisions. Srinagapatam was stormed, Tippu was slain. Did Britain annexe Mysore? Not a bit. It sought in the dust for that expelled Rajput family, planted the heir of state and wealth once more on the throne of his father. And because the Madras Government takes care of its relics, you may see the palace as it was when Lord Wellesley stormed it, and when Arthur Wellesley was Military Governor thereof. It and the uplands of Mysore are worth going to see, and you can reach it from Bangalore, the cantonment of the British force that was created to protect Mysore from more vicissitudes.

The Blue Mountains

And when you have seen Madras, Queen of Cities, and ruined Srinagapatam, and the red-tiled villages and the coco palms, unless indeed you want to see the engineers at work making great trade ports at Visianagram in the west and Quilon in the east, it but remains to you to say, 'I will see the Blue Mountains'. Then if you have a Madrassi servant or any other servant, he will say 'What master pleases' or '*jo hukm*', and make arrangements accordingly. It is all too easy. You will go by the broad-gauge train, and early in the morning you will see blue hills far above you capped perhaps in cloud. And you will come out of the 'Blue

Mountain' express, as the Madras Railway likes to call its none too rapid train, and you will take your seats in a baby train, a front seat in the leading carriage with window at the front. Then off you will go to quite a different fairyland to the Himalaya—up amid palms, to coffee and tea estates through thick forests by the way, that keep tigers, above an ancient *droog*, a fortress, whence Tippu hurled his prisoners to their death. Somewhere about noon your funny little sixpenny nursery train will run you into a sun-kissed, cool-breezed station, Conoor, the 'Mountain of Sunlight', a place of neat white houses with red-tiled roofs and coffee trees all in a row. The fresh hill air will enchant you. And perhaps you will get out and drive to a hotel and find yourself amid half-English houses, and tea planters and old colonels. You will drive on next day by car twelve miles or so of almost Sussex country to the great Downs of Ootacamund, where they hunt the hounds in pink, and you play golf on greens and there are trout in the river and woodcock in the spinneys and somehow you've lost India. Yet the Indian sun brings you the scent of eucalyptus from all the groves that stud the hill-top, like great dark pine forests. You have reached a goal that few people dream of, among those clever old planters and settlers and colonels aforesaid, and those who plant schools and orphanages and convents in happy surroundings.

Now that is the end of my story save a little bit on the continent and its future, and White Papers and prosaics, before the King comes up the gangway and the battleships fire their great guns.

CHAPTER XXIII

JOHN BULL TO BRAHMINI BULL
(A PEEP INTO THE FUTURE)

THE WHITE PAPER

SINCE this book was first conceived, lo! the White Paper has appeared, and the British public is all a-wonder. It was not intended to touch herein on what must be called 'Political India' since it is an India singularly inevident to the ordinary visitor and sojourner, while the mass of the people want trade and rain and shine in due season.

It is not till you reach some of the commercial scholastic centres with thousands of young men educated beyond their prospects and chances, that you realize a driving force behind the politician—young men who dream of countless schoolmasterships and inspectorships and everything else that will enable them to live on a salary. But it is all so natural. There are the sons of the big merchants who see something of the West, and who dream dreams if they don't see visions, and there are these countless lesser intelligentsia, whose parents of humble trading class have saved and scraped in the hope that the education they give their children must bring wealth.

But when you have taken off all the froth and discounted the folly, it is but natural that the desire for westernized progress in some form should arise. By some egregious mistake of our own, but by whom made and at what precise epoch it is hard to say, we, the British who have rebuilt this edifice, have succeeded in allowing an anti-British element and atmosphere to grow up. There are more flower-beds, no doubt, where the pro-British friendly understanding and trust grows even more strongly and profusely, but in India public opinion is very timid; a few voluble and bomb-inclined people will terrorize and dominate just as in Ireland. The wise old heads that knew India, and would not be put off by hot air and flummery, have always said, 'Advance as much as you like, encourage and help as much as you can, but the moment you see enmity hit it on the head. You can't placate the implacable. Let a rivulet run, it will grow up a torrent.' The hot-air merchant has said, 'These nice kind people who speak such good English, and quote the best authors, they would not hurt a fly, and of course, they can manage millions. Besides it is hard for one race to be dominated by another.'

Now has come the White Paper full of good stuff, and with just enough mischief let into the corner as may easily lead to the loss of India or at least a sharp campaign to restore order to prevent bloodshed and hostility.

The people of Great Britain, having regard to all they have done, intend to insist on a friendly and ultimate predominance in the form of a Condominium. It is because they feel that the White Paper, while purporting to give this, fails in spite of all its brave words to secure it, that so many are determined to see it modified and modified even more in the interests of India than of Britain. That is why Dominion Status, which incidentally has been altered since Lord Irwin's injudicious use of the word, by the statute of Westminster, seems so unsuitable a phrase. A phrase that we use of six million white Australians, a million and a half New Zealanders, ten million Canadians, is not the one that applies to 353 millions of all colours and creeds. Nor does the fact that five million English and French-Canadians federalized eighty years ago, and now are ten millions of many races, help us to handle this problem.

But except for the ultimate paramountcy, everything that shall produce content and prosperity while preserving British interests, is very dear to British hearts. For the sake of the bravery of the martial races they will even forget, and pretend that it never happened, the hostile treachery of some of the very leaders who now assemble at the round tables. Unfortunately, these very martial races who can give the goods, but are deficient in facility, are not those who will get a fair share of what is going. The country is not organized so that like Henry III. the ruler can sit fair on his chair of

People and priests and lords and crown.

The chair will tilt horribly and the interests will not be balanced for many a year yet. The important matter about such changes as are coming, so far as many of the chapters of this book are concerned, is what will be the future for Europeans in India. Lord Willingdon, the strong Governor, the man who will have no rot or tomfoolery as regards law, order and treachery, has a very 'Liberal' heart. He believes that all will be happier and better than ever, that India will eagerly share her future with the British, that all the chicanery and dishonesty which so easily come through in many forms of Indian life will disappear and not matter, and that all will be well.

Those who are doubtful say, 'Yes, *if* you and your successors have the real power to steady the machine, with something more civilized than a whiff of grape . . . something that will enable you to keep the Patels and De Valeras and their impudences in their place before it comes to push of pike'.

If that is secured by some clever alteration in the draft proposals, then with Lord Willingdon we can see a great future of *camaraderie*. On the other hand, the forces of mischief and of inefficiency are so strong that they may grow out of all knowledge and His Excellency be powerless to stop it. To prevent this, to enable the future to be one of success and not failure, is the goal to which every Briton should direct his attention. It is perhaps as well to realize that a cauldron of 353 million souls seethes and overbalances fairly easily and gets beyond the power of all the King's horses and all the King's men to put right.

No Viceroy has any idea of what goes on and has always gone on under the surface. The district officer knows how easily and how quietly innocent situations ferment and boil over, and how virulent can be the simmering at times from spore and microbes that are age-old. The Moguls knew, and when they failed to keep it in hand, it destroyed them. The Indian Civil Service know, Viceroys and Secretaries of State do not, nay cannot. For donkey's years have the magistrates watched for trouble, taken securities for good behaviour, turned the excitable into special constables in good time, and put in, in fact, that stitch-in-time which few even hear of.

Watchman, what of the Night?

What then does the visible future seem to promise? Watchman, what of the night? 'Is it plaguy dark and does it smell of cheese?' I quote from antiquity, and I am inclined to answer—'Not too dark but undoubtedly smells of cheese'. With India in upheaval, according to the popular idea, with agricultural India quiet and content enough as it really is, with the intelligentsia starved for a future, with politics run wild and the curse of the cowardly secret gun-man let loose on the land, and Secretaries of State producing constitutions; again, 'what of the night?' No one can think and talk of India to-day without looking forward.

We must make some assumptions and I will venture to make a few. First I will assume that the good British, who are a sovereign people, will steer a straight course, between the specious arguments of what the *Daily Mail*, perhaps horribly, calls 'the yes-men' and the harder-thinking folk who have to face facts and hold the baby. I will assume that from the parturition of the great minds we shall have a constitution embodying all the good points of the White Paper, while putting in 10 per cent more of the stiffening of reality into some of the frame-work—the British, as Colonel Josiah Wedgwood has urged, to have *some share in the Federation*, some *ad hoc* representation for all they have given and endured; that something shall be done to ensure the future and the honour of that wonderful police, of which the 'yes-men' know so little. It need not be much, but it must be done by right thinking. Further, I will assume that the one essential of modern civilization, nay of all civilization, shall be assured, the independence and incorruptibility of the judges—so easy to talk about, so hard to attain—which the White Paper proposes to destroy, and leave to some leaven born of underground temples and an unclean rite. Only lately did the writer hear an important American, declaring that every man had his price, refuse to accept the English belief in the incorruptibility of English judges. We who know the care taken for centuries and long process of evolution believe, nay know beyond the foundations even of belief, that our judges are incorruptible. If white America doubts, then white and black India will not only doubt, but will intrigue to make the judiciary corruptible. Indian judges must have the security of the Crown behind them. But then again do I presume that wisdom will prevail over the intrigues of the Indian pleader.

We then start with the assumption of an eventual British paramountcy benevolent but assured, founded on Britain's Imperial position, and we assume that there will be enough British personnel to ensure the probity of the services, and their working with something of the high standards of the last century. Given these starting points, we will now proceed to make a few more assumptions, not unwarranted let us hope, but essential not only for progress, but to prevent a slipping back. These are they and are almost the same that God spoke in the Twentieth Chapter of Exodus:

That Indian Ministers shall work for the good of India and not of race and religion, and be spared, at any rate, the Eastern ramification of Western political intrigue and vice.

That the great plan for developing all India's genuine needs and waiting advancements shall go forward steadily.

That the Indian schools, medical, scientific, engineering, etc., shall be sufficiently high in standard and free from dishonesty to be accepted throughout the Empire.

That attempts to undermine Army and Police, so that the great pillar shall crash, be as sternly repressed in the future as in the past.

That widows shall not be burned alive, children sacrificed to cure singers' sore throats, child wives crucified (*vide* Indian Press of 1932).

That constables' heads shall not be cut off, especially while they are living, to intimidate them, and to make a dacoit holiday.

With some of these assumptions, and a few more, accepted, especially in such matters as the manufacturing of false evidence, false complaints and false suits, one may with the more pleasure look at the India for which one dreams dreams.

The Dreams that I Dream

Now that I have lulled my brain with somewhat daring assumptions, I will permit myself to dream dreams for the India in which I have spent so many happy years, where I have had so many friends, and for the people for whom I have so great an affection. I see the great Provinces going on as part of a Condominium, in which the proportion of British officers in each service are able to work in the most complete *camaraderie* with their Indian *confrères*, in which the twice-born races recognize themselves as a white people, and act accordingly. I look to some school systems, that shall be better than the Seton Hutchinson fiasco, and the ineptitudes and chinoiseries that accompanied it. I look to see the pattern set by the Army that the Simon Commission so applauded followed everywhere, and schools such as St. George's Schools, and Colleges, the Military Academy at Dera Dun, or the Aligarh University of ancient renown, becoming a pattern. I look for no immense commercial and industrial development because I don't believe the wealth and resources and the needs for resources, are there, but steady improvement in the profits of agriculture and slow developments in industry. I fear for education, lest it scatter the land with sour half-starved schoolmasters who hatch

Bolshevism in their meagre little hearts, and I think that the educational policy must be most carefully adapted to the needs of an agricultural people who can never aspire to anything more than getting the best that science can give them out of a land that is poor and a climate that is hard.

I look for a gentry, especially in the North, that shall more and more devote themselves to their estates and agriculture, aspiring to send some of their sons to Army and Civil Service. I hope to see the magnificent yeoman peasantry getting more from their land, doing better by co-operation, limiting their families to what the land can carry, and also sending some of their young men to all those Government services where 'guts' and character are needed for the State.

I look to an Indian Army, a Crown Army, in which the great efforts of the British to produce a fighting chivalrous officer may be successful. I very much doubt that the intelligentsia type which we are allowing to try their hand will ever have the courage, character and stamina to take this place, but they are having the chance, and if the British officers succeeded in making soldiers of them, it will be such a feather in their cap as practical men have never hitherto dreamt of. I imagine that it is still the yeoman farmer and the small landowner who will hold his own in the soldier world, the man who the Simon Commission tells unpractical India will once again unduly dominate, unless the British discipline keeps some check over aspirations and opportunity.

But I like to think of the young intelligentsia of India showing the world how excellent are their brains and their capacity in so many walks of life, eschewing such ways as Bolshevik schools in Russia, or hate societies in the United States, because those lead no ways except to the 'place called stop', where John Bull eventually awaits those who will not listen. There is so much better fun in the world for them if they will but look for it, and there is no one to whom Brahmini Bull may better listen to than cousin John of the same Aryan family.

I wonder often as to what religious life may be in store

for India. I deplore the extraordinary *volte-face* that happens here when Hindu and Moslem students in the West hobnob together, and say that all that their fathers thought was tosh, even if their mothers put it across them when they go Home. We go through it all ourselves here in England, pretty often, but we get back again to what was done for us in the old time afore. In the Army in India we expect a Moslem soldier to be good Moslem, and a Sikh soldier to be a good Sikh, for that way runs faithfulness and peace at the last. We hope that a good Hindu is also a *good* Hindu, though we know less as to how to teach him to be so. But the Hindu teaching has so much that all the world can but venerate and admire, that I dream of it still keeping the white folk white and improving the black folk of the older India, and wonder if the Gandhi vision for the depressed classes can come to pass without destroying the whole structure of Indian life. I don't dream at all on the subject of Christianity in India, for who can trace God's purpose, and when we have spread the News we have done our share.

The ploughman diggeth his plough
More deep in the grudging sod,
The wheat and the soil is all my care
And the rest is the will of God.

Whichever of the 'many mansions' the people of India are to dwell in, is outside my ken or vision, and the dream refuses to go that way.

I see that the hot-air merchants and the murder fiend together may so easily misinterpret the dream, that I shudder once again, remembering that Warren Hastings said: 'India may be as easily lost as the North American Colonies, on the floor of the House of Commons' . . . lost through folly and lying, and nine-tenths of India all the while praying that it shall not be. But sometimes I think of wise old Jeremiah, who said, 'The prophets prophesy falsely, and the priests bear rule by their means; and'—here comes the rub—'my people love to have it so'.

I Dream Truer and Better

Turning on the other side, I remember how Britain upheld the whole world in the World War, and feel that fate means us a better turn than to let India fall either to pieces or from us. I remember that David Lloyd George was not the only man who won the War, that soldiers and sailors and workers of the whole Empire did it too, and that together in condominium we shall go forward from strength to strength. But it is not by always saying yes to 'Daddy, mayn't I drive the car?' that great machines are kept in the centre of the road.

Alexander of Macedon, Asoka, mighty Harsha, Akbar, Warren Hastings and George Curzon did not prosper Empires by always saying yes. Perhaps here I might quote, as I so often venture to do, from two of the men who both dream dreams and see visions:

EX OCCIDENTE VOX (Lyall)

West to East

'Fast and Pray', said the sages of Ind;
'We know not what penance and prayer may give.'

. . . . . .

Let the temples moulder in gathering sand,
Let the stones lie strewn in the cedar grove;
Ye shall rule like gods in a glorious land;
Ye shall live by knowledge, and peace, and love.

and then—

East to West

O men of the wandering sea-borne race,
Your venture was high, but your wars are done,
Ye have rent my veil, ye behold my face;
What is the land that your arms have won?

And lest our minds get too full of the things that do not always come to pass, let us close with the practical thought from the 'Galley Slave', for it takes dreams and facts together to make the sort of world that the British can handle, and it envisages the Condominium:

Oh! gallant was our Galley from her carven steering-wheel
To her figurehead of silver and her beak of hammered steel.

. . . .

But no Galley on the waters with our Galley could compare.

INDEX